CRITICAL INSIGHTS

Lord of the Flies

CRITICAL INSIGHTS

Lord of the Flies

Editor
Sarah Fredericks
University of Arizona

SALEM PRESS
A Division of EBSCO Information Services, Inc.
Ipswich, Massachusetts

GREY HOUSE PUBLISHING

Publisher's Cataloging-In-Publication Data
(Prepared by The Donohue Group, Inc.)

Names: Fredericks, Sarah, editor.
Title: Lord of the flies / editor, Sarah Fredericks, University of Arizona.
Other Titles: Critical insights.
Description: [First edition]. | Ipswich, Massachusetts : Salem Press, a division
          of EBSCO Information Services, Inc. ; Amenia, NY : Grey
          House Publishing, [2017] | Includes bibliographical references
          and index.
Identifiers: ISBN 978-1-68217-567-5 (hardcover)
Subjects: LCSH: Golding, William, 1911-1993.Lord of the flies. | Golding,
          William, 1911-1993--Criticism and interpretation. | Airplane
          crash survival in literature. | Social groups in literature.
Classification: LCC PR6013.O35 L63 2017 | DDC 823/.914--dc23

First Printing

Contents _____

Resources

Dedicated with deep affection and respect to Robert C. Evans, exemplary scholar, prodigious writer, tireless mentor, enthusiastic teacher, and kind friend.

With warm thanks also to my dear friend Stephen Paul Bray.

About This Volume

Sarah Fredericks

In the first decade after its publication, *Lord of the Flies* grew into a veritable literary phenomenon. By 1962, *Time* boldly proclaimed it "Lord of the campus." Although William Golding's most famous novel has since fallen from the spotlight, this thrilling adventure story still offers readers a chilling glimpse of human nature's potential for evil.

The present volume begins with an essay by Stephan Schaffrath which connects representations of violence in *Lord of Flies* to the real-world experience of violence and the resulting trauma. Contextualizing *Lord* within Golding's own military experience in World War II, Schaffrath demonstrates how the brutalities of war—and the resulting psychological damage—permeate the novel. Schaffrath's application of *killology*, or the psychology of killing, introduces fresh and relevant insight into one of the most notable themes in *Lord*, the innate capacity for evil within all human beings. Of particular importance is Schaffrath's insightful exploration of "posturing" both in the escalation to violence and in the exertion of control by means of violence. Schaffrath's essay demonstrates *Lord*'s enduring relevance to readers living in a world marked by individual acts of violence, war, and the shocking depths of human depravity.

Next, Courtney Lane offers a succinct overview of William Golding's life and career, from his early life at home and school to his various vocational forays, including his experiences in the British Navy during World War II, and, finally, to his rise to critical acclaim as an author and world-renowned novelist. Lane draws on John Carey's definitive and extensive biography *William Golding: The Man Who Wrote Lord of the Flies,* which itself makes use of both Golding's personal correspondence and previously unpublished archival material in addition to objective, fact-based material curated by Carey as well as numerous other scholars.

Lane's biographical essay probing the contradictions in Golding's personal and professional life provides a solid foundation for Brian Ireland's discussion of the historical context of *Lord of the Flies*. Emphasizing the sheer savagery that occurred during World War II, Ireland begins his essay by outlining the massive death toll and various atrocities committed upon soldiers and civilians alike—especially women and children—in Europe, Russia, and the Pacific. Golding's own experiences in the war, Ireland asserts, fundamentally reshaped his notion of good and evil and caused him to question whether civilization constrains or cultivates the human capacity for evil. *Lord* was more than just a reaction to WWII, however; Ireland demonstrates the ways in which Golding's novel is also a product of the Cold War and thus engages with other dystopian novels and 1950s science fiction. In numerous ways, he concludes, *Lord* reflects the inherent and pervasive darkness that characterized the first half of the twentieth century.

The second essay in the critical contexts section, by Robert C. Evans, advocates the necessity of *critical pluralism*, the notion that multiple critical interpretations are required when analyzing a complex work of literature and that no single theory is definitive. Focusing on *Lord*'s most frequently critiqued passage, its abrupt ending, Evans offers numerous critical interpretations of the novel's conclusion based on more than twenty different approaches to literary criticism. Evans illustrates how a single paragraph, sentence, or even word can sustain multiple critical readings. From a pragmatic perspective, Evans advocates critical pluralism by exhibiting that the more literary theories with which one is familiar, the richer one's interpretation of *Lord* (as well as literature in general) will be. Following Evans's essay is perhaps the most theoretically innovative chapter in this volume, an interpretation of *Lord* using cognitive criticism by Nicolas Tredell. Tredell uses the concept of *motor resonance* or *kinesis* to explore how the reactions of a reader's nervous system to the events occurring in *Lord* (and when reading in general) mimic reactions to similar real-life situations—while of course stopping short of taking action in response to that fictional stimulus. Tredell's careful attention to *Lord*'s language, such as its phrasing, syntax, and use of various tenses, elucidates the characters' (and the readers') visceral experiences, not only in terms of physical sensations, but also in the embodiment of thoughts and emotions as well as the distortion of "delayed decoding." Tredell concludes with an insightful discussion of *mind reading* (the attempt to discern the thoughts and feelings of another) and the limits and impotence of various characters' *self-knowledge* (the attempted reading of one's own mind).

The critical contexts section concludes with an essay by Rafeeq O. McGiveron that compares/contrasts Golding's depiction of human nature in *Lord of the Flies* with that in Robert A. Heinlein's science fiction novel *Tunnel in the Sky* (1955). McGiveron challenges Golding's fundamental conclusion about the boys' inevitable descent into savagery, arguing that the boys' ages—the biguns are no more than twelve or thirteen years old—undermine Golding's basic assumption about inherent evil since the characters in *Lord* are too immature and lack the necessary skills to demonstrate true human potential. *Tunnel in the Sky,* on the other hand, features older boys who are more familiar with the adult world and thus, because of their maturity and self-sacrifice, are able to overcome challenges even greater than those faced by the boys in *Lord*. Golding, McGiveron concludes, set up the boys in *Lord* to fail by making them too young, thereby skewing the results of his thought experiment.

One of the challenges readers face when engaging with critical commentary is contextualizing any given critique within ongoing critical conversations. Oftentimes critics frame their arguments in response to other critical interpretations, and without knowledge of this larger discussion, readers glean only a partial understanding of the conversation, potentially resulting in incomplete, flawed, or unoriginal interpretations. Unfortunately, when it comes to well-known and frequently discussed classics such as *Lord of the Flies*, the sheer volume of critical commentary can make it difficult for even the most studious researcher to develop a full sense of the critical conversation. The first four essays in the critical readings section provide essential, succinct overviews of the most significant and substantial critical articles addressing *Lord of the Flies*. Robert C.

Evans begins with a thorough summary of the critical commentary on *Lord*, both academic and in the popular press, during the first fifteen years after the novel's publication—the height of its popularity. Evans catalogues, among other elements, aspects of *Lord* reviewers praised or critiqued; the numerous literary works with which *Lord* has been compared; significant analyses of the novel's characters, setting, and language; possible interpretations and meanings; key symbols and themes; and discussions of the book's craft and artistic merit.

Evans's chapter offers readers insight into *Lord*'s rise to critical popularity while the next chapter, by Sarah Fredericks, summarizes the following twenty years of criticism (1970-1989) during which *Lord* fell into relative obscurity, at least in the United States. Fredericks's chapter, like Evans's, offers a chronological overview of major critical articles (or book chapters later published as stand-alone essays) on *Lord*. Some of the articles Fredericks discusses challenged previous criticism, especially those that critiqued *Lord* as an oversimplified allegory; some assessed the then-current state of declining interest in Golding's most famous work; and still others offered new interpretations of *Lord*, many of which attempted to highlight its continuing relevance as the twentieth century came to a close. The third and final essay in the trilogy of summaries of critical articles, by Kelley Jeans, summarizes critical articles from the last decade of the twentieth century and the first decade of the twenty-first. Jeans's overview reveals three key trends: (1) increased critical comparisons between *Lord* and literature and myths of the ancient world, (2) renewed attacks against what some critics saw as racist or imperialist agendas in *Lord*, and (3) repeated attempts to reinvigorate critical interest in *Lord* by applying various theories to the text. Even as interest in *Lord* within the English-speaking world continued to decline, Jeans concludes, the novel nevertheless enjoys sustained critical interest outside America and especially in the United Kingdom.

Although most literary criticism on *Lord* is written in the English language, there is nevertheless a significant number of critical essays on Golding's most famous novel that are written in languages other than English. Unfortunately, monolingual English speakers have little access to these articles, as few are offered in translation. The fourth essay in the critical readings section, by Grace Chen, summarizes some of the most significant articles on *Lord* written in foreign languages including Spanish, German, and French. Offering readers a thematic sampling of international criticism, Chen outlines varied pedagogical, theoretical, historical, and biographical approaches to *Lord*. Chen observes two noteworthy trends: first, the frequency with which Simon, his death, and his role as a savior figure is analyzed; and, second, enduring critical interest in the form, genre, and structure of *Lord*. This chapter offers readers insight into how *Lord* has been introduced to new audiences and discussed critically around the world.

It is difficult to discuss the character Piggy without mentioning his weight (after all, his name in the novel constantly calls to mind his obesity). The next chapter, by Robert C. Evans, closely examines the novel's treatment of Piggy's fat body, both in the ways that Ralph and other characters disparage it as well as the frequency with which the narrator references it. Evans challenges the assertion that *Lord* censures such prejudicial contempt for overweight people. In fact, Evans argues, the narrator frequently participates in denigrating Piggy, a fact which complicates a frequent critical claim that the narrator portrays Piggy as a "hero." The novel's near-constant mockery of an obese child can make *Lord* difficult to read or teach, but Evans encourages readers to probe the rhetorical intentions behind Golding's choice to make readers uncomfortable.

In 1954, two novels were published with similar titles: Golding's *Lord of the Flies* and J. R. R. Tolkien's *The Lord of the Rings*. Nick Groom explores connections between these novels, their themes, critical reception, readership, and authors, especially within the context of postwar England and its literary and cultural movements. Groom highlights further connections between Golding's and Tolkien's bodies of work, including Golding's *The Inheritors*, *Circle under the Sea*, and *Darkness Visible*, and Tolkien's *The Lost Road*. Whereas Groom considers *Lord of the Flies* in connection to its literary contemporaries, in the next chapter Christopher Baker analyzes the film adaptations of *Lord* by Peter Brook (1963) and Harry Hook (1990) in relation to Golding's text. Contrasting the two films' divergent visions and social commentary, Baker argues that Brook's black-and-white, documentary-style film evokes the novel's rich symbolism and pervading dreadfulness of human nature while Hook's prismatic, plot-driven film hearkens back to R. M. Ballantyne's adventure novel *The Coral Island*. This distinction between symbolic and metaphoric interpretations is most evident, Baker argues, in the two films' differing depictions of Simon's death.

While it is generally accepted that *Lord* demonstrates characteristics typical of a dystopian work of fiction, few scholars have done more than assign it a cursory label as such. In the next chapter, Joan-Mari Barendse closely reads the novel to determine whether *Lord*, as a dystopia (or *bad place*), qualifies as a *classical dystopia*, in which there is no hope for fundamentally transforming the society, or as *critical dystopia*, in which the society can potentially change into a *eutopia* (or *good place*) or at the very least feature a eutopian enclave. Barendse analyses various symbols of hope in *Lord*, such as the conch shell and Piggy's glasses, and questions whether the arrival of the naval officer at the novel's conclusion offers the boys true rescue from their dystopia. Next, the penultimate chapter of this volume offers readers the rare opportunity to engage directly with foreign language criticism on *Lord*. Gérard Klaus translates and updates his 1984 article "Jeu et Sacré dans *Lord of the Flies* de William Golding." Questioning Golding's own claims about good and evil in the novel, Klaus closely examines patterns of play and the treatment of fun and games. Klaus argues that the disintegration of society on the island and the boys' ultimate rejection of law and order is actually a "natural" regression to a primordial state, granting them primitive access to the sacred. In the final chapter in the critical readings section, Eric Wilson, like Klaus, expands upon earlier work, here exploring the ways in which *Lord* functions as political and religious drama and satirizes Thomas Hobbes's *Leviathan* (1651). Society and morality in *Lord,* Wilson asserts, are fundamentally destabilized by social and existential envy, and Wilson attributes the failure of the boys' fledgling democracy to Piggy's function as a double.

THE BOOK
AND
AUTHOR

On *Lord of the Flies*: Representations of Violence-Induced Trauma

Stephan Schaffrath

"Today the existence of our species and of all life on this planet may depend on our not just seeing but knowing and controlling the beast called war—and the beast within each of us." (Grossman 95)

As William Golding's first and perhaps best-known novel, *Lord of the Flies* is a staple in many Western high school humanities curricula. My own first encounter with the novel was as a teenager, when I was assigned the work in my German high school, where I read it in translation. Without doubt, since its debut in 1954, *Lord of the Flies* has affected many a young mind across many nations and cultures. With violence not abating but rather on the rise in the real world, Golding's fictitious treatise of the primordial evil that lurks in all of us is still very much relevant and pertinent, and it may never lose its relevance. A closer look at Golding's first work betrays the author's uncanny grasp of the nature of violence as it occurs in the real world, especially in circumstances of warfare. A comparison of the treatment of violence and ensuing trauma as it is depicted in *Lord of the Flies* with what noted academics and other experts have written about violence-induced trauma sheds renewed light on the relevance and applicability of Golding's work.

As a British Navy veteran of World War II, Golding was no stranger to the terrors of willful violence. He knew death and understood what the act of killing entailed. This novel was crafted with the relatively fresh memory of the horrors of war, less than a decade after the close of World War II. *Lord of the Flies* is unambiguously about violence. The overall circumstance of the novel is war. The narrative is set in the not-so-distant future of the novel's year of creation, 1954. Young boys find themselves stranded on a tropical island. Through conversations between some of the children, we can piece together that they had been evacuated by plane after a nuclear attack on their homeland in Britain. When their plane eventually came under attack as well, the pilot released the passenger cabin (a technical detail that places the novel slightly in the science fiction genre). Said passenger cabin then crash-landed on the island. The cabin leaves behind what Golding calls the *scar*, apparently the area where the cabin tore through the island's lush vegetation, but the cabin itself is not found. It must have been dragged out to sea by natural forces, conceivably by a parachute, which had also enabled its relatively soft landing. Notably, the novel's general circumstance is war, an occasion of state-decreed violence, typically on a large scale. Soon, the idyllic peacefulness of their new location, a wondrous tropical island that supplies plentiful fruit from unidentified trees, turns into a locale of violence as well. It all begins arguably harmlessly with the children claiming possession of the island, in tradition with what generations of grown-up Britons have done before them.

There is some violence among the children early on, most notably the verbal and psychological abuse that one overweight boy is subjected to. The next level of violence is against nature by means of burning large swaths of the island's vegetation, albeit somewhat by accident. The children's thirst for violence and domination quickly evolves into violence against the island's wild pig population, which is hunted for food, despite the easy reach of several plant-based forms of nutrition and some easily picked sea creatures. The hunters of animals then evolve (or devolve) into hunters of humans, specifically those humans who do not readily subject themselves to the will of the boy who becomes the island's tyrant, Jack. After at least two children's deaths and a large forest fire, the crew of a British Navy cruiser takes notice of the island. They send a landing party that discovers the children and marvels at their savagery before taking them back to the better organized and more orderly savagery of the grown-ups' war. The British Navy arrives just in time to end the most gruesome and willful murder of one child by other children. The ending begs the question: "And who will rescue the adult and his cruiser?" (Epstein 204).

The novel lends itself beautifully to a violence-themed plot summary, as I just attempted here. However, it is the way in which

Golding describes and builds the circumstances of violence that drives the narrative. It is that lens of a man who knows what it is like when the civilized part of us makes way for the primordial forces that lurk in all of humanity. It is tempting to give in to a Freudian reading that discusses the representations of the id, superego, and ego in this novel. And, with so much violence against Mother Nature, an ecocritical or ecofeminist reading seems appropriate as well. But there is more to it. This novel warrants more than a merely theoretical discussion of human mores. As an active participant in World War II, William Golding is what Karl Marlantes would call an initiate in the "Temple of Mars," someone who has stepped over the threshold that separates the few from the many.

One of the novel's earliest critics, E. L. Epstein, already picked up on this work's symbolic nature (204). *Lord of the Flies* is essentially a theoretical narrative that is nevertheless based on what happens in real-life violent situations. Golding's keen eye for the chaos of war keeps us well grounded in the here-and-now of flesh-and-blood humanity. It is an interesting thought experiment about what would happen if preadolescent boys were left to their own devices, with sufficient fresh water and food but no adult supervision or even any instructions or any immediate prospects for rescue. It is also a book about growing up, a story depicting aspects of developmental psychology, in a shockingly concrete manner. And, because of its symbolic yet highly concrete nature, it informs us of human nature in general.

How People Become Killers and the Trauma of Killing

David Grossman is well known in military and other security-related professional circles for his work on the psychology of killing, what he terms *killology*. One of Grossman's most interesting findings is that almost all humans have an innate and fierce resistance to killing, regardless of the circumstances. Even in combat, when soldiers face an armed enemy and when they are sanctioned by their own government to take other people's lives, the vast majority either do not fire their weapons or simply just pretend to fire them at the enemy; that is, until modern armies developed ways to condition soldiers to kill. Weapons training alone is not enough to make most ordinary people into killers on the battlefield, and much less so outside of situations that involve state-sanctioned violence. However, most people can be conditioned by rigorous drills to fire a deadly weapon at another human being or even to apply the more gruesome methods of closeup killing that involve stabbing, slashing, and breaking parts of another human's body. Grossman also warns us of how modern media (in particular shooter-style video games) can inadvertently condition especially young people to become killers, and without any of the safeguards that military training builds into its training programs.

In the case of the boys on the island, readers at first witness playful and fairly harmless reenactments of warlike situations, such as when Ralph pretends to be "a fighter-plane, with wings swept back, and machine-gunned Piggy," the one obese boy on the island and the one main character whose real name remains elusive to us (11). Soon after, some of the older boys set out in the vein of conquerors to take possession of the island: "they savored their right of domination" (29). This conquest game is arguably a result of the type of conditioning a British schoolboy in the 1950s would have received as part of his formal education, considering that postcolonial critique was still not part of mainstream sentiments in that era. Having recently vanquished the evil axis powers of World War II, Britain—despite its less-than-spotless human rights record as a colonial power—must have seemed a largely benevolent force to the majority of Britons at the time. Nostalgia for the slowly disintegrating British Empire would not have been met with quite as many frowns as today.

But Golding understood that Britons were far less than innocent. Golding's cynical attitude towards his fellow countrymen would not have been shared by many of his contemporaries, though. According to Golding, writing *Lord of the Flies* "was simply what seemed to be sensible . . . after the war, when everybody was thanking God they weren't Nazis. And I'd seen and thought enough to realize that every single one of us could be Nazis" (qtd. in Biles 3). So, taking possession of an uninhabited island, as harmless and even as necessary as it may seem under the circumstances, is in truth a step towards violence, since one must defend one's dominion, with deadly force if necessary. More importantly, the boys are exerting their will upon what is presented to readers as a virgin paradise, an idyllic and pristine piece of nature.

Early on, Jack, the leader of the choirboys and eventually the island's tyrant, expresses his faith and pride in his nationality, when the children establish sets of rules: "After all, we're not savages. We're English, and the English are best at everything" (42). This sense of British cultural superiority is echoed by the Navy officer who discovers the children at the end of the novel: "I should have thought that a pack of British boys—you're all British, aren't you?—would have been able to put up a better show than that" (201-2). In short, even though the young boys are not conditioned to be killers, their upbringing in British society at the time would have conditioned them to think of themselves as superior to other nationalities, to believe themselves virtually immune to savagery, to impose their interests on nature without a second thought, and to readily lay claim to foreign territory. Golding was less than sympathetic towards those who thought themselves better than others, simply because they were British: "I could listen to people talking about 'bloody Nazis,' people who I knew *were* Nazis. Do you see, they were in fact Nazis; only they didn't happen to live in the Nazi social system" (qtd. in Biles 35-6).

The aforementioned education and cultural influences are not sufficient to make the boys into killers, though. In fact, there are several instances when their upbringing keeps them from willfully hurting one another. The most telling and simultaneously disturbing example is when Roger, the most sadistic of Jack's hunters, stalks one of the younger boys, but eventually catches himself before hurting him (60-2). In the absences of the military-style conditioning that produces efficient killers, the boys however undergo stages that slowly drive them closer and closer to that same end. Grossman explains that in addition to the commonly noted "fight-or-flight model to stress in combat" another two possible reactions can be seen in both animal and human behavior: "When we examine the responses of creatures confronted with aggression from their own species, the set of options expands to include posturing and submission" (5). In *Lord of the Flies* readers can see all four, which is another indication of Golding's insight and initiation to the world of lethal combat. The fight-or-flight response is perhaps best represented by Ralph's reaction to Jack when he engages in a spear fight with his nemesis (177) and then shortly after hides and eventually flees across the island away from the newly formed tribe. Still, there are other examples, in particular the ones involving the imagined beast of the island. Posturing plays an even bigger role. Early on, Jack and his choirboys-turned-pig-hunters put on a show of how fierce they are. In fact, posturing has its genesis before the narrative begins, as much of Jack's power is derived from his status as the leader of the paramilitarylike choir who march "in step in two parallel lines" (19). Moreover, Piggy and presumably several other boys are quickly "intimidated by [Jack's] uniformed superiority" (21). Once on the island, Jack's choir quickly transforms into Jack's hunters and eventually Jack's henchmen and most likely then Jack's murderous mob, although the last stance is somewhat based on conjecture because of the deus-ex-machina-style appearance of the British naval officer that puts an end to Jack's "game." We never find out exactly what Jack intended to do to Ralph with the "stick sharpened at both ends," although readers must surely remember that the head of the first killed pig was impaled and propped up on exactly such a stick. At any rate, Golding at one points goes out of his way to tell readers that Jack's choir "wore the remains of a black cap and ages ago they stood in two demure rows and their voices had been the songs of angels," which is surely a thinly veiled reference to the fallen angels of Judeo-Christian tradition (133). Are readers to think that the choirboys turned into little devils?

As part of that transformation and as an essential aspect of posturing, Jack's followers always carry spears and later paint their faces to appear more warriorlike, which give them the appearance of "anonymous devils' faces" (181). This posturing is no different from what violence-bent political regimes do when they put on grandiose military parades or pump footage of live-fire military exercises through popular media. In a best case scenario, such posturing serves as a means to avert actual violence, which is typically a good thing. Posturing can also be used to intimidate and psychologically weaken one's adversary. Posturing "actions are designed to convince an opponent, through both sight and sound, that the posturer is a dangerous and frightening adversary" (Grossman 6). Submission in *Lord of the Flies* is best exemplified when the twins Sam and Eric submit to Jack's demand that they leave Ralph and join his tribe, a decision which quite possibly saved their lives, although it comes with negative mental and physical consequences.

Another example of posturing in *Lord of the Flies* are "mock battles," as Grossman refers to them (6), when the boys play hunting. In fact, when one of the boys, Robert, plays the part of the pig, the other boys become so excited that Robert falls victims to the other boys' rising enthusiasm for inflicting pain. Robert is almost killed. Even Ralph, who is not part of Jack's hunters, succumbs to the temptation:

> Ralph, carried away by a sudden thick excitement, grabbed Eric's spear and jabbed at Robert with it.
> "Kill him! Kill him!"
> All at once, Robert was screaming and struggling with the strength of frenzy. Jack had him by the hair and was brandishing his knife. Behind him was Roger, fighting to get close. The chant rose ritually, as at the last moment of a dance or a hunt.
> "Kill the pig! Cut his throat! Kill the pig! Bash him in!"
> Ralph too was fighting to get near, to get a handful of that brown, vulnerable flesh. The desire to squeeze and hurt was over-mastering. (Golding 114-5)

After this "game" the boys discuss how to enhance their experience for the next time to "do it properly." Roger suggests a real pig as a victim, and Jack jokes that one of the little boys would do as well (115). This mock battle or hunting game starts out as a form of entertainment, but it quickly turns into a tool for desensitization from the innate as well as trained inhibitions that keep the children from doing harm to their fellow human beings. However, the boys quickly discover that the excitement that comes from violence can be intoxicating.

Grossman (a psychologist), Marlantes (a Vietnam War Marine Corp veteran), and Hedges as well as Junger (both war correspondents) report that excitement is part of deadly violence, and it is often what makes it so dangerous to victims, perpetrators, and bystanders alike. It should be noted here that all four writers warn of the immense psychological dangers of putting especially young adults into circumstances in which they are expected to kill other human beings.

Grossman tells us how those who kill in combat experience the "exhilaration stage," which is followed first by the "remorse stage" and then by the "rationalization and acceptance stage." Although this is obviously a gross simplification of the complex psychological processes that are at the basis of how well a combat participant may or may not readjust to life in peaceful society, it shows us that exhilaration is a common and even natural first response to killing (233-47). One may argue with whether or not one should feel bad about experiencing this type of emotional reaction after killing an animal or another human being. Regardless of the should and ought of the matter, it is important to know that this response is not out of the ordinary. Karl Marlantes, who is the only one of the four who has actually killed other human beings in combat, explains his own emotional experience after killing: "When I was fighting—and by fighting I mean a situation very different from launching a cruise missile—either I felt nothing at all or I felt exhilaration akin to scoring the winning touchdown" (26). He further responds to people who tell him how he should have felt: "And it makes me angry when people lay on me what I ought to have felt. More important, it obscures the truth. What I feel now, forty years later, is sadness" (27). And he above all understands the complexity of these difficult situations, as he walks his readers through the minutiae of one particular combat example (27-30). He then elaborates: "Suppose it was one of my sons, Peter or Alex, trapped, filled with fears as these huge American Marines, known to be ruthless, even crazy, came relentlessly from out of the jungle, swarming up the hill, killing his friends in their holes around him" (31). Marlantes's honesty is refreshing, instructive, and terrifying all at the same time. Considering the complex circumstances of combat, his own emotional response after all these years is perhaps the most appropriate: "Oh, the sadness [. . .] And, oh, the grief of evil in the world to which I contributed" (31). Marlantes continues to explain that sadness is an important ingredient in his own healing of these old wounds over several decades (32).

Hedges, a longtime war correspondent and an experienced observer of deadly violence, echoes Marlantes's thoughts: "However much soldiers regret killing once it is finished, however much they spend their lives trying to cope with the experience, the act itself, fueled by fear, excitement, the pull of the crowd, and the god-like exhilaration of destroying is often thrilling" (171). Sebastian Junger, another war correspondent, puts the allure of combat (i.e., deadly violence) this way:

> "Combat isn't where you might die—though that does happen—it's where you find out whether you get to keep on living. Don't underestimate the power of that revelation. Don't underestimate the things young men will wager in order to play that game one more time." (144-45).

It seems that it is not by coincidence that Golding's thought experiment is about children at play. And when the group of boys decide on which games are most exciting, hunting, playing castle, and warrior tribe easily win over building shelters and keeping the signal fire going. Considering the male-dominated nature of this discourse, it would be fascinating to see a similar thought experiment with preadolescent girls unfold on a writer's pages.

Another thing that the early Golding critic and mentor Epstein picked up on was the way in which the hunters' killing of a sow is described "in terms of sexual intercourse" (206). And it is no coincidence that this and other pseudosexual acts that the novel describes are all acts of violence, to a degree that the term *sexual intercourse* is misleading, beginning with the passenger cabin that plows a "scar" into the virgin forest, shortly prenarrative. Sexual assault is never really sexuality; it is about thrills derived from power and domination, not unlike the exhilaration that killing may elicit. The threatening nature or perversity of such violence, especially in context with prepubescent sexuality, in this novel is shockingly apparent. "In developmental psychology there is a general understanding that an individual must master the twin areas of sexuality and aggression (Freud's Eros and Thanatos) in order to have truly achieved adulthood. In the same way, the maturation of the human race necessitates our collective mastery of the two areas" (Grossman xxiv). Jack, who is one of the most physical among the boys, has not even begun to figure this out yet, although he seems to be the one who experiences most intensely what violence does to the violent. When Jack and his hunters come upon a sow, who, "sunk in deep maternal bliss . . . was fringed with a row of piglets," the boys manage to severely wound her and take chase upon her. Then "the sow staggered her way ahead of them, bleeding and mad, and the hunters followed, wedded to her lust, excited by the long chase and the dropped blood." Finally, Roger with a spear and Jack with his knife take center stage in this tragic scene (143-5). The ambiguous language that queasily marries meanings of violence with that of sexuality are without doubt intentional:

> Roger found a lodgment for his point and began to push till he was leaning with his whole weight. The spear moved forward inch by inch and the terrified squealing became a high-pitched scream. Then Jack found the throat and the hot blood spouted over his hands. The sow collapsed under them and they were heavy and fulfilled upon her. (135)

And to rob any of his readers of any notions or illusions that this was just about hunting for food, Golding adds the following language:

> Roger began to withdraw his spear and boys noticed it for the first time. Robert stabilized the thing in a phrase which was received uproariously.
> "Right up her ass!" (135).

Instead of simply securing another food source, these preadolescent boys descend into a very disturbing place within the human psyche. They engage in what amounts to gang rape, bestiality, and something that certainly must have felt like murder. Yes, the victim was a *mere* animal, but among hunters there are rules to spare mothers whose young depend on them, against bestiality, and against an animal's unnecessary suffering. Golding clearly suggests that young boys are capable of what amounts to an atrocity. And, let us not forget that this novel was published in the 1950s, long before the age of depictions of gratuitous violence in the media.

Decades later, Grossman wrote about the ranges of killing, postulating that the closer the range of killing, the more severe the traumatic effects on the person who engages in the act of killing. "It has long been understood that there is a direct relationship between the empathic and physical proximity of the victim, and the resultant difficulty and trauma of the kill. This concept has fascinated and concerned soldiers, poets, philosophers, anthropologists, and psychologists alike" (97). Beyond the "hand-to-hand combat range" where "resistance to bayoneting or stabbing becomes tremendously intense" there is "the macabre region at the extreme end of the scale, where sex and killing intermingle"—killing at "sexual range" (98). The penetration of the animal's anus, the spilling of bodily fluid (blood, in this case), and the postclimactic collapse on top of the dead victim/object-of-desire are clear indications of what Golding was driving at, long before psychologists tackled this subject in their discourse. Ironically, the event that caused the children's evacuation from the British homeland in the first place, a nuclear weapon attack, ranks at the opposite end of the killing distance spectrum, where traumatic effect on the killers are least significant, unless perhaps they are later meaningfully confronted with the evidence of what horrors they wrought.

Pigs prove no longer sufficient as prey shortly thereafter. At least two of the boys who were stranded on the island become victims of homicide. There is a third boy (the one with the mulberry birthmark on his face) who apparently perishes in the first human-made forest fire early in the novel. The first properly recorded homicide happens by accident or by mistake, although it is unclear to what extent the killers actually knew what they were doing. Simon, initially one of the choirboys, is the only child who discovers the true identity of the monster, or "the beast," that haunts the island. First, Simon experiences a vision that shows him that the true beast is within each of us (143). Later, he further discovers that what some of the boys have identified as one or *the* monster was in fact the remains of a dead pilot whose body was still connected to a parachute that jerked his lifeless limbs with each squall of wind. When Simon rushes to the beach to tell the others about his discovery, he happens to catch them at the end of a pig-feasting-induced ritualistic hunter dance that quickly turns into a Dionysian orgy of violence.[1] Simon finds himself in the middle of the frenzy and is quickly misidentified as the beast itself:

> The beast [i.e., Simon] struggled forward, broke the ring and fell over the steep edge of the rock to the sand by the water. At once the crowd surged after it, poured down the rock, leapt on to the beast, screamed, struck, bit, tore. There were no words, and no movements but the tearing of teeth and claws. (153)

Some of Golding's words suggest that the killing of the beast/ the murder of Simon may have included acts of cannibalism. Yet again, unlike the battles of the grown-up (i.e., nuclear attacks and aerial battles), readers are confronted with an example of killing at "sexual range." And the tantric dancing and chanting that helped put the boys into a trancelike state that facilitated (if not conditioned) killing, again allude to primal and even sexual motives.

The second homicide is the first and only clear case of conscious murder of another human being. When Roger "with a sense of delirious abandonment" dislodges a boulder from the Castle Rock and watches it deal a blow to Piggy, who then falls down the cliffs onto rocks in the churning sea (180-1), readers are not faced with the disturbing details of killing within "sexual range." However, with the range still being fairly close—perhaps at "handgrenade range" or "close range" on the Grossman scale (112-7)—and, more importantly, as a case of premeditated murder, the boys have now moved on to another level of killing conditioning. Consciously and willfully killing another human being is no longer just a fantasy. Immediately after Piggy's death, Jack does not even hesitate to "viciously, with full intent" throw a spear at Ralph. Jack has clearly moved beyond a game of posturing. And, if the naval officer had not shown up on the island, readers are to assume that Jack and his tribe would indeed have killed Ralph with clear intent and in the most brutal way.

Many things have led to this point of homicide, starting with seemingly innocent child's play on the beach and what British society taught the boys about certain peoples' domination over another (i.e., Eurocentric imperialism), with little discussion on the ethics of such practices and histories. And, early on, all the boys apply societal preferences for body aesthetics to rationalize their constant harassment of Piggy for his large size and his asthma. None of them even bothers to find out his real name. This and the repeated threats and abuse by Jack slowly but surely lead to Piggy's eventual death. He is the perfect "other." It has been common practice to make one's enemies an *other* to make it easier to kill them. Cultural, societal, political, racial, and other types of acts of ostracizing and marginalization contribute to the psychological illusion of the enemy as someone less than human, which in turn reduces one's innate inhibition to kill that no-longer-person (Grossman 148-70). "This dissociation of one's enemy from humanity is a kind of pseudospeciation. You make a false species out of the other human" (Marlantes 40-1). Another important factor in killing in *Lord of the Flies* is the phenomenon of anonymity and group absolution (Grossman 151). When Jack's tribal members all paint their faces and style their messy long hair in the same way, there is no longer an individual who can be held accountable for their collective deeds. This group dynamic further decreases individual inhibitions to violence.

Conclusions—An Aftermath Untold
The website for the magazine *Psychology Today* explains trauma in practical, easily accessible, and professionally vetted terms:

"Psychological trauma may set in after a distressing or life-threatening event. Sufferers may develop extreme anxiety or PTSD, or they may have ongoing problems with relationships and self-esteem" ("Trauma"). Although Golding tells us a little bit about the kids' anxiety, especially the littluns who seem to suffer from constant nightmares, the true aftermath of the horrors that transpired in a relatively short period of time is left to the readers' imagination. After Simon is killed when the group mistakes him for the "beast," there is the inception of psychological quasitherapy when Piggy and Ralph discuss the unmentionable details of that night. Ralph, who took part in what Golding suggests was an atrocity, insists to Piggy that they had better not ignore what happened, that they need to deal with it:

> "You didn't see what they did—"
> "Look, Ralph. We got to forget this. We can't do no good thinking about it, see?"
> "I'm frightened. Of us. I want to go home. Oh God. I want to go home." (157)

Ralph realizes that they are in dire need of rescue, and not just from being stranded on an island far away from British civilization. They need to be rescued from what they have become.

There is little indication that the boys will receive the type of therapeutic help that they require. Ralph's emotions pour out when the naval officer arrives, although the officer turns away from Ralph to give him and the others "time to pull themselves together" (202). This does not seem helpful for the children's emotional recovery from trauma. Grossman tells us that American World War II soldiers benefited from spending weeks together with their units on the sea voyage home from their respective places of combat, as they were able to digest together what they had experienced together (288-9). Since their homes were destroyed by a nuclear weapon, and since the grown-up warrior struggles to understand the depth of Ralph's emotional trauma, Ralph in particular may never return to normalcy, either physically or psychologically.

Still, readers may find solace in *Lord of the Flies*. Kate Rowley, a high school English teacher, tells us that Golding's work brings solace to many of her "high-needs" students who can relate to the hardships and violence the novel depicts (10). Golding's work endures as valuable insight into some of the less appetizing recesses of our humanity. It may not offer tangible solutions, but it continues to make us aware of our frailties, so that we may stumble less.

Note
1. See Mark Roncace for an insightful discussion on Dionysian elements in *Lord of the Flies*.

Works Cited

Biles, Jack I. *Talk: Conversations with Golding*. Harcourt Brace Jovanovich, 1970.

Epstein, E. L. "Notes on *Lord of the Flies*." *Lord of the Flies*, by William Golding. Perigee, 1954, pp. 203-8.

Golding, William. *Lord of the Flies*. Perigee, 1954.Grossman, David. *On Killing: The Psychological Cost of Learning to Kill in War and Society*. Revised edition. Back Bay, 2009.

Hedges, Chris. *War Is a Force That Gives Us Meaning*. Anchor Books, 2003.

Johnston, Arnold. *Of Earth and Darkness: The Novels of William Golding*. U of Missouri P, 1980.

Junger, Sebastian. *War*. Twelve, 2010.

Marlantes, Karl. *What It Is Like to Go to War*. Atlantic Monthly, 2011.

Redpath, Philip. Preface. *William Golding: A Structuralist Reading of His Fiction*. Vision and Barnes & Noble, 1986, pp. 9-10.

Roncace, Mark. "*The Bacchae* and *Lord of the Flies*." *Classical and Modern Literature*, vol. 18, 1997, pp. 37-51.

Rowley, Kate. "Coming of Age in the United States: A Case for Differentiating Curriculum as a Response to Trauma." *California English*, vol. 22, no. 1, Sept. 2016, pp. 10-11. EBSCO*host*, proxy-iup.klnpa.org/login?url=http://search.ebscohost.com/login.aspx?direct=true&db=eue&AN=117833221&site=ehost-live.

"Trauma." *Psychology Today*, 19 Apr. 2017, https://www.psychologytoday.com/basics/ trauma

---

William Golding: A Life of Contradictions____

Courtney Lane

William Gerald Golding was born on September 19, 1911, in Cornwall, England, the second and final child (after brother Joseph) of Alec and Mildred Golding. Alec was a schoolteacher by trade, a profession that seems to have influenced his sons, each of whom became teachers themselves. Mildred, six years older than her husband, was a suffragist.

The Goldings were progressive in their political and religious views, unabashedly "atheist, socialist, and rationalist" (Smith). They deplored the class distinctions endemic in British society. Mildred and Alec shared a passion for music (both were talented at a variety of instruments including the piano, viola, and flute), and Golding inherited it as well: His proficiency at piano while at Oxford was enough to merit a potential career as a professional musician.

In September 1921, Golding began his education at Marlborough Grammar School, where Alec taught. His gift for music, passed down from Alec and Mildred, began to blossom, and he began an intense study of the piano. It is also during this time that he began his first efforts at writing—poetry—and copied out several of his compositions in his diary.

After he turned nineteen in the fall of 1930, Golding was accepted into Oxford, with a plan to study botany (an appeasement to his scientifically minded father) at Brasenose. Instead, he spent most of his time in Oxford's bookshops and concert halls, indulging his two true passions of writing and music. After his fifth term, in the spring of 1932, he was "sent down" (temporarily expelled) for his almost complete lack of work towards his botany degree. It was then determined that Golding should return to Oxford and take the final part of his science examination (he passed) before changing his course of study to English literature. Even these studies, which would seem to be tailor-made for Golding's interest in writing, did not truly pique his interest, and his work towards his degree was perfunctory.

Golding had continued to write poetry off and on through college, and a friend recommended some of his poems to a Macmillan editor, who agreed to publish them in the Macmillan's Contemporary Poets series. W. G. Golding's *Poems* was published in fall of 1934. Golding was disappointed that this achievement got so little notice and wondered whether writing was really the career for him. He pondered life as an actor or as a professional pianist, but ended up taking a teaching position at Michael Hall in 1935, likely garnered through the auspices of a friend (Carey 64).

Golding's early career as a teacher showed him to be ineffective and apathetic. He became casually engaged to Mollie Evans, a girl he had known in high school and idealized in some of his early poetry. Spurred by his concerns about earning a living to support a family, he decided to return to Oxford for a teaching qualification, which he completed in the summer of 1938. He then secured a teaching job at Maidstone Grammar School, where his musical ability and published poetry gave him a certain status.

As 1938 progressed, the potential for war with Hitler and Germany became more and more likely. Golding joined several political groups, where he met Ann Brookfield, whose left-wing politics and razor-sharp intelligence were a match for his own. Golding wrote in an unpublished manuscript later in life: "I ditched the girl I was going to marry and married Ann instead" (qtd. in Carey 76). They married on September 30, 1939, only five months after their first meeting.

Their first few months of marriage were difficult for the Goldings: Ann became pregnant, and Golding lost his teaching position at Maidstone Grammar School, almost certainly for alcoholism (Smith). Luckily he was recommended by a friend for a teaching post at Bishop Wordsworth's School, where he started in April 1940. The Goldings' son, David, was born on September 9, 1940. The boy was somewhat sickly and suffered from a club foot, a condition that was eventually medically corrected.

World War II had a profound impact on Golding's life; he joined the Navy in December 1940, trained in weapons and minesweeping, and took part in the D-Day invasion of Normandy. He commanded a bombing ship at the Battle of Walcheren against one of Hitler's strongholds in Belgium, and while the outcome of the battle placed Walcheren in Allied hands, it left him shaken. "World War II was the turning point for me," Golding recalls, "I began to see what people were capable of doing" (qtd. in Lambert). In August 1945, Golding was demobilized and released from service.

When he returned to his teaching post at Bishop Wordsworth's School, he also returned to a larger family than he had left; in July 1945, Ann had given birth to their daughter Judy. His sojourn at the school remained as unhappy as it had been before the war, being "neither a dedicated nor a gifted teacher," as a colleague put it (qtd. in Carey 115). However, his interactions with the students provided inspiration for his most seminal work, *Lord of the Flies*.

At this time Golding had begun writing in earnest, finishing three books, all of which were returned by the publishers to whom he sent them. Spurred by his time in the Navy, he also picked up hobby sailing and was rarely without a boat for family excursions. Both his naval combat and his sailing experiences would feature in multiple stories and books he later wrote.

The seed of *Lord of the Flies* grew from a conversation with Ann, discussing how the children had responded to island adventure tales such as *Treasure Island* and *The Swiss Family Robinson,* and pondering how a group of unsupervised children would behave if they were stranded on such an island. He wrote the book during school hours. According to his journal, Golding began writing the book in 1951 and completed it sometime during 1952 (Carey 150).

What follows is part of the legend of *Lord of the Flies*: It was rejected 21 times (Lambert) and relegated to the reject pile at Faber and Faber, where it was rescued by Charles Monteith, who had been at the company a scant month. Monteith contacted Golding in October 1953 to let him know that Faber and Faber were considering the book for publication. He and Golding collaborated closely on the suggested edits to the manuscript. It was the beginning of a lifelong friendship and working relationship between the two.

Faber and Faber formally accepted the book for publication in February 1954 and it was released on September 17 of that year. Although Monteith had not been able to excite much advance publicity for *Lord of the Flies*, it became an almost instant critical darling (although only a modest seller) upon its publication. It was accepted for American publication by Coward-McCann in April 1955.

In November 1954 Golding completed a draft of what would become his second published novel, *The Inheritors*. The novel, about a struggle between Neanderthal and *Homo sapiens* tribes, was published on September 16, 1955. Reviews were generally enthusiastic; Golding, however, was pessimistic and constantly concerned about sales numbers: He was desperate to be able to support himself entirely by writing so that he could give up teaching.

Golding struggled through several drafts of what would become *Pincher Martin*, about a sailor who survives the sinking of his ship. It was published on October 26, 1956, and the reviews seemed to justify Golding's insecurities about all of his writing: The book was generally panned by the press. However, Frank Kermode, an influential literary critic, lobbied hard for the book, calling it "greatly superior" to Golding's other novels (Carey 201). Published in America by Harcourt, Brace & Co. under the title *The Two Deaths of Christopher Martin*, the book rallied slightly from a strong *New Yorker* review, but sales of both *Pincher Martin* and *Lord of the Flies* remained sluggish, and *The Inheritors* had not been published in America at all.

Lord of the Flies won third prize in the International Fantasy Award in 1957 (the winner was Tolkien's *Lord of the Rings*). By then Golding was at work on the novel *Free Fall* (published October 23, 1959). As with *Pincher Martin*, reviews were generally negative; however, the book did very well in its first year of sales. To augment his income from book sales, Golding spent 1959 to 1961 as a book reviewer and literary journalist, making but little headway on a new novel (*The Spire,* published in 1964).

Golding and his family spent 1961 to 1962 in America, where Golding was writer-in-residence at Hollins College in Virginia and accepted lecture appointments all across the country. During this time Golding's work at last became popular and widely distributed in America.

Golding continued his streak of publishing with a collection of essays and reviews called *The Hot Gates* (1965), a novel titled *The Pyramid* (1967), and a film script called "The Jam" (never produced). But in 1969 his concerns lay with his household rather than his publisher: His son, David, suffered a nervous breakdown, prompting an increase in Golding's drinking. In 1971, Golding returned to Faber and Faber's publication list with *The Scorpion God*, a collection of three short novels. Also in 1971, Golding's daughter, Judy, married Terrell Carver, an American student at Oxford.

From 1971 to 1975, "Golding's creativity hibernated" (Carey 339). Finally, he returned to work on what would become *Darkness Visible*, published in 1979. Concurrently he worked on *Rites of Passage* (1980, which was awarded the Booker Prize for fiction), the first book in a trilogy; the subsequent books in the series were *Close Quarters* (1987) and *Fire Down Below* (1989). Between these titles he published *A Moving Target* (1982) and *The Paper Men* (1984).

Despite Golding's unfailing feelings of inadequacy in his writing, he had by then become regarded as part of the British literary elite. This accomplishment was validated by his being awarded the Nobel Prize for Literature in October 1983. His travels after winning the award spurred the writing of *An Egyptian Journal* (1985).

Despite his early deploring of class distinctions, Golding lobbied for a knighthood, which he received in 1988. It was 1993 before he started work on a new novel, having spent the intervening years traveling for pleasure and for speaking engagements. The novel he conceived would eventually be published as *The Double Tongue*. Unfortunately, that publication would be posthumous. Sometime in the early hours of June 19, 1993, Golding died at his home after attending a party with his family and a number of literary luminaries. Upon learning of his death, his wife, Ann, suffered a stroke from which she never fully recovered. Golding was buried in the cemetery at Bowkerchalke, and a memorial service was held November 20, 1993 at Salisbury Cathedral.

Ann died on January 1, 1995, and was buried beside her husband. *The Double Tongue* was published that summer and dedicated to Charles Monteith, who had died in May of that year. Now the man who had written *Lord of the Flies*, the woman who had encouraged it, and the publisher who had believed in it were gone.

Works Cited

Carey, John. *William Golding: The Man Who Wrote Lord of the Flies.* Free Press, 2009.

Lambert, Bruce. "William Golding Is Dead at 81; The Author of *Lord of the Flies*." *New York Times*, June 20, 1993, http://www.nytimes.com/learning/general/onthisday/bday/0919.html. Accessed Apr. 28, 2017.

Smith, Wendy. Review of *William Golding: The Man Who Wrote* Lord of the Flies, by John Carey. *Washington Post*, Aug. 1, 2010, http://www.washingtonpost.com/wp-dyn/content/article/2010/07/30/AR2010073002549.html. Accessed Apr. 30, 2017.

CRITICAL CONTEXTS

William Golding's *Lord of the Flies* in Historical Context_____

Brian Ireland

Many critics have explored the theme in *Lord of the Flies* (1954) of a group of children's descent from civilization to savagery; of a loss of innocence on an Edenic island, where a mysterious and fearful "beast" causes the children to divide into factions, with murderous outcomes. The novel is, though, multilayered and complex: its plot, characterization, symbolism, and themes invite analysis of opposing dualities such as Christianity and paganism, innocence and guilt, childhood and adulthood, civilization and anarchy, collectivism and individuality, and democratic values as opposed to tyranny. The context of the novel's production, release, and reception was the immediate post-World War II era and the Cold War clash of ideologies between East and West. Author William Golding had been a junior officer in the Royal Navy during the war and witnessed firsthand its violence and cruelty. These experiences caused him to ponder the origins of violence and humanity's capacity for good and evil. This essay will explore these ideas and make particular reference to the novel's historical context, in a period British poet W. H. Auden called the *Age of Anxiety*.

World War II
Auden's 1947 poem explored themes of identity, materialism, isolation, and anguish in the postwar world. It was Auden's response to a war that had exposed the fragility of civilized society and given vent to atrocities that were as epic in scale as they were in barbarism. Nazi Germany systematically rounded up millions of Jews from all over Europe and Russia, stripped them of their possessions, transported them in freight trains to concentration camps, and then murdered them with poison gas. Disease, malnutrition, and brutality accounted for those who initially survived the mass exterminations. Nazi tactics included bombing cities and targeted civilians in places

---

such as Guernica in 1937 during the Spanish Civil War. Rotterdam suffered similar treatment in April 1940 as German bombs blitzed the city center, killing hundreds. Later that year the Nazis subjected Coventry in England to aerial bombing and hundreds more were killed. From September 1940 to May 1941 the Germans blitzed British cities, killing thousands in London, Liverpool, Manchester, Cardiff, Belfast, Glasgow, and many other large urban centers. The Royal Air Force retaliated by developing a heavy bomber force, which would target dozens of German cities including Berlin, Hamburg, Cologne, Munich, Essen, Bremen, Kiel, and Mannheim. This onslaught of destruction culminated in the 1945 bombing of Dresden, an attack that destroyed the medieval city while killing at least 35,000 civilians, many of them refugees from the Russian drive eastwards (Grayling 259).

Civilians suffered in other ways: in 1942, the Nazis destroyed the Czech town of Lidice in reprisal for the assassination of a Nazi official. All men in the town were executed immediately and the women and children sent to concentration camps, where most died. A small few of the children were adopted by SS families for "Germanisation." Altogether, around 340 innocent civilians died as a result of the destruction of Lidice (Goshen 870-72). As the war turned against Nazi Germany, similar atrocities took place in a number of French towns, most infamously in June 1944 at Oradour-sur-Glane where approximately 640 civilians—the majority of whom were women and children—were murdered by members of an SS Panzer group (Hastings 185-98). In another notorious event, in March 1944 German troops executed more than 300 Italian civilians in Rome in retaliation for a deadly ambush by Italian partisans (Mikaberidze 24-5). These are indicative examples; many thousands of civilians lost their lives in similar retaliatory atrocities. Russian civilians were particularly vulnerable given Nazi ideology, which adjudged them as *Untermensch* (subhuman). Over 20 million Russians died in World War II, representing by far the biggest loss of life on the Allied side. Russian troops took their revenge on German civilians: Perhaps as many as two million women were raped as Russian troops rolled through Axis towns and cities in the war's final days, and in its immediate aftermath (Wheatcroft). German troops made prisoners of war by the Russians also suffered terribly: for example, only around six thousand of the 90,000 German troops captured at Stalingrad survived Russian incarceration to return home after the war (Roberts 134).

In the Pacific theater, casualties may have been fewer but the war was prosecuted just as fiercely: in 1941, Japanese Imperial forces killed more than 2000 American military personnel and civilians in a sneak attack on the American territory of Hawaii. In the war that followed, both sides committed atrocities. Perhaps because the Japanese lacked the ability to strike at the US mainland, their forces directed their anger and frustration at Allied troops and also towards the civilian populations of territories they conquered. Indeed, Japanese cruelty was one of the most notorious aspects of the war. For example, soon after the Pearl Harbor attack, the Japanese executed five America airmen captured after a raid on Tokyo. They tortured prisoners, used forced labor, and forced Korean women into acting as sex slaves for Japanese troops. A section of the military codenamed Unit 731 carried out lethal medical experiments on Chinese civilians and on prisoners of war (Dower 33-73). Japanese soldiers acted fanatically, carrying out suicidal attacks on their enemies, the most infamous being kamikaze attacks on US ships. Other suicidal attacks took place in the Aleutians and on Saipan. Both Japanese soldiers and civilians committed suicide in Okinawa rather than surrender to American forces. Japanese forces began and ended the war in the Philippines in barbaric fashion: in 1942, Japanese imperial forces captured approximately 75,000 American and Filipino troops on the Philippine island of Luzon. In what became known as the Bataan Death March, these troops were force-marched 65 miles to prison camps, with many thousands dying of exhaustion and dehydration, or killed by Japanese bayonets because they could not go on. When American troops retook the Philippines in 1945, perhaps 100,000 of capital city Manila's 700,000 population were killed in the fighting. During this period the Japanese Army tortured and murdered around 1,000 Christian hostages in an act referred to by one Filipino inhabitant as "soldiery gone mad with blood lust" (qtd. in Dower 45).

In turn, the actions of the Japanese fueled American hatred towards them. In the United States, beginning in early 1942, 110,000 Japanese-Americans were incarcerated in concentration camps (Dower 79-80). In ferocious battles on tiny islands in the Pacific, American troops mutilated Japanese bodies for souvenirs, attacked hospital ships, refused to take prisoners or shot prisoners of war, and shot Japanese civilians in what one historian has called a "war without mercy" (Dower 62-70). A Marine who fought on Okinawa reflected that the "fierce struggle for survival ... eroded the veneer of civilization and made savages of us all" (qtd. in Dower 63). US strategic bombing was no less merciless: in *The Fog of War* (2003) Robert S. McNamara, an officer in the US Air Force during the war and later US Defense Secretary during the Vietnam War, explained that from 1941-45, but before the atomic bombings of Hiroshima and Nagasaki, the American aerial bombing campaign against Japan killed "50 to 90 percent of the people of 67 Japanese cities." McNamara called the US-Japanese war "one of the most brutal wars in all of human history." And of course the war ended when President Harry Truman authorized the use of atomic bombs on two Japanese cities, killing immediately between 190,000 to 230,000 people in what remains the only use of such weapons in anger (Bradford 608).

Good and Evil

It was in this maelstrom that William Golding learned harsh lessons about war and about himself. Originally from Cornwall in England, Golding studied at Oxford, publishing a book of poetry while attaining his BA degree in English Literature. He married in 1939 and was a school teacher when the war broke out. His rural upbringing and gentle middle class background left him ill-prepared for the horrors of war. Nevertheless, he enlisted in the Royal Navy in December 1940, initially serving aboard HMS *Galatea* in the North Sea. After a short period of time aboard *Galatea*, during which he participated in the search for the German battleship *Bismarck*, Golding transferred to HMS *Wolverine*. This was a fortunate move: not long after, many of Golding's friends and ex-crewmates were killed when a German submarine sank the *Galatea* in the Mediterranean. HMS *Wolverine*'s main role was as an escort for Atlantic convoys—a hazardous and difficult mission, often undertaken in dreadful weather and harsh seas. Golding would later recall conditions onboard *Wolverine* as "cramped, crowded, and unavoidably liable to [lice] infestations" (qtd. in Carey 87). In October 1941, Golding was transferred to the Royal Naval Barracks at Portsmouth, where he survived a terrifying Luftwaffe bombing raid. Soon after, he successfully applied for an officer commission, eventually learning to pilot a troop landing craft. He took part in the Normandy landings in June 1944, and at Walcheren in the Netherlands, where his boat was one of only a few to survive an Allied assault on the heavily defended island (Reiff 27-8). As John Carey notes, "Memories of Walcheren haunted him for the rest of his life" (108).

Golding's war experiences caused him to question the roles of good and evil in the world, and to examine humanity's capacity for violence—two important themes of *Lord of the Flies*. He recalls his experiences at sea on the *Galatea* as "misery, humiliation and fear" (Carey 83) and he believed the lessons to be learned from war were about the nature of humanity rather than about nationalism and competing political or economic ideologies (Meitcke 2). "One had one's nose rubbed in the human condition," he explained (qtd. in Gindin 4), and he came to realize that both sides in the conflict were capable of terrible acts of violence and cruelty. These things, he explained, "were not done by the headhunters of New Guinea or by some primitive tribe in the Amazon. They were done skillfully, coldly, by educated doctors, lawyers, by men with a tradition of civilization behind them, to beings of their own kind." Man "produces evil," he concluded, "as a bee produces honey" (qtd. in Sandbrook 344). To use a biblical analogy, humanity was not an innocent in the garden, corrupted thereafter by civilization; rather, humanity always had the capacity for evil and civilization could be a way to temper that inherent trait. Golding believed, for example, that only "certain social sanctions" or "social prohibitions" separated the Allies from the Nazis (Gindin 4-5; Reiff 29).

These were controversial ideas and he pondered how he might express them in a work of fiction. As a youth he had read R. M. Ballantyne's *The Coral Island* (1858), about a group of young castaways on a South Pacific island. Major themes of Ballantyne's novel are the importance of Christianity, the civilizing influence of Christian missionaries, and the superiority of Anglo-Saxon values (Baker intro.). In *The Coral Island*, the boys encounter evil in the form of pirates and cannibalistic Polynesian natives. But what might happen, Golding wondered, if evil was within? He had observed how soldiers—many of them youths or barely out of their teens (Fussell)—had behaved in the war. How then might a group of "civilized" Western youths really behave if castaway and left to their own devices?

To achieve this didactic aim, Golding's island is deserted; it has no indigenous inhabitants. In previous novels such as Ballantyne's, Robert Louis Stevenson's *Treasure Island* (1883), Daniel Defoe's *Robinson Crusoe* (1719), or Herman Melville's semifictional *Typee* (1846), and in movies such as *The Idol Dancer* (1920), *Hula* (1927), *Bird of Paradise* (1932), and even *King Kong* (1933), natives are portrayed in ways that encourage readers/audience to deride native practices such as cannibalism, permissive sexual behavior, and "heathen" religious beliefs. In these stories, shipwrecked sailors or explorers typically maintain Western values, underpinning the superiority of Western civilization. However, the message is clear in these tales: while natives are expected to be heathen and savage, civilized Westerners exposed for too long to native practices may become corrupted. Golding avoids this possibility by removing natives from his tale. As the original title of the book—*The Stranger Within*—indicates, the children are left alone to discover that "the savage" resides within themselves. They abandon democratic ideas, split into factions, and create their version of a hunter-gatherer society. The children become superstitious, and nervous talk about a monster reifies into a protoreligion in which they provide sacrifices to the beast, even as they seek it out to kill it. Fear leads them to gravitate towards the strong—those who can provide food and protection. In the process, they forget their humanity, turning on each other and losing the trappings of civilization.

Civilization and Savagery

This process unfolds gradually; initially Golding gives them the opportunity to enact familiar forms of self-government, but this endeavor eventually falls apart. In the story, the conch serves as the main symbol of authority and of order. The sound of the conch calls the children to an assembly where an election is held for leader between Ralph and Jack Merridew. Jack had demanded to be leader because he is "chapter chorister and head boy," but the children insist on a vote. The conch proves to be the deciding factor: "The being that had blown that, had sat waiting for them on the platform with the delicate thing balanced on his knees, was set apart" (Golding 19). Ralph triumphs because the children rely on the democratic process they had known in their past lives. In turn, Ralph acts sensibly and responsibly, directing the children to gather food, build shelters, and tend to a fire in the hope that smoke will attract a passing ship and therefore effect rescue. This rational and logical approach is the kind of Victorian can do attitude that marked the children's behavior in Ballantyne's *Coral Island*. Unanimity soon falls apart, however; Jack remains envious of Ralph's authority and works to build his own support. He reassigns the choir to the role of "hunters," realizing intuitively that as time passed and the children got hungry and afraid, they would respond to a show of strength. Ralph happily, but naïvely, agrees to this arrangement—a show of appeasement that would end tragically.

Golding accomplishes the journey from civilized to savage in a number of ways. For example, the children discarding their school uniforms is an obvious symbol of the stripping away of a layer of civilization. The first person in the novel to strip naked is Ralph, in response to the heat of the island and the heaviness of his clothes, which are unsuited to this environment. However, in this early encounter with the island, Ralph is not yet ready to abandon past conventions and he collects his scattered uniform and reclothes. We are told that Ralph finds this "strangely pleasing," as if his school uniform provides some security and familiarity (Golding 12). In a similar vein, when Piggy meets Jack for the first time he is reduced to silence, intimidated by Jack's "uniformed superiority" (Golding 17). Soon though, near-nakedness becomes a powerful totem and it is the painted camouflage of Jack's hunters—white and red clay and black charcoal—that gives them a group identity and allows them to play the role of the savage.

The characterization of the novel's four main protagonists, Ralph, Jack, Piggy, and Simon, provides a clear distinction between rationality/civilization and irrationality/savagery. Ralph represents order and reason; in advocating a signal fire, he is the one most focused on rescue, and the only one of the children who has a plan to make that happen. Elected leader, he resists any urges towards despotism, preferring instead consultation and cooperation. Of all the children, he is the one most representative of the civilized world from which they are now estranged. The closest he has to an ally in this regard is Piggy, a subject of ridicule from most of the children because he is overweight, shortsighted, and suffers from asthma. Nevertheless, Piggy supports the election process to choose a leader, follows Ralph's instructions, is aware of the democratic power of the conch, and makes suggestions based on logic and reason.

In opposition to them is Jack, who has a strong sense of his own self-importance. He demands to be leader and is frustrated when the children choose to elect Ralph instead. Unlike Ralph, Jack regards the acquisition of power as an end in itself: he has no concern for the children and no plans to escape the island. He fuels the children's fear of a beast so they will be drawn to him for protection. And when he eventually establishes his own camp and followers, he behaves in tyrannical fashion, enacting fearful rituals and brutal acts of violence. He represents the savage, the "stranger within" that Golding saw evidence of during the war.

The final main protagonist is Simon, a sensitive child who serves as the emotional and spiritual heart of the novel. Envisioned by Golding as a Christlike figure (Gindin 24), Simon bravely faces up to the beast, discovering that it is merely the corpse of a parachutist.

This causes him to reflect on the divisions among the children and he realises the truth in what he had earlier suggested to the group: "maybe there is a beast . . . maybe it's only us" (Golding 82). Before he is able to reveal this, however, Jack's hunters strike him down in a frenzy of sacrificial violence. With this, Golding reveals, the savage has won and the beast has been exposed as an intrinsic part of human nature.

One by one, then, the symbols that underpin civilization are removed—the children's clothes; the parliamentary authority of the conch; Ralph's elected leadership; Piggy's glasses (a symbol of the kind of bookishness that seems unnecessary on the island); the extinguishing of the signal fire (the ability to make fire is one trait that distinguishes humans from all other animals); Christian values; and finally all rationality and reason as the island becomes a scene of destruction, anarchy, and murder. These are the lessons, Golding believes, humanity must learn not only about the war but about itself (Meitcke 2). Golding admitted that his war experiences motivated him to write the novel: "It was simply what seemed sensible for me to write after the war when everyone was thanking God they weren't Nazis. I'd seen enough to realize that every single one of us could be Nazis" (qtd. in Shaffer 54). This point wasn't lost on one literary critic, Walter Ernest Allen, who compared events in the story to "the vilest manifestations of Nazi regression" (289). Furthermore, the two forms of leadership Golding proffers, through the democratic figure of Ralph and authoritarian Jack, engage with discussions that were then current about the origins of conflict and the "authoritarian personality" (Adorno).

The Atomic Age

As well as World War II, a second major context of the novel is the Cold War. The atomic bombings of Hiroshima and Nagasaki marked the end of the former and beginning of the latter. This was apparent immediately. For example, an American radio broadcaster reacted to the bombing on August 7, 1945, saying "There is reason to believe tonight that our new atomic bomb destroyed the entire Japanese city of Hiroshima in a single blast.... It would be the same as Denver,

Colorado, with a population of 350,000 persons being there one moment, and wiped out the next" (qtd. in Boyer 5). This realization of a Pyrrhic victory against the Japanese, and the understanding that the next war would be fought with atomic bombs, contributed to a mood of "triumphalist despair": the "blinding light" of atomic warfare "had revealed in victory perils almost as terrifying as in defeat, holding out not the promise of an American Earth, but of no Earth at all" (Engelhardt 9, 55). *Lord of the Flies* was released in the final year of the Korean War, fought by United Nations forces including Great Britain and the United States against communist North Korea and its allies Russia and China. Both Presidents Truman and Eisenhower considered using atomic weapons, and as Niall Ferguson explains, the American public was very much in favor of that: "Asked if they favored 'using atomic artillery shells against communist forces ... if truce talks break down,' 56 percent of those polled said yes" (105).

This was the age of science fiction become science fact, with the total destruction of entire cities now possible. Developing missile technology quickly brought the United States in range of Soviet weapons, and vice versa. The immediate context of the novel is therefore the existential threat of atomic warfare, and this is included in the plot. Although all is not completely explained, it seems the boys were being evacuated from Great Britain to Australia because of the threat of war. This was likely inspired by a real-life evacuation of British children, under the auspices of the Children's Overseas Reception Board, during the early years of World War II (Dangar). When Ralph insists his Navy father will rescue them, Piggy replies "Didn't you hear what the pilot said? About the atom bomb? They're all dead" (Golding 11). In addition, the detachable cabin in which the children land safely on the island is a piece of technology that did not exist in the 1950s. These novelties led critic Usha George to conclude that *Lord of the Flies* belongs to "the sub-genre of science fiction" (14). Indeed, when Golding first sent his manuscript to Faber publishers, the in-house reader responded: "Time: the Future. Absurd & uninteresting fantasy about the explosion of an atom bomb on the Colonies" (Cohen 223).

Lord of the Flies can be considered therefore as a dystopian novel, set in a world in which atomic warfare is a reality. Such was the impact of Hiroshima, Nagasaki, and the Cold War on society that literary treatments of these subjects were not uncommon. For example, Golding's work sits alongside other postapocalyptic novels such as George R. Stewart's *Earth Abides* (1949), John Wyndham's *The Day of the Triffids* (1951), Nevil Shute's *On the Beach* (1957), Pat Frank's *Alas, Babylon* (1959), and Walter M. Miller Jr.'s *A Canticle for Leibowitz* (1961). Aside from Piggy's comment about the atomic bomb, direct references to nuclear catastrophe are absent. However, fiery conflagrations sweep the island on two occasions, once when sparks from the signal fire ignite some nearby dry timber; and again when Jack starts a large fire in an attempt to flush out Ralph from his hiding place. The first fire possibly kills one child, who is never seen again on the island; the second fire does great damage to the environment and threatens to spread out of control. Fire is an important symbol in the novel. It represents the children's best chance of escape, but it is also a threat to life. In a sense also, it represents both the hopes and fears of humanity about the nuclear age: would atomic energy create unlimited, clean energy or would it extinguish all life on the planet? As Ian McEwan observes, "The boys set fire to their island paradise while their elders and betters have all but destroyed the planet" (159).

Lord of the Flies was created and released at a time when memories of World War II were recent and when humanity was still trying to understand how and why the world had descended so quickly into anarchy. Attempts had been made to underpin the rule of law: war crimes tribunals were set up at Nuremburg and Tokyo; and in 1945 a new organization, the United Nations, was established with the aim of peacefully solving future international disputes. The atomic destruction at Hiroshima and Nagasaki made such measures essential but in the atomic age it was difficult to judge the value of this new technology, or to predict how the future would unfold. Would the lessons of the last war have any value in this new science fiction age? Golding aspired to explicate his views on the universal human condition based on his experiences in World War II, which helped formulate those views. As Whitley points out, Golding was "concerned to flesh out his truth as accurately as possible" (10) so while the atomic age might be the context and the future for both the children in his novel and his audience, he remained focused on the human condition. There are, therefore, no science fiction monsters in Golding's work—no creatures created by radioactive fallout or mutation—only ordinary children but within whom the capacity for evil resides. Because of that recurring motif, *Lord of the Flies* has more in common with Robert Louis Stevenson's *Strange Case of Dr. Jekyll Mr. Hyde* (1886) than it does with most 1950s science fiction literature. However, the novel offers a warning similar to that sounded in other postapocalyptic works of fiction: that in the absence of the structures of accountability and mechanisms of law and order, the children's descent into savagery may also be the fate for wider civilization.

The novel ends with a rescue, of sorts, and in an anticlimactic fashion. Readers do not get to experience the violent demise of Ralph with which they had been teased throughout the final chapter. At the moment where his capture seems imminent, Ralph flees onto the beach, where he discovers an immaculately dressed Navy officer and a boat. When he turns to his pursuers, fierce savages just moments before, there is a shift in perspective—they are now just a "group of painted boys" and his nemesis Jack a "little boy" (186) too afraid to speak. Soon the children dissolve into tears at the realization of what they have done, and, as the author tells us, for their loss of innocence. The officer looks embarrassed: "What have you been doing? Having a war or something?" (185), he asks. The officer is shocked at Ralph's response that two children have died. What the officer had previously referred to as "fun and games" (185) has had tragic consequences. He gazes at his ship, perhaps realizing that his profession is merely a grown-up version of these children's "fun and games," and he will soon take them back into a world in which an atomic war is unfolding (11). The boys may be naked and savage, disappointing the Navy officer who expects a group of "British boys" to "put up a better show" (186), but despite his neat, trim uniform and clean appearance, the killer also resides within him. The unveiling of that horrific knowledge is Golding's greatest achievement, and it is difficult to pick fault with Dominic Sandbrook's observation about *Lord of the Flies*, that "few books better capture the dark side of the century that saw two of the bloodiest conflicts in human history, as well as the Holocaust and the nuclear arms race" (344).

Works Cited

Adorno, Theodor W. *The Authoritarian Personality.* Norton, 1950.

Allen, Walter Ernest. *The Modern Novel in Britain and the United States.* Dutton, 1964.

Baker, James R., and Arthur P. Ziegler Jr., editors, *Lord of the Flies*, by William Golding. Casebook Edition. Perigee, 1988.

Boyer, Paul. *By the Bomb's Early Light: American Thought and Culture at the Dawn of the Atomic Age.* U of North Carolina P, 1994.

Bradford, James C., editor. *International Encyclopedia of Military History.* Routledge, 2006.

Carey, John. *William Golding: The Man Who Wrote Lord of the Flies.* Faber, 2012.

Cohen, Richard. *How to Write Like Tolstoy: A Journey into the Minds of Our Greatest Writers.* Oneworld, 2016.

Dangar, Joyanta. "The Nightmare Beast, War and the Children in William Golding's Lord of the Flies". *PSYART: A Hyperlink Journal for the Psychological Study of the Arts.* http://psyartjournal.com/article/show/dangar-the_nightmare_beast_war_and_the_children. Accessed April 18, 2017.

Dower, John. *War Without Mercy.* Pantheon, 1993.

Engelhardt, Tom. *The End of Victory Culture.* HarperCollins, 1995.

Ferguson, Niall. *Colossus: The Rise and Fall of the American Empire.* Penguin, 2012.

The Fog of War: Eleven Lessons from the Life of Robert S. McNamara. Dir. Errol Morris. Sony, 2003.

Fussell, Paul. *The Boys' Crusade: The American Infantry in Northwestern Europe, 1944-1945.* Modern Library, 2003.

Gindin, James. *William Golding.* Macmillan, 1988.

George, Usha. *William Golding: A Critical Study.* Atlantic, 2008.

Golding, William. *Lord of the Flies*. Casebook Edition. Perigee, 1988.

Goshen, Seev. "Lidice." *Encyclopedia of the Holocaust*, vol. 3. Edited by Israel Gutman. Macmillan, 1990, pp. 870–72.

Grayling, A. C. *Among the Dead Cities*. Bloomsbury, 2007.

Hastings, Max. *Das Reich: The March of the 2nd SS Panzer Division Through France, June 1944*. Pan Macmillan, 2012.

McEwan, Ian. *William Golding, The Man and His Books: A Tribute on his 75th Birthday*. Edited by John Carey. Faber, 1986.

Meitcke, W. *William Golding: Lord of the Flies*. Barron's, 1984.

Mikaberidze, Alexander, editor. *Atrocities, Massacres, and War Crimes: An Encyclopedia,* vol. 1. ABC-CLIO, 2013.

Reiff, Raychel Haugrud. *William Golding: Lord of the Flies*. Marshall Cavendish, 2009.

Roberts, Geoffrey. *Victory at Stalingrad: The Battle That Changed History*. Routledge, 2013.

Sandbrook, Dominic. *The Great British Dream Factory: The Strange History of Our National Imagination*. Allen Lane, 2015.

Shaffer, Brian W. *Reading the Novel in English 1950-2000*. Blackwell, 2006.

Wheatcroft, Geoffrey. "How good was the Good War?" *The Boston Globe* May 2005.

Whitley, John S. *Golding: Lord of the Flies*. Edward Arnold, 1970.

The Conclusion of *Lord of the Flies*: Multiple Critical Perspectives_____

Robert C. Evans

One especially famous and controversial passage from Golding's *Lord of the Flies* consists of its last few paragraphs. In those, a British naval officer suddenly appears, as if from nowhere. He arrives just before young Ralph seems about to be murdered by the other boys, who once elected him their leader. Led by the vicious hunter, Jack, the boys have set the island on fire to pursue Ralph more effectively. Just when they seem about to catch and kill him, the naval officer appears.

His sudden arrival has been criticized as a mere gimmick (see, for example, Friedman 29). It has also been both attacked and defended by being compared to the sudden arrival of a *deus ex machina* (literally, god from a machine) in various classical Greek tragedies (see, e.g., Dickson 15). The suddenly changed perspective the officer introduces has been hailed as necessary and effective but has also been condemned as desperately inartistic (for the former view, see, e.g., Haldar 133; for the latter, see, e.g., Bowen 608).[1] Certainly his appearance provides a reasonably happy ending, otherwise the novel might have concluded with yet another brutal death of an innocent boy. Simon and Piggy have both been murdered, and the anonymous officer arrives just in time to save Ralph from a similar gruesome fate:

> "We saw your smoke. And you don't know how many of you there are?"
>
> "No, sir."
>
> "I should have thought," said the officer as he visualized the search before him, "I should have thought that a pack of British boys—you're all British, aren't you?—would have been able to put up a better show than that—I mean—"

"It was like that at first," said Ralph, "before things—"
He stopped.
"We were together then—"
The officer nodded helpfully.
"I know. Jolly good show. Like the Coral Island."

Ralph looked at him dumbly. For a moment he had a fleeting picture of the strange glamour that had once invested the beaches. But the island was scorched up like dead wood—Simon was dead— and Jack had ... The tears began to flow and sobs shook him. He gave himself up to them now for the first time on the island; great, shuddering spasms of grief that seemed to wrench his whole body. His voice rose under the black smoke before the burning wreckage of the island; and infected by that emotion, the other little boys began to shake and sob too. And in the middle of them, with filthy body, matted hair, and unwiped nose, Ralph wept for the end of innocence, the darkness of man's heart, and the fall through the air of the true, wise friend called Piggy.

The officer, surrounded by these noises, was moved and a little embarrassed. He turned away to give them time to pull themselves together; and waited, allowing his eyes to rest on the trim cruiser in the distance. (Golding 224-25)

Whether or not this passage effectively concludes the novel, it definitely lends itself to interpretation from numerous critical perspectives. These include just about every kind of critical theory commonly studied, from the most ancient to the most recent. The passage thus provides a good test case of what is sometimes called *critical pluralism*—the idea that no single kind of criticism is necessarily right or wrong and that no single perspective can begin to do justice to complex literary texts. Critical pluralists believe that readers benefit from keeping numerous interpretive possibilities in mind when analyzing any work. Doing so (pluralists contend) helps prevent narrow, dogmatic readings by fostering valuable critical conversation not only among different readers but also within each reader's mind.[2]

Consider, for example, the officer's first statement: "We saw your smoke." **Formalist** critics, who value how each part of a work contributes complex unity, might note the officer's unintended irony. He doesn't realize that one of the book's main themes has involved Ralph's desire to be rescued by keeping a large, smoky fire constantly lit. Often that fire has died, much to Ralph's frustration. Jack has shown little interest in keeping the fire (symbolically associated with civilized life) continually burning. But Ralph has been hoping fire might be seen by a passing ship. This, ironically, is precisely what has now happened, leading to his rescue at the last possible minute. The other boys, by setting fire to the island, have created such a massive blaze that a passing cruiser has come to their rescue. The fire intended to kill Ralph has now led to their common salvation. The need to keep a visible fire burning has been one of the book's key motifs and would thus intrigue **thematic** critics, who are especially interested in the central ideas that pervade and help unify complex texts.

Two Words: "No, Sir"

Ralph's two-word response to the officer's question—"No, sir"—lends itself to interpretation from many points of view. **Plato**, for instance, would almost certainly admire Ralph's deference. Ralph embraces the hierarchy on which (according to Plato) well-ordered societies depend. By subordinating himself to a wise adult, he behaves as everyone should. Although Plato generally disdained literature for frequently promoting irrational behavior, he probably would admire Ralph's behavior here. **Aristotle**, Plato's pupil (and a great defender of literary art) might admire how Ralph's reply is consistent with his character. Ralph has long sought adult intervention and shown a real respect for proper authority. His reply thus perfectly reflects the character and personality he has consistently displayed. Aristotle admired writers who could create characters whose consistency contributed to a work's overall unity.

Horace, the great Roman poet deeply influenced by Aristotle, might also praise Ralph's consistency. Yet Horace, who believed that writers should try to please broad audiences, might also note that Ralph behaves in ways consistent not only with Ralph's individual character but with the character of boys (or children) in general when they interact with adults. In other words, Ralph behaves not only consistently as an individual but also as children *in general* usually do. Horace believed that writers, to succeed, needed to create characters who seemed credible to audiences who expected certain *kinds* of people to behave in predictable ways. Meanwhile, another great classical theorist, **Longinus**, might have the least to say about Ralph's reply. Longinus thought literature should inspire, uplift, and elevate readers; it should prove irresistibly powerful, like a bolt of lightning, and should bring out the best, morally and even spiritually, in audiences. Ralph's behavior here is certainly ethical (and Longinus would therefore admire it), but this particular moment is not especially inspiring or uplifting.

Traditional historical critics, interested in how literature reflects typical values and behavior of its time, might note that Ralph's response completely illustrates the sort of reply a boy of his background, era, and upbringing could have been expected to offer. **Thematic** critics, interested in the various ideas emphasized in a text (and that help give it unity), might note how Ralph's respect for adult authority reflects a major theme of the whole novel. Ralph himself began as an authority figure among the boys; he was, in a sense, the adult among them. He sought to return to the world of adult supervision. Now he shows his typical respect for adults. Because his response not only reflects his consistency of character but also contributes to the book's thematic unity, his reply would also interest **formalist** critics. They are intrigued by the ways even the slightest details of well-written works contribute to a work's overall coherence. Formalists see even a text's tiniest parts as resembling pieces of a highly complex jigsaw puzzle. Ideally, each piece, by fitting perfectly, contributes to a complex unity.

Psychoanalytic critics, influenced by Sigmund Freud, tend to see human minds as involving complex interactions involving the id, ego, and superego. The id is associated with the emotional, impulsive, pleasure-seeking aspects of the mind. The ego is associated with the rational, logical parts of the psyche that must cope with the world as it really is (not as we might wish it to be). The superego conforms to the dictates of conscience, morality, and social expectations. By deferentially calling the officer "sir," Ralph follows rules laid down by the ego and superego. In contrast, the other boys have just been following the irrational impulses of their ids. **Archetypal** critics, meanwhile, are also interested in ways literature reflects and stimulates the human psyche. They, however, are less interested in individual minds than in the so-called *collective unconscious*. They might argue, for instance, that almost all humans share deep-seated impulses to acknowledge legitimate authority as well as equally deep-seated desires to avoid any chaos resulting from an absence of legitimate authority. Almost all children (archetypal critics might argue) turn to adults for help when they feel threatened in times of need, so Ralph is behaving here in a perfectly natural way.

    Marxist critics, influenced by Karl Marx, might be tempted to question Ralph's ready deference to authority, especially any authority associated with the British Empire. Marxists would definitely see that Empire as a central force promoting the imposition of capitalism on the rest of the world. Marxists (especially any wishing to ignore Marxism's own record in twentieth-century communist practice) might suggest that Ralph, like the soldier himself, has been trained up as a good little follower. Marxists would tend to interpret this moment, like most moments in literature, in political and economic terms. In contrast, **structuralists** would try to be more neutral and self-consciously scientific. They would note that humans structure existence by imposing binary codes on it. These codes consist of related self-reinforcing opposites that build an overarching structure. Thus, the boy is small while the officer is large. The small boy enjoys relatively little power while the adult male enjoys much more power. The small, relatively powerless boy must defer to the adult, relatively powerful officer who expects and receives deference. And so on. Ralph's behavior here reflects a particular social structure. To interpret that structure and this text correctly, one must know the codes that underlie both the structure and the text. **Deconstructors**, on the other hand, would show how the neat structures posited by structuralist critics are full of inevitable contradictions. Some pieces of the structure don't smoothly fit. Thus, the officer may be more powerful than Ralph, but he is less powerful than his superiors. His power, then, is only relative. Even more interesting might be the possible deconstructive claim that Ralph is now wiser, more insightful, and less naïve than the adult to whom he defers. Ralph has recently come to realize that neat categories and structures easily break down and collapse, while the officer, presumably, still has faith in neatly structured hierarchies. Ralph has had to *live* through a kind of deconstruction, a breakdown of cultural codes. For him, all the old certainties have suddenly become uncertain. His attempt to return to the old ways will never be complete or secure; he will never be able to forget his terrifying deconstructive experience. That experience has helped him see into the abyss that civilized codes tend to overlook or obscure.

Feminist critics might note that the officer to whom Ralph defers is a *male* addressed as a male ("sir"). He is the most powerful male in a book lacking a single female character who is actually present (although Piggy's "Auntie" is often mentioned). The officer represents a largely male power structure and is part of a war largely involving males fighting males. Both Ralph and the officer behave as typical males of their era. (A feminist might wonder how this episode would differ if the officer were a woman rather than a man. Would a woman officer address Ralph and the other boys as the male officer does? Would Ralph react the same way to a woman officer as he reacts to this imposing, unemotional, no-nonsense male?) **Reader-response** critics might argue that answers to these questions, and indeed to almost any questions about any literary text, would greatly depend on the specific traits of individual readers or groups of readers. Readers with military experience or who had had no-nonsense parents of either sex (for instance) might respond in one way to this episode, while readers without military experience or who had had especially indulgent parents might respond differently. One's reactions to any text, then, would reflect either one's personal traits or the traits of a group to which one belongs. For reader-response critics, readers determine texts' meanings; texts can be interpreted in widely varying ways depending on the readers doing the interpreting.

Dialogical critics, however, who are interested in a text's various voices, might be interested in the ways Ralph's simple "No, sir" echoes uses of that phrases both in real life and in prior texts, both literary and nonliterary. For dialogical critics, few uses of language are utterly original; almost all uses echo prior uses. "No, sir" is demonstrably one of the most common phrases in English; a search in Google Books turns up well over two million examples. (Interestingly enough, a search for "no, ma'am" turns up roughly one-tenth as many, a fact that would definitely interest a feminist critic.) Ralph's two simple words imply a completely different tone than comparable expressions such as "nope," "nah," or "uh-uh" would have conveyed. Dialogical critics are as interested in the tones of voice a text implies as they are in any so-called "basic meanings."

New historicist critics, on the other hand, tend to be interested in relations of power, often among individuals but also between and among different kinds of groups. Merely by adding "sir" to his prior word "no," Ralph immediately signals his inferior status, not only because the officer *is* an officer but also merely because he is an adult. Paradoxically, by acknowledging his relative lack of power vis-à-vis the officer, Ralph is likely to win the officer's respect and thus enhance his own power. If he had addressed the officer disrespectfully, he might have temporarily asserted his independence, but he would almost certainly have lost power by offending a superior. For new historicists, status and power are central questions in any relationship and in any culture. Such status and power are almost always in flux (at least potentially) and are up for constant negotiation and renegotiation. Power is rarely stable, as Ralph has already discovered and as Jack is about to discover as well.

Multicultural critics, interested in ways literature reflects and appeals to the interests and traits of various subcultures, might argue that Ralph's response to the officer's query reflects (1) the relations between polite children and adults in Ralph's culture, (2) the relations between boys and adult males in that culture, (3) the relations between schoolboys and authority figures in that culture, and so on. Ralph and all the boys are presumably white boys on an island populated (strangely enough) solely by white boys, and they are about to be taken onto a warship surely populated almost entirely by adult white males. For the most part (with the possible exception of Piggy), Ralph and his onetime friends seem to share the same basic socioeconomic background, but they quickly devolve into two separate and opposed subcultures consisting of hunters and fire-keepers. The boys are also divided into subcultures based on age: the older boys and the littluns. Samneric, the twins, constitute their own tiny subculture, while Piggy is discriminated against by almost everyone, largely because of his weight. In short, even within this tiny microcosm of boys on an island, various subcultures definitely exist.

Postmodernist critics, like deconstructors, look for any signs of fundamental contradictions, inconsistencies, and instabilities. They also tend to celebrate such traits rather than merely calling attention to them. Like deconstructors, they might suggest that the officer, in a sense, is less mature than Ralph now is—that the officer is behaving more like a boy than Ralph is likely to behave in the future. But postmodernists are vulnerable to the charge that their wholesale skepticism gives them precious little room to criticize anyone for anything. Critics of postmodernism might argue that if there are no real solid, objective standards, there are no legitimate, consistent reasons to fault anyone's values or behaviors, no matter what they may be. This, at least, is a charge commonly leveled at postmodernists.

Of very recent kinds of theorists, **Darwinists** might have the most to say about Ralph's reply of "No, sir." Darwinists (influenced by Charles Darwin) believe that certain very basic traits are common to most humans and are literally bred into people in genes that have evolved over millions of years. The need to defer to authority—to adapt to the so-called pecking order—is one such trait, especially when that order involves subordinate and dominant males. Among many mammals, especially primates, young males quickly realize the need to defer to older, dominant males, although much older males may eventually lose their dominance in competition to younger, stronger males. *Lord of the Flies*, a Darwinist might argue, shows what happens when "civilized" behavior breaks down and people revert to the kind of competition often associated with so-called *social Darwinism.*

The Rest of the Passage

As we move through the novel's final paragraphs, the particular usefulness of various critical approaches becomes obvious. Thus, when the officer says "I should have thought," he speaks as **Horace** would expect an educated Englishman of his time to speak. That is, the officer fits a stereotype that has become familiar partly because it has been used so often and partly because it seems so accurate. His specific diction would also interest a **dialogical** critic, since dialogical critics are interested in the varied voices, both literal and metaphoric, a text employs. Meanwhile, a **formalist** would admire how the rest of this sentence—with its pauses, questions, and trailing off at the end—successfully mimics actual speech. Paradoxically, Golding uses resources of art to make the officer's speech sound artless and spontaneous. Because the officer speaks in ways typical of someone of his particular historical era and specific social class, his words would interest both a **traditional historical critic** and a **Marxist**. Both would probably also be interested in his reference to the specifically *British* character of the boys. Britain, after all, consists of several nations, not just one. Though dominated by England, Britain also consisted, in Golding's era, of Scotland, Wales, and Northern Ireland. The officer speaks not simply as an Englishman but as a representative of the British Empire—an empire that was beginning to fall apart even as Golding wrote. The officer considers the boys British and seems disappointed that they have not behaved as better representatives of the empire. A **multicultural** critic might argue that the officer thinks the boys have betrayed the values of their particular British culture. But an **archetypal** critic might argue that they have simply behaved as all humans might under similar circumstances, and a **Darwinian** critic might agree. From a Darwinian point of view, they have reverted back to the law of the jungle, in which survival of the fittest is the key concern. And, from a **psychoanalytic** point of view, they have collectively allowed their ids to overrule their egos and superegos. In other words, from all three of these perspectives they have behaved not as a failed "pack of British boys" but as a group of typical human beings, subject to primal forces that are more fundamental than the dictates of national identity or imperial pride. In any case, a psychoanalytic critic might see the officer as the embodiment of the Freudian superego: He is the voice of authority, of conscience, of society's expectations of its individual members. In that sense, he also speaks as **Plato** might speak—with a disappointed sense that the boys have fallen short of ideal behavior.

Ralph's reply—with its pauses and its abrupt cessations—would interest both **dialogical** and **formalist** critics. Both would appreciate Golding's ability to capture, convincingly, a particular tone of voice—a tone **archetypal** critics would probably say is typical of anyone, anywhere, at any time who feels confused and embarrassed by what he is trying to communicate. Meanwhile, Ralph's words imply one of the novel's major motifs (the breakdown of community) and would interest **thematic** critics for that reason. The fact that the officer nods "helpfully" makes him sound, at least briefly, more like a father figure than a distant voice of impersonal authority. That one adjective helps complicate his character and would, for that reason, interest a **formalist**, since formalists believe that reality is complex and that the best texts reflect and convey that complexity. Yet a formalist might find the officer's ensuing sentences ("I know. Jolly good show. Like Coral Island.") enormously ironic. Formalists tend to admire irony because almost by definition it implies complexity. A formalist might respond to the officer's words by saying that he really *doesn't* know what the boys have been through, that the "show" they experienced has been anything but jolly or good, and that their experience has been exactly the opposite of the experience of the boys in R. M. Ballantyne's 1858 romantic adventure novel *The Coral Island*, with its reassuring depiction of British boys behaving remarkably well when faced with numerous unexpected challenges. Both **traditional historical** critics and **dialogical** critics would be interested in Golding's allusion to Ballantyne's book. Traditional historical critics would identify the allusion and explain its significance, while dialogical critics would note the ways (here and elsewhere) *Lord of the Flies* engages in a kind of intertextual dialogue with the earlier novel. Meanwhile, a **multicultural** critic might note that "jolly good show" is (or was) likely to be used far more often by British speakers of English than by Americans, while a **Marxist** critic might suggest that the phrase is typical of upper-class speakers or speakers hoping to be considered upper class.

Ralph's response to the officer's comment (Ralph "looked at him dumbly") might interest a **formalist** because this comment can be interpreted in at least two ways. Either Ralph can't think of an appropriate reply, or he finds the officer's comment so completely inadequate that he decides to stay silent. (This potential ambiguity might interest **deconstructors** and **reader-response** critics as well.) The officer, at this moment, seems far less wise than Ralph, a possibility that would interest not only **new historicist** critics (because Ralph in that sense is now more powerful than the officer) but also **deconstructive** critics (because in this respect the clear boundaries between *adult* and *child* have become blurred). Meanwhile, both **Aristotle** (interested in the skillful design of well-wrought works) and **formalists** (interested in the same thing) would admire how Ralph's memory of the once strangely glamorous beaches recalls the very beginning of the book, thus giving the novel a nice sense of symmetry that also helps emphasize, by contrast, just how much things have changed.

The fact that the island is now "scorched up like dead wood" would interest both **thematic** and **formalist** critics (because the need to maintain fire has been one of the novel's constant themes, and also because, ironically, the same fire that has finally led to the boys' rescue has also destroyed their temporary island paradise). **Archetypal** critics might note that fire has often symbolized, in human cultures all over the world and throughout time, both civilization as well as destruction, and that it is used in both ways in Golding's books. **Ecocritics**, concerned with humanity's obligations to nurture and preserve the planet, might note how the boys have visited destruction on a largely idyllic environment, much as the adults have done the same to the planet at large through atomic warfare. Meanwhile, **Aristotle**, concerned especially with the nature and causes of tragedy, might note the reference to Simon's death. Simon was killed by the very people he was trying to help—the very people who had been his friends. His death (the terrible, pitiful, and fear-inspiring death of a good person) illustrates Aristotle's definition of tragedy almost perfectly.

Ralph's eventual descent into tears would interest various kinds of critics. **Psychoanalytic** critics might say that his outburst indicates that his emotional id has overwhelmed his rational ego. **Archetypal** critics might argue that he is merely responding as most humans do when their grief becomes too hard to bear. **Horace** might say that Ralph is responding as we might expect almost any person— especially any young boy—to respond in such a situation. **Feminists** might note that by finally crying, Ralph is responding as females have stereotypically been thought to respond at moments of crisis, although feminists might also note that women are actually often far better than men at coping with extreme pain. Until now, Ralph has been trying to control his emotions (his ego has been trying to control his id). Now, however, he lapses into "great, shuddering spasms of grief that seemed to wrench his whole body." **Formalist** critics, who value details of phrasing as much as (if not more than) details of meaning, would admire the sheer sounds and rhythms of the words here.

Ecocritics would note that the once-Edenic island has now been turned, in a way all too typical of humans, into a "burning wreckage," while **archetypal** and **psychoanalytic** critics (along with **Horace**) might note how quickly and easily the recently fearsome "little boys" revert to the typical behavior of sniveling children. A **formalist** would admire the vivid, detailed, rhythmic description of Ralph's "filthy body, matted hair, and unwiped nose," while **thematic** critics, interested in the ideas a work explores, might especially focus on the statement that "Ralph wept for the end of innocence, the darkness of man's heart, and the fall through the air of the true, wise friend called Piggy." It is as if Golding, in the novel's penultimate sentence, wanted to emphasize as many of its major themes as possible, and as explicitly as possible: "the end of innocence," "the darkness of man's heart," the virtue of wisdom, and the value of friendship. **Formalist** critics, along with **Aristotle**, might note how this sentence helps tie the entire book together as well as bring it full circle: At the beginning of the novel, Ralph had despised Piggy, but now he recognizes and acknowledges Piggy's worth. A **multicultural** critic might suggest that Ralph has now learned, belatedly, to value the fat boy he had once mistreated. He has learned to appreciate Piggy's value as an individual rather than condemning him for not fitting a preconceived, prejudicial stereotype.

The story's final two sentences (especially the very final one) have often been discussed. **Psychoanalytic** and **archetypal** critics might be especially interested in the fact that the officer feels both "moved and a little embarrassed." Psychoanalytic critics might say that his ego briefly gives way to his id but then tries to regain control. Archetypal critics might argue that his compassion is natural when adults see children suffering. **Aristotle** and **Horace** might also say that his mixed feelings are typical of human nature, while **Longinus**, with his interest in elevation and nobility, might say that the officer's compassion makes him seem more admirable than he would seem if he merely kept a completely stiff upper lip. Longinus might argue that the officer's kindness in turning away from the boys reflects an admirable nobility of character, although a **multicultural** critic might argue that his conduct reflects a stoicism typical of his class, rank, and culture and that people with different cultural backgrounds might respond with far more compassion to the boys than the officer actually demonstrates. Instead of trying to comfort them (some might argue) he merely looks away.

In any case, the book's final words (its reference to the "trim cruiser in the distance") has been interpreted from many different perspectives and can be interpreted from many more. **Plato** might argue that the "trim cruiser" symbolizes the kind of order and discipline the boys have abandoned. **Aristotle** might suggest that the reference to the cruiser ties into all the book's earlier references to possible rescue ships, thus giving the novel a strong sense of final coherence. **Horace** might say that such a ship is exactly the sort of vessel we might associate with this officer, just as the officer himself is almost a stereotypical officer of the British Navy. **Longinus** might have little to say about the ship per se unless he saw it as a symbol of the kind of lofty, civilized values he admired. A **traditional historical critic** might be able to describe almost exactly the kind of ship Golding probably had in mind. Ships called "cruisers" have existed for centuries, but the term "cruiser," in the years before and following World War II, had very particular characteristics. Such a critic might also note that Golding himself was a British naval officer during the war. Meanwhile, a **thematic** critic might note the cruiser's relevance to the themes of rescue and war that run throughout the book.

A **formalist** critic might zero in on the adjective "trim," which implies such other adjectives as *compact, tidy, clean, clean-cut, attractive, symmetrical, sleek, graceful* and so on—all connotations that make the ship the symbolic opposite of the burned-out island and the filthy boys. The cruiser can be seen as symbolizing order rather than chaos, power rather than weakness, and competence rather than incompetence. On the other hand, a formalist might also see irony in the reference to the "trim cruiser." Many formalist critics have in fact argued that the ship symbolizes an adult version of the very forces of hostility and warfare the boys have unleashed on the island. Far from symbolizing reason and civilization, the ship can be seen as symbolizing just the opposite (a fact that would also interest **deconstuctors**). A **psychoanalytic** critic might see the "trim cruiser" as a symbol of the well-ordered ego; an **archetypal** critic might see it as a symbol of the kind of disciplined, efficient military power that has long been valued in most cultures throughout the world; while a **Marxist** critic might see it as a symbol of the ruthless, domineering British Empire. A **structuralist** critic might note that the word "trim" associates the ship with a whole host of similar adjectives (many of them mentioned in italics above), while a **feminist** might see the ship as stereotypically male: an efficient killing machine. A **reader-response** critic might argue that for anyone familiar with the Royal Navy or navies in general, the reference to the cruiser might have special resonance, while **multicultural** critics might note that people with such backgrounds and interests form a subculture within the larger culture. The reference to the cruiser might, for a **dialogical** critic, remind readers of other texts in which ships rescue people in need, while **new historicist** critics might see the cruiser as a symbol of Britain's power in the 1950s—power that rapidly diminished thereafter. The cruiser— with its rules, regulations, and standard design—might seem the opposite of the sort of thing **postmodernists** value, just as **ecocritics** might see it as symbolizing humans' tendency to wreak destruction on each other and on the natural environment. Finally, **Darwinians** might see the ship as just another symbol of the kind of inbred aggressiveness that is one of the most persistent traits of human nature.

Even single details of particular texts, therefore, can be interpreted in astonishingly numerous ways. Familiarity with literary theory arguably makes the reading of any work a richer, more complex experience than the experience that results by relying merely on "common sense." The more kinds of criticism a reader knows, the less that reader is to find any single one of them either wholly satisfying or completely sufficient.

Notes

1.   Numerous other examples of all these claims could easily be cited; see the critical survey articles by Evans, Fredericks, and Jeans in the present volume.

2.   For solid introductions to the various kinds of criticism discussed in this essay, see, for instance, the various introductory works cited below.

Works Cited

Bowen, John. "Bending Over Backwards," *Times Literary Supplement*, Oct. 23, 1959, p. 608.

Dickson, L. L. *The Modern Allegories of William Golding*. Tampa: U of South Florida P, 1990.

Friedman, Lawrence S. *William Golding*. New York: Continuum, 1993.

Golding, William. *Lord of the Flies*. Introduction by Stephen King. 1954. Faber, 2011.

Haldar, Santwana. *William Golding's Lord of the Flies*. New Delhi: Atlantic, 2006.

Additional Works Consulted

Barry, Peter. *Beginning Theory: An Introduction to Literary and Cultural Theory*. 3rd ed. Manchester UP, 2009.

Garner, Christina M. "Appendix: The Kinds of Questions Different Critics Ask." *Perspectives on Renaissance Poetry*, by Robert C. Evans. Bloomsbury Academic, 2015, pp. 194-207.

Guerin, Wilfred L., et al. *A Handbook of Critical Approaches to Literature*. 6th ed. Oxford UP, 2011.

Hall, Donald E. *Literary and Cultural Theory: From Basic Principles to Advanced Applications*. Houghton Mifflin, 2001.

Parker, Robert Dale. *How to Interpret Literature*. 3rd ed. Oxford UP, 2015.

Tyson, Lois. *Critical Theory Today: A User-Friendly Guide*. Garland, 1999.

Knowing the Beast: *Lord of the Flies* and Cognitive Literary Criticism_____

Nicolas Tredell

William Golding's first novel, *Lord of the Flies* (first published in 1954), has proved a potent and controversial work that has been variously read as an allegory of original sin, a demonstration of the capacity of human beings for cruelty, an all-out attack on the idea of childhood innocence, and an anatomy of the political process by which societies form, produce leaders, establish hierarchies, and collapse (see Page and Bloom). All these interpretations have persuasive elements, but they tend to move away from the visceral effects of the novel into abstractions. Of course, this is necessary and inevitable in any interpretation of a literary text; the critic draws back from its immediate texture to try to perceive overall patterns. But it is also necessary to return often to the texture to try to grasp how it is woven and how it works on the reader, and cognitive literary criticism can help us to do this (see Stockwell).

Drawing especially on Terence Cave's recent *Thinking with Literature* (2016), this essay applies key concepts and approaches of cognitive criticism to *Lord of the Flies*, with the aim of understanding more fully the power of Golding's novel to engage the reader, to provoke controversy, and to generate multiple interpretations. It examines the novel in terms of "motor resonance" or "kinesis," the way in which the reader's nervous system responds to fictional scenes as it might to real events, although, given the reader's awareness that they are reading a fiction, it stops short of translating those responses into action (Cave 28-9; Tredell 55). It analyzes the portrayal of the perpetration and correction of cognitive error in *Lord of the Flies*. It explores the novel in terms of "mind reading," the attribution of mental states and intentions to others, which human beings constantly practice in real life and in relation to characters in fiction and which fictional characters are portrayed as practicing in relation to one another (Cave 26-8; Tredell 55). It also discusses the novel's representation of reading one's own mind, of self-knowledge. In conclusion, it considers *Lord of the Flies* in terms of "underspecification" (Cave 2; Tredell 55)—the way in which it does not specify its meanings fully, leaving the reader to draw them out and permitting a range of interpretations—and looks at the novel in light of the idea of "mirror neurons" which, closely linked to the concept of "motor resonance," posits that the neurological reactions of human beings to the situations of other human beings form the basis of empathy (Cave 36, 164-5 n10).

Motor Resonance
Cognitive criticism holds that, in reading literary texts, the reader's nervous system responds to the situations the words evoke as it would to similar situations in actual life; this response is not carried through into action because the reader knows the situation portrayed in the text is not real in the same way that an actual situation would be, but it is nonetheless a vital aspect of the reading process, a crucial element in the way readers identify with and are gripped by a fiction. *Lord of the Flies* works to make the reader feel, on and in their body and nerves, the sensations the characters feel. In Chapter 1, for example, Ralph jumps down off the palm terrace onto the beach:

> The sand was thick over his black shoes and the heat hit him. He became conscious of the weight of his clothes, kicked his shoes off fiercely and ripped off each stocking with its elastic garter in a single movement. Then he leapt back on the terrace, pulled off his shirt, and stood there among the skull-like coco-nuts with green shadows from the palms and the forest sliding over his skin. He undid the snake-clasp of his belt, lugged off his shorts and pants, and stood there naked, looking at the dazzling beach and the water. (Golding 10)

This passage conveys the physicality of Ralph's experience by its selection and placement of language. It stresses the heavy, constraining forces of both Ralph's clothing and the natural world, and Ralph's vigorous resistance to these. The more usual phrasing of the first clause, "The sand was thick over his black shoes," would be "The sand was thick *under* his black shoes" (italics added); the change of preposition from "under" to "over" emphasizes that the sand dominates both the natural movement of Ralph's feet and the shoes that are a synecdoche of the civilization from which he has come: Inert nature seems more powerful than animate nature or culture. The second clause of the first sentence personifies the heat as striking Ralph and the alliterative monosyllables of "heat hit him," coming down like the strokes of a hammer, strengthen the sense of a blow being delivered. In the second sentence, the noun "weight" adds more heft to the impression of constraint conveyed by the shoe-covering sand in the first sentence.

Countering this constraint and aggression are the active and sometimes phrasal verbs that denote Ralph's responses: "kicked," "leapt," "pulled," "ripped off," "lugged off." The second sentence accentuates these with adverbs and adverbial phrases: "fiercely," "in a single movement." We can legitimately develop interpretations of this passage in terms of more abstract oppositions such as nature and culture or freedom and constraint, and we may link these interpretations to more general readings of the themes of the novel, but these interpretations begin in the motor resonance of the reader whose nervous system responds to these stimuli as if, within the willing suspension of disbelief necessary to the appreciation of fiction, they were real.

In Chapter 4, when Ralph is running to try to see the ship that may be on the horizon, "He did desperate violence to his naked body among the rasping creepers so that blood was sliding over him" (Golding 73). Here, the nakedness that was a sort of liberation when he tore off his clothes on the beach becomes a site of vulnerability. With its connotations of a coarse file for use on hard materials such as wood and metal, "rasping" brings home the harshness of the creepers in their abrasive friction with human flesh unprotected by clothing, while "sliding," a rather unusual present participle to apply to blood—"flowing" or "pouring" would be more common— suggests the viscous quality of its passage over his skin as it starts to congeal.

While the rasping of the creepers and the sliding of the blood are tactile sensations, felt on the skin, the last words of the quoted passage focus on the visual sense, on "looking," and the adjective "dazzling," applied to the beach and water, is one of many references to visual disturbance in *Lord of the Flies*. In Chapter 1, for instance, Piggy says "We may stay here till we die" and with his last word, which might in other circumstances suggest the chill of death, "the heat," paradoxically, "seemed to increase till it became a threatening weight and the lagoon attacked them with a blinding effulgence" (Golding 15). This personifies both the heat and the lagoon as aggressive, the heat taking on menace and mass and the lagoon assuming the aspect of an attacker armed with a brightness that blinds the eyes. The use of the Latinate noun "effulgence" here might seem an evasive euphemism—why not say "blinding brightness"?—but it also references classical epic and tragedy, with their vividly portrayed martial conflicts and eyeless protagonists. The adjective "blinding" is another example of a motif of visual impairment that runs through *Lord of the Flies*.

Even when representing inner thoughts, Golding gives them a physical, bodily dimension. Thus in Chapter 5, seeing Percival Wemys Madison, Ralph recalls the boy with the birthmark on his face who disappeared in the fire in Chapter 2: "Ralph remembered another small boy who had stood like this and he *flinched away* from the memory. He had *pushed* the thought *down* and *out of sight*" (94, italics added). Here, thoughts are embodied by the use of the phrasal verbs "flinch away" and "push down," which suggest bodily actions of quick withdrawal and forceful thrusting, and by the sensory metaphor of being "out of sight"—a phrase that invokes the commonplace saying "out of sight, out of mind" and takes on an extra dimension of significance in a novel so concerned with visual and cognitive error.

Visual and Cognitive Error

Perceptual distortions and apparitions feature notably in *Lord of the Flies*. Like Prospero's isle in Shakespeare's *The Tempest*, the boys' coral island is full of noises and sights, both natural—"The air was thick with butterflies, lifting, fluttering, settling" (Golding 30)—and apparently preternatural, "magicked out of shape or sense" (Golding

27) by the seemingly miraculous metamorphoses of mirage evoked in Chapter 4:

> Strange things happened at midday. The glittering sea rose up, moved apart in planes of blatant impossibility; the coral reef and the few, stunted palms that clung to the more elevated parts would float up into the sky, would quiver, be plucked apart, run like rain-drops on a wire or be repeated as in an odd succession of mirrors. Sometimes land loomed where there was no land and flicked out like a bubble as the children watched. (Golding 63)

The mirage, like a hall of mirrors, seems to possess the power to multiply phenomena (such as palm trees and coral reefs) and even to create ex nihilo (out of nothing) the solid substance of land; but its apparitions prove fragile, evanescent, as the simile of the bubble demonstrates. Piggy, the voice of scientific rationalism—as he says "expansively" in Chapter 5, "Life [...] is scientific" (Golding 92) – "discount[s] all this learnedly as a 'mirage'" and the children get used to the "mysteries" and ignore them (Golding 63). But the evocation of the mirages establishes, early in the novel, a sense of the island as a place where illusions flourish and may mislead.

Lord of the Flies is marked by evocations of cognitive error, of "delayed decoding," to borrow Ian Watt's term from his 1981 study of Joseph Conrad. According to Watt, "delayed decoding," in Conrad's fiction, puts

> the reader in the position of being an immediate witness of each step in the process whereby the semantic gap between the sensations aroused in the [fictional] individual by an object or event, and their actual cause or meaning, [is] slowly closed in his consciousness. (Watt 270)

For instance, in Conrad's 1902 novella *Heart of Darkness* (which *Lord of the Flies* often echoes), the main narrator, Charlie Marlow, then captain of a steamboat on an African river, suddenly becomes aware that "Sticks, little sticks, were flying about" and some moments and three sentences pass before he correctly decodes this strange sensory phenomenon, realizing that the flying sticks are "Arrows, by Jove! We were being shot at!" (Conrad 75). Golding's form of "delayed decoding" does not, however, adhere as closely as Conrad's to the movement of an individual mind from the apprehension of a sensory phenomenon towards an accurate understanding of it. In an early example from Chapter 1 of *Lord of the Flies*, the "delayed decoding" is not attributed to a specific character, but to a generalized "eye," implying that anyone (any "I") may make such an interpretive error.

> The children who came along the beach, singly or in twos, leapt into visibility when they crossed the line from heat-haze to nearer sand. Here, the eye was first attracted to a black, bat-like creature that danced on the sand, and only later perceived the body above it. The bat was the child's shadow, shrunk by the vertical sun to a patch between the hurrying feet. (Golding 20)

The "black, bat-like creature" that the eye first perceives is a component of Gothic fiction, preparing the reader for the horrors to come; but the misinterpretation is quickly corrected by an authoritative narrative voice which might be that of an adult Piggy, presenting a rational, scientific explanation. But no *character* in the novel possesses such authority: Piggy may be the voice of reason and of a popular idea of science but carries little weight. Ironically, this is partly because of his surplus of physical weight, his fatness, which together with his shortness, asthma, and spectacles, and his accent and use of English that mark him as lower class in the eyes of the other boys, undermine his standing.

Although the eye is generalized in this example, the eyes most often mentioned in *Lord of the Flies* belong to Piggy and his visual deficiencies are stressed, in a way that draws the reader into a world of reduced vision. In Chapter 2, Piggy says that, without his spectacles, "I can hardly see!" (Golding 44), a phrase he echoes and expands soon afterwards: "Jus' blurs, that's all. Hardly see my hand—" (Golding 45). In Chapter 4, Piggy reiterates his ocular limitation: "I know I can't see very much" (Golding 72); although here the verb "know" signals his awareness of his myopia, it demonstrates a degree of self-knowledge. Later in the same chapter, Jack smacks Piggy's head, making his glasses fly off, with the result that one of their lenses shatters against rocks: Piggy protests "Now I only got one eye" (Golding 78). This might invoke the Cyclops, the monocular giant in Book 9 of Homer's *Odyssey*, or "the one-eyed merchant" whose back bears an enigmatic burden in the "wicked pack of cards" of Madame Sosostris in T. S. Eliot's *The Waste Land* (1922; 1974, 64; part 1, lines 52, 46); but Piggy lacks the power of a giant or a portentous Tarot symbol; he is only an asthmatic, fat, myopic, short, socially awkward schoolboy, whose sole strength is his intelligence, and who strikes no physical fear into his companions.

Soon afterwards in Chapter 4, Ralph takes Piggy's glasses, with their one remaining lens, to light a fire, leaving Piggy "islanded in a sea of meaningless colour" (Golding 79). The adjective "islanded" provides an image of Piggy's individual isolation as an outsider, stranded on the island of himself, but it also makes him a microcosm of the isolation of the boys taken as a whole on the coral island— they are all, as a group, "islanded," outsiders physically and morally set apart from society; while the adjective "meaningless" shows how Piggy, shorn of his spectacles, lacks the cognitive capacity to perceive shapes and to name and identify objects, immersed in a formless and illogical world "magicked out of shape or sense," like the world the mirages create.

In *Lord of the Flies*, the most potent instance of "delayed decoding," the greatest cognitive error, based on a misinterpretation of partial visual data, occurs when the twins, known collectively as Samneric, mistake a dead parachutist, a victim of an aerial battle fought at a height of ten miles who has drifted down onto the shattered rocks of the mountaintop, for "the beast."

> [T]he figure sat, its helmeted head between its knees, held by a complication of lines. When the breeze blew the lines would strain taut and some accident of this pull lifted the head and chest upright so that the figure seemed to peer across the brow of the mountain. Then, each time the wind dropped, the lines would slacken and the figure bow forward again, sinking its head between its knees. So as the stars moved across the sky, the figure sat on the mountain-top and bowed and sank and bowed again. (Golding 105)

This description enables the reader to imagine, not only what it would look like, but also what it would feel like to be pulled and released in this way—and this motor resonance generates a sense of pathos because the reader knows that the apparently animate form that seems to be experiencing and even initiating such movement is in fact dead. The description also places the reader in a privileged cognitive position of knowing what the beast really is; even so, the description of the dead man repetitively raising his head and then sinking has an uncanny quality, and it is easy to understand how, in the supercharged state of mind generated by rumours and fears of a beast, Samneric, glimpsing the corpse in the light of their signal fire, believe that it is the beast itself.

When Samneric rush back to Ralph and Piggy, their description of what they think they have seen soon overcomes the doubts of their listeners and strikes terror into them. "Soon the darkness was full of claws, full of the awful unknown and menace" (Golding 108). In this sentence, the use of the noun "claws," as a metonymy for both an actual, unspecified creature such as a tiger, wolf, or crab and a vision of nature as savage rather than soothing— "red in tooth and claw," in the phrase made famous in Tennyson's poem *In Memoriam A. H. H.* (1850; 1975, 243; part 56, line 15)—gives body to a formulation that might otherwise seem too vague: "the awful unknown and menace."

It is not Samneric who move towards a realization of the true nature of the beast they believe they have seen, who reach the stage where they can correctly decode the sensory phenomena they have experienced; rather, it is Simon who decodes it in Chapter 9, quickly grasping, once he gets close enough, the reality of the beast and exploding the cognitive error made by Samneric: "He crawled forward and soon he understood" (Golding 161). In a final, grotesque simulacrum of a sentient act, the entangled, wind-stirred figure "lifted, bowed, and breathed foully at him" (Golding 162); Simon's visceral response is to vomit "till his stomach was empty," purging the misunderstanding. But he feels it imperative to pass on the result of his successful decoding to his fellow boys: "The beast was harmless and horrible; and the news must reach the others as soon as possible" (Golding 162). His attempt to tell them leads, however, to his own death as the boys, in a frenzy, take Simon himself for the beast. His cognitive clarity about the nature of the beast is not matched by a similar clarity about the nature of the collective beast the boys have become; he does not read their joint mind correctly.

Mind Reading

Mind reading is another key concept of cognitive literary criticism and, like motor resonance, it posits a continuity between everyday experience and the experience of reading. Just as the reader's nervous system responds to situations represented in fiction as it might to situations in actual life, while being aware that they are not real and thus stopping short of action, so the reader tries, in reading fiction, to read the minds of the characters as one does all the time in actual life—not in a telepathic sense, but by inferring their thoughts, feelings, and intentions from their words, actions, and situations. Moreover, the reader of fiction works on the implicit assumption that fictional characters are likewise engaged in trying to read one another's minds (even in avant-garde work that rejects conventional realistic characterization, such as Samuel Beckett's *The Unnamable* (1953), this assumption is likely to persist in a fragmentary, partial way).

Lord of the Flies is a novel with a third-person narrator who is, in principle, omniscient, all-knowing, aware of what is happening in the thoughts and feelings of each and every character. In practice, this omniscient narrator, even if theoretically all-knowing, does not reveal all, but offers selective glimpses into different viewpoints and sometimes refuses omniscience, seeing a character from the outside and showing other characters in the novel, like the reader, engaged in mind reading as they try to infer that character's thoughts and feelings. Consider, for example, the moment near the end of Chapter 1 when the boys read Jack's mind just after he has stopped short of killing the pig: "They knew very well why he hadn't: because of the enormity of the knife descending and cutting into living flesh; because of the unbearable blood" (Golding 34). Here the narrator, rather than entering Jack's mind (as in principle he could), enters the collective consciousness of the boys who observe Jack, showing them engaged in a unanimous act of mind reading that results in a sense of cognitive certainty rendered by a colloquial locution—"They knew very well … "

One of the key strands in *Lord of the Flies* is the story of Jack's overcoming of this initial inhibition. In Chapter 3, for instance, the narrator does briefly enter his mind when words fail him, to show his mounting inner urge to engage in lethal hunting:

> "I went on," said Jack. "I let them [the rest of the hunters] go. I had to go on. I—"
> He tried to convey the compulsion to track down and kill that was swallowing him up. (Golding 55)

Significantly in the symbolic pattern of the novel, the "compulsion" is imaged here as a consuming beast, "swallowing him up." The narrator goes less extensively into Jack's mind than into Ralph's, perhaps because to do so might arouse a sympathy for Jack that would alter the moral proportions of the novel (imagine how *Lord of the Flies* would read if the whole story were told from Jack's viewpoint).

Lord of the Flies registers the gulfs that can exist between characters, and these are similar to the gulfs that can exist between people in real life and set limits to accurate mind reading in actuality as in fiction. Near the end of Chapter 3, Ralph and Jack, walking along, are called "two continents of experience and feeling, unable to communicate" (Golding 60). There is an implication here that not only Ralph and Jack, but each boy on the island, is a continent of "experience and feeling, unable to communicate." In an ironic twist to the geographical imagery of the novel, the island is peopled, metaphorically, by isolated continents—which does not prevent them from acting collectively and sometimes brutally.

Piggy, in this as in other respects, displays and claims a certain cognitive superiority, which he attributes, ironically, to the ill health that limits his physical effectiveness. In Chapter 5, he tells Ralph, "I been in bed so much I done some thinking. I know about people. I know about me. And him [Jack]. He can't hurt you: but if you stand out of the way he'd hurt the next thing. And that's me" (Golding 102). Here Piggy's reading of Jack's mind is perspicacious and prescient. But in the immediate context of life on the island, Piggy's mind reading can go wrong. In Chapter 4, Piggy suggests making a sundial to serve as a clock; Ralph replies sourly and Piggy responds seriously, making Ralph smile involuntarily. The smile misleads Piggy into an erroneous reading of Ralph's mind:

> Piggy saw [Ralph's] smile and misinterpreted it as friendliness. There had grown up tacitly among the biguns the opinion that Piggy was an outsider, not only by accent, which did not matter, but by fat, and ass-mar, and specs, and a certain disinclination for manual labour. Now, finding that something he had said made Ralph smile, he rejoiced and pressed his advantage. (Golding 70)

But Piggy's advantage is illusory, based on faulty mind reading; Ralph tells Piggy to shut up and moves away, changing the subject.

As well as the knowledge of others that can come from observation and mind reading, there is also self-knowledge. One of the oldest cognitive injunctions is "Know thyself," inscribed on the forecourt of the ancient Greek temple at Delphi. *Lord of the Flies* dramatizes the issue of the limits of self-knowledge, suggesting that the "self" is a fragile, unstable construct that is difficult to know, especially when caught up in collective misperceptions. Putting on a mask, for example, may create a different self, as Jack finds in Chapter 4 when he looks at his reflection in the mirror provided by the water in the coconut shell:

> He looked in astonishment, no longer at himself but at an awesome stranger. He spilt the water and leapt to his feet, laughing excitedly. Beside the mere, his sinewy body held up a mask that drew their eyes and appalled them. He began to dance and his laughter became a bloodthirsty snarling. He capered towards Bill and the mask was a thing on its own, behind which Jack hid, liberated from shame and self-consciousness. (Golding 69)

Involvement in collective activity may also create a different self or a merging of selves into a single group self. This is evident in the hunting and killing activities in which the boys engage. The italicized chant that helps to bond the group self—"*Kill the beast! Cut his throat! Spill his blood*"—recurs at key points in the novel (Golding 75, 126, 167, 168, 205) and although its precise wording varies—most notably, *pig* in the first instance, gendered as female, turns male in the second instance and in subsequent examples shifts from the porcine to the bestial, becoming the more amorphous and unidentifiable beast, gendered as male—its insistent rhythm remains and becomes, by the twelfth and last chapter of the novel, "familiar" (Golding 205). Significantly, it features five times (Golding 167, 168) in the crucial scene in Chapter 9 in which Simon, returning from the mountaintop to correct the boys' cognitive error and tell them that the beast is really a dead parachutist, falls victim to a lethal case of delayed decoding error when he himself is mistaken for the beast. Golding's description here is likely to arouse a motor resonance in the reader that, disturbingly, shifts between identification with the victim and with the killers, splitting the reading subject in two:

> "*Kill the beast! Cut his throat! Spill his blood! Do him in!*"
> The sticks fell and the mouth of the new circle crunched and screamed. The beast was on its knees in the centre, its arms folded over its face. It was crying out against the abominable noise something about a body on the hill. The beast struggled forward, broke the ring and fell over the steep edge of the rock to the sand by the water. At once the crowd surged after it, poured down the rock, leapt on to the beast, screamed, struck, bit, tore. There were no words, and no movements but the tearing of teeth and claws. (Golding 168)

In the final phrase we may notice, once again and more fully this time, the allusion to Tennyson's "Nature, red in tooth and claw"—but this time the "Nature" is not outside humanity, threatening it, but within humanity itself.

The killing marks the limits of self-knowledge, or at least its impotence to inhibit action. For Ralph, and, above all, Piggy, the primary embodiment of cognitive perspicacity in the novel, have joined in this slaughter, even if Piggy stayed on the outside of the killing circle; and in Chapter 10, Piggy, in his urgent exchange with Ralph afterwards, does not want to acknowledge their complicity. Here, significantly, the narrator does not try to enter the consciousness of either of them but relies largely on dialogue, leaving the reader to read their minds. When Ralph declares that Simon's death "was murder," Piggy "shrilly" retorts "You stop it" (Golding 172). When Ralph demands "Didn't you see […]?" Piggy replies "Not all that well. I only got one eye now" (Golding 173), giving new significance to the commonplace phrase "turning a blind eye." Piggy insists that Simon's death was "an accident" and even resorts to victim blaming: "he had no business crawling like that out of the dark. He was batty. He asked for it" (Golding 173). He stresses to Ralph that he should not "let on that we was in that dance," and when Ralph exclaims "But we were!" he persuades Ralph to agree that they were not in the inner circle: "We was on the outside. We never done nothing, we never seen nothing" (Golding 174). Here Piggy is no longer the representative of correct cognition but of what the Norwegian dramatist Henrik Ibsen called, in his play *The Wild Duck* (first published in 1884), "the saving lie" (Ibsen 243, 244): the kind of untruth that is justified by the claim it is necessary in order that individual and social life may continue (Ibsen's original Norwegian neologism, "livsløgnen," literally means "the life-lie"). It is significant that soon after this, near the end of Chapter 10, Jack steals Piggy's glasses, with their one remaining eye; this confirms and symbolizes Piggy's sacrifice of his cognitive and moral perception in his earlier refusal to acknowledge his complicity, and that of Ralph and Samneric, in the killing of Simon. Without his glasses, Piggy, at the start of Chapter 11, feels he has been "blinded" (Golding 187), the classical punishment for moral transgression. Like Oedipus at Colonus and Samson in Gaza, he is eyeless on Golding's island.

To compare Piggy to Oedipus and Samson may seem an excessive and incongruous inflation of a fat, short, asthmatic, myopic schoolboy, but it is one of the achievements of *The Lord of the Flies* that, as the narrative unfolds, the reader, embroiled physically and imaginatively in the compelling action, ceases to think of its characters as children. It is only at the end, with the arrival of the naval officer in Chapter 12, that the reader's sense of scale readjusts and its figures shrink back to child size—the fearsome Jack, for example, is a "little boy who wore the remains of an extraordinary black cap on his red hair and who carried the remains of a pair of spectacles at his waist" (Golding 222). But this cognitive correction is not enough to make all that has gone before flick out like a bubble, as if it were a mirage, and return the reader to a comforting normalcy; after this, there must be a new normal that can incorporate the experiences that Golding has dramatically evoked in the novel.

Conclusion: Underspecification and Mirror Neurons

In *Wartime and Aftermath* (1993), his survey of wartime and postwar English writing from 1939-60, the critic Bernard Bergonzi offers a succinct appraisal of *Lord of the Flies* which remains, with a range of qualifications and nuances, widespread. There is, Bergonzi acknowledges, "good reason" for its worldwide fame: It provides "a gripping and exciting narrative" while "at the same time raising profound questions about the nature of civil society and the limits and possibilities of human nature." But, he contends, it "has the limitations of a moral fable, with elements of both rigidity and thinness; Golding seems to have had a very clear idea in his own mind of what everything stood for, and the underlying ideas are too explicit" (Bergonzi 191). But there is already an implied contradiction in Bergonzi's appraisal: How can an overly explicit novel raise "profound" questions—surely it could only raise them in a superficial way? The kind of evaluation Bergonzi exemplifies depends on abstracting from the text at a distance rather than engaging with its texture. It is of course the case that the precision of Golding's prose enables him to suggest, with unusual clarity, a sheaf of philosophical and political positions and problems; but he does *suggest* rather than state these, leaving the reader to make inferences about their exact nature and proportions. Throughout the novel, while characters and situations are vividly and concretely evoked, the ideas to which they may give rise are underspecified; it is the

---

reader, or the critic, who may then specify more closely but such specifications do not exhaust the text, as the multiple interpretations it has generated and continues to generate show.

Bergonzi makes, in parenthesis, one other point worth addressing: that the novel's "pessimism [...] made it unpopular with progressive humanists" (Bergonzi 191). Cognitive literary criticism offers, not a means of rehabilitating it for progressive humanism or for any other ideology, but of mitigating, or at least complicating, what might seem to be its pessimism, through the idea of *mirror neurons*, which posits that the human nervous system contains components that mirror the situations of other human beings and that form the basis of empathy. In this respect, consider the scene in Chapter 1 in which Ralph reveals Piggy's nickname (we never know his proper name) to the assembled boys: "A storm of laughter arose and even the tiniest child joined in. For the moment the boys were a closed circuit of sympathy with Piggy outside: he went very pink, bowed his head and cleaned his glasses again" (Golding 23). Here the reader is able both to identify with the laughing boys— with the physical and psychological group response generated by neurological and cognitive similarities between individuals—and to feel empathy for Piggy, to share his embarrassment as it affects his body and to read his mind, intuiting his feelings of humiliation and isolation from his situation and his change in skin color. This solicitation of empathy is a recurrent element in the novel, so that, at the end, the reader can feel for and with Ralph as he weeps "for the end of innocence, the darkness of man's heart, and the fall through the air of the true, wise friend called Piggy" (Golding 223). The "end of innocence," with its biblical implications, the "darkness of man's heart" (with its echo of Conrad's *Heart of Darkness*) and even "the fall through the air" (with its allusion to the Fall of humankind and the Fall of Lucifer) are potent but abstract phrases: Ralph's final feeling for Piggy activates a response in the reader that is the basis of a compassion that counters and complicates, though it does not cancel, the cruelty the novel has so powerfully portrayed.

Works Cited

Bergonzi, Bernard. *Wartime and Aftermath: English Literature and Its Background 1939-1960.* Oxford UP, 1993.

Bloom, Harold, editor. *William Golding's* Lord of the Flies: *Bloom's Modern Critical Interpretations.* Chelsea House, 2008.

Cave, Terence. *Thinking with Literature: Towards a Cognitive Criticism.* Oxford UP, 2016.

Conrad, Joseph. *Heart of Darkness* with *The Congo Diary.* Edited with an introduction and notes by Robert Hampson. Penguin, 1995.

Eliot, T. S. *The Waste Land. Collected Poems, 1909-1962*, Faber, 1974, pp. 61-86.

Golding, William. *Lord of the Flies*, Faber, 1977.

Ibsen, Henrik. *The Wild Duck.* Translated by Una Ellis-Fermor. *Hedda Gabler and Other Plays.* Penguin, 1950, pp. 139-260.

Page, Norman, editor. *William Golding: Novels, 1954-1967: A Casebook.* Palgrave Macmillan, 1985.

Stockwell, Peter. *Texture: A Cognitive Aesthetics of Reading.* Edinburgh UP, 2014.

Tennyson, Alfred. *Poems and Plays.* Edited by T. Herbert Warren, revised and enlarged by Frederick Page. Oxford UP, 1975.

Tredell, Nicolas. "Fireflies and Field." *PN Review 234* (Mar.-Apr. 2017), vol. 43, no. 4, pp. 54-5.

Watt, Ian. *Conrad in the Nineteenth Century.* U of California P, 1981.

"Until the Grownups Come" versus "To Found a New Nation": Human Nature in Golding's *Lord of the Flies* and Heinlein's *Tunnel in the Sky*_____

Rafeeq O. McGiveron

William Golding's *Lord of the Flies* (first published in 1954) is justly revered for its investigation of the evil inherent in all humanity. Of course, regardless of whether one approaches the topic from a religious point of view, an evolutionary perspective, a psychoanalytical stance, or even a position informed merely by everyday experience, the observation that every person intrinsically has the capacity for both good and ill is far from new. The power of Golding's novel lies instead in the awful depth of the evil he portrays in seemingly ordinary schoolboys of only twelve or thirteen years old, who descend into literally murderous savagery when marooned on an island far from an adult civilization that itself has descended into an exponentially murderous nuclear World War III.

Still, the very aspect that makes the book so shocking—its characters' youth, which at first might suggest an innocence more likely to lead to hijinks and adventure than to superstition, torture, and beheading—in fact on reexamination should undercut the relentless pessimism of the tale's logic. We can see this perhaps most clearly when comparing Golding's bleak classic with Robert A. Heinlein's *Tunnel in the Sky* (first published in 1955), a contemporaneous young adult science fiction novel about teenagers who, due to failure of a transdimensional gate, are stranded in the dangerous wilds of a distant alien planet. Heinlein's work pits his protagonists not just against hunger and thirst and predatory life forms but also against each other, and yet its triumphant ending stands as a literary rejoinder to Golding's grim world-view. Golding in the dystopic *Lord of the Flies* has rigged a crucial variable of his plotting to miss the true potentials of humanity, for he uses characters too young to have gained crucial knowledge and skills, whereas Heinlein, with an optimism that actually is based in great pragmatism, recognizes that social stability requires a maturity and self-sacrifice that must, and indeed can, be carefully learned on the long path to adulthood.

Golding's Novel

Lord of the Flies begins immediately following an air crash—actually, the jettison of the passenger cabin (Golding 8) by a transport under enemy attack, although the result is little less violent—that strands upon a remote Pacific island dozens of schoolboys evacuated from a Britain now under atomic attack. When Ralph, the fair-haired lad with the shoulders of a boxer-to-be but the "mildness about his mouth and eyes that proclaimed no devil" (10), in the opening pages of Chapter 1 first realizes that the shoot-down has left the boys without even the pilot to tell them what to do, "the delight of a realized ambition overc[omes] him" (8). Doing a headstand, he "grin[s]" at the plump, ungrammatical, but sometimes-perceptive boy called Piggy, exclaiming, "No grownups!" (8). Ralph is only "twelve years and a few months," after all, old enough to have lost his baby fat but "not yet old enough for adolescence to have made him awkward" (8). The sight of a pretty conch gleaming in the rippling water still brings "a delighted smile" to his face (15), just as might the boyish entertainment of running with arms swept back like a fighter jet's wings and strafing his companion with a "Shee-aa-ow!" (11). "[T]he reality of the island"—meaning its freedom from adults with their school lessons and rules and curfews—makes him laugh "delightedly," stand on his head again, cavort nakedly and luxuriously in the warm sand, and finally gaze out at the ocean "with bright, excited eyes" (10). Entranced in "the vivid phantoms of his day-dream" (16), Ralph at first does not quite seem to understand the import of Piggy's suggestion that he blow the conch to summon any other survivors (16). After a few false starts, though, including those in which the resultant "low, farting noise" convulses the pair with "bouts of laughter" (17), the two call the other boys in from the jungle.

The castaways begin to realize that without adults, they shall "have to look after [them]selves" (22). It is quite a step up from fart jokes and name-calling, although of course these latter amusements

---

seem never to pale.[1] At Ralph's notion of needing "a chief to decide things" (22), Jack, the seemingly worldly-wise leader of a group of choirboys, "with simple arrogance" claims himself as best qualified: Aside from being "chapter chorister and head boy," he also "can sing C sharp" (22). The assertion appears made without self-consciousness or embarrassment, but the observed habits of the adult world, in which, as Piggy puts it in Chapter 5, people "meet and have tea and discuss" (94), suggest that nominations and a general election may be in order instead. In "[t]his toy of voting" (22), then, Ralph receives the majority of ballots, gaining even the good-natured applause of the choir, who had voted in a bloc for their own leader. Indeed, despite Jack's first "blush of mortification" and abortive movement to leave, the vanquished accepts defeat as civilly as any twelve-year-old might (23), and the two even form, essentially, a coalition government.

We should not forget, however, that these gestures of civil organization are just that—gestures, without a real understanding of the ideals they should represent. Jack's self-aggrandizement may be obvious, but it seems doubtful that Ralph's assertion of the group's need for a chief was meant to imply any candidate besides himself. As the plot demonstrates, Ralph is more even-tempered and more thoughtful than Jack, but he nevertheless quietly enjoys the prestige of his position. When in Chapter 2, for example, he institutes the parliamentary rule that any boy holding the conch during meetings may speak, "[a]nd he won't be interrupted," at the same time he naturally adds, "Except by me" (33), thus consciously or unconsciously claiming that prerogative not for the office of the chief in general but for himself in particular. Later, in Chapter 4, when Jack's hunters let the signal fire go out just as a ship was spotted in the distance and rescue might have been possible, Ralph's bitter accusation points less at duty per se than at the fact that he himself has been let down, even ignored: "I was chief, and you were going to do what I said" (70). Even at the end of the novel, after Piggy has been killed and all the other biguns, or older children, have joined the rival tribe Jack has started, when the rescuing British naval officer asks who the leader of the boys is, Ralph answers swiftly and "loudly," before his rival can: "I am" (201).

Such boyish motivators, from the joy of tramping through the wilds in the "glamour" of exploration (25) to "[t]he humiliating tears" (127) of losing face before one's peers, abound. In Chapter 3, Ralph complains disgustedly of the immaturity of his fellow castaways: "Meetings. Don't we love meetings? Every day. Twice a day. We talk.... I bet if I blew the conch this minute, they'd come running. Then we'd be, you know, very solemn, and someone would say we ought to build a jet, or a submarine, or a TV set. When the meeting was over they'd work for five minutes, then wander off or go hunting" (51). The chief is correct, and yet at times he dimly senses that he actually is only a step or two removed from this level of irresponsibility as well. In Chapter 5, for example, Ralph silently admits to himself that unlike Piggy, who "could go step by step inside that fat head of his," he himself "can't think" (78). It is a sobering realization when such evaluation, planning, follow-through, and self-restraint are precisely what are needed for survival, and ideally not just from the chief's prime advisor but all members of the group.

Of course, the community actually has been founded almost less upon the need for survival—both physical and perhaps emotional— than simply the need for easy gratification. In Chapter 2, when Ralph at the group's second meeting agrees with Piggy that since no one at home knows where they are, the boys "may be here a long time," the silence is "complete" (34). The chief immediately reassures the assemblage, however, with promises of fun:

> "But this is a good island. We—Jack, Simon, and me—we climbed the mountain. It's wizard. There's food and drink, and—"
> "Rocks—"
> "Blue flowers—"
> Piggy...pointed to the conch in Ralph's hands, and Jack and Simon fell silent. Ralph went on.
> "While we're waiting we can have a good time on this island."
> He gesticulated widely.
> "It's like in a book."
> At once there was a clamor.

"Treasure Island—"

"Swallows and Amazons—"

"Coral Island—"

Ralph waved the conch.

"This is our island. It's a good island. Until the grownups come to fetch us we'll have fun." (34-35)

Certainly fun is fun, and there might be time for it now and then even in potentially difficult survival situations, but Ralph definitely emphasizes the recreational aspects of their stranding rather more than is healthy for the group. Even when Jack "crie[s] excitedly," "We'll have rules! ... Lots of rules!" this is not so that the boys actually may accomplish anything but instead for the "Bong!" and "Doink!" of the punishments to be meted out "when anyone breaks 'em" (37). Ralph sums it all up with "We want to have fun. And we want to be rescued" (37), an attempt at balance that still falls woefully short of conveying how much more than mere play will be required of them if they are to survive.

The youths simply do not have the self-restraint and foresight needed for basic tasks like constructing shelters or keeping a signal fire burning, let along governing themselves as a true community. What makes the island "good," it seems, is the freedom for fun, from the "play, aimless and trivial," of the six-year-olds building elaborately decorated sandcastles (59), as seen in Chapter 4, to the pig hunting of those around age twelve or thirteen, a quasi-sexual act Golding describes in Chapter 8 as a "lust" that culminates with "hot blood spouting," leaving the victors "heavy and fulfilled upon" a great sow's belly (135). All play and no work makes Jack a sullen boy, at least when called to answer for it, and when he fractures the group in Chapter 8, his announcement to Ralph, punctuated with "humiliating tears" after calling unsuccessfully for a vote of no confidence, is couched in the language of boyhood: "I'm not going to play any longer. Not with you" (127). Later, in trying to attract more recruits, Jack explains that what he and his "tribe" do is "hunt and feast and have fun" (140), a boast he echoes in Chapter 9, asking, "Who'll join my tribe and have fun?" (150).

In addition to the boys', well, *boyish* focus on the short-term goals of the instant gratification of play, neither have they yet developed the empathy necessary for the give-and-take required to create and sustain a community. For example, throughout the book, Piggy is treated as "an outsider" (65) and made an object of ridicule, and despite some occasional leanings towards friendship, it is only at the very end of Chapter 12, after Piggy's murder, that Ralph supposedly realizes him as a "true, wise friend" (202). Perhaps more tellingly, when Percival, one of "[t]the smaller boys...known by the generic title of 'littlun,'" in Chapter 4 falls into a pitiable state of madness, "crawl[ing] into a shelter and stay[ing] there for two days, talking, singing, and crying," the older boys show no sympathy or even concern; indeed, they call him "batty" and are "faintly amused" (59). Such attitudes are unfortunate, but they are not unexpected in children still so far from adulthood.

With an immature outlook that sees play as the goal and yet fails to see other humans as worthy of consideration, it should not be surprising that the breakaway schoolboys of Jack's new group, freed from the order of the conch, descend into a dictatorship far less benevolent than Ralph's. The broad contours of Jack's reign would have been very familiar to Golding's contemporary readers who recalled a world war fought against Adolf Hitler, Benito Mussolini, and Emperor Hirohito just a decade earlier. On an island without the makings for uniforms, the fiercely proud boy first uses clays and charcoal to paint his face as camouflage for hunting, and yet, as Golding reminds us in Chapter 4, "the mask [i]s a thing on its own, behind which Jack hid[es], liberated from shame and self-consciousness" (64). By Chapter 8 this "stark naked[ness] save for the paint" has become, essentially, a uniform that, combined with a "howling" charge, can make the smaller children "fle[e] screaming" (140). The new tyrant is accompanied by storm troopers with fire-sharpened sticks for spears, minions who might punctuate his pronouncements by raising their weapons theatrically and intoning, "The chief has spoken" (141). Jack in Chapter 6 has already denigrated the freedom of speech denoted by possession of the conch, claiming, "We know who ought to say things. ... It's time some people knew they've got to keep quiet and leave deciding things to the rest of us" (102). Now, of course, it is only he who does the deciding in his tribe, for by Chapter 9 "authority s[its] on his shoulder and chatter[s] in his ear" (150), allowing any whim or urge to become law.

Even being "taken prisoner by the Reds," Ralph and his last allies agree in Chapter 10, would be preferable to capture by Jack (162). In Chapter 9, after all, when the dreamy Simon staggers out of the dark jungle and into the "demented" firelit ritual dance that mimics pig hunting, the others end up killing him, not only with clubs and spears but also with "the tearing of teeth and claws" (153). It is not simply a case of misidentification, however, as the shamefaced and horrified Ralph, who with Piggy has attended the feast, admits in Chapter 10; despite the confusion of the darkness and storm, and despite the intoxication of "that bloody dance," they still recognized Simon, and it "was murder" (156). Jack and his second-in-command, Roger, are "terrors" (189), the unwillingly conscripted twins Sam and Eric tell Ralph in Chapter 12: "what's sense" is "gone" (188), replaced by orchestrated mob violence and willingness, even eagerness, to murder. Roger has already killed Piggy by toppling a boulder upon him in Chapter 11 (181), and in Chapter 12 he "has sharpened a stick at both ends" (190), meaning that after Ralph is driven out of hiding, he can be beheaded, and his head placed on the spike as an offering to the imagined "beast" of the island, as first was done with the sow's head in Chapter 8 (136-37).

I myself have some doubt that children even as old as twelve or thirteen would descend to this level of utter savagery—not just cruelty and even beatings but willful murder and decapitation— without a nudge from the adult world.[2] Regardless of the exact extent to which the social structure actually might break down in such a circumstance, however, it is clear that the problem is exacerbated by the characters' youth, with its concomitant lack of social development. In fact, although the older boys may pose at being almost grown up[3] and thus very competent, the narrative here and there makes them seem even younger, or at least less mature and hence more underprepared, than their chronological ages might suggest.

It is not particularly unusual, for example, for children of ten or twelve or so to refer to their parents as Mummy or Daddy; still, when speaking with someone outside the family, it would be far more customary to shift to "*my* daddy," since that parent is not the listener's father. Although Ralph in Chapter 2 uses the public phraseology when explaining, "My father's in the Navy" (37) to establish his own bona fides, just a few sentences later he slips into the more childish pattern when suggesting, in a hopefulness that envisages the most improbable coincidence, that "[i]t might even be Daddy's ship" that rescues them (37). In fact, Ralph's first reference to his father, in speaking with Piggy in Chapter 1, seems even more little-boyish: "I could swim when I was five. Daddy taught me. He's a commander in the Navy. When he gets leave he'll come and rescue us" (13). In addition to using the language of young childhood, the boy demonstrates astonishing naïvety in imagining that a private citizen in the middle of an atomic war could mount an expedition searching the South Seas for his vanished son. It is the stuff of adventure books, but hardly, I would think, the sort of thing a twelve-year-old would believe.

Ralph's childlike outlook is revealed as well in his simplified notion of the British government being run by "the Queen," who "has a big room full of maps," he asserts reassuringly in Chapter 2, with "all the islands in the world...drawn there. So the Queen's got a picture of this island" (37). And in Chapter 7, privately, he reminisces about his former home, back when "Mummy had still been with them and Daddy had come home every day," "[w]ild ponies" had come in from the moors, he observed with the focus of a small child the minutiae of "the plate with the little blue men," and he had had the treat of "a bowl of cornflakes with sugar and cream" at bedtime (112). The shelf beside his bed had held familiar books:

> They were dog-eared and scratched. There was the bright, shining one about Topsy and Mopsy that he never read because it was about two girls; there was the one about the magician, which you read with a kind of tied-down terror, skipping page twenty-seven with the

awful picture of the spider; there was a book about people who had dug things up, Egyptian things; there was *The Boy's Book of Trains*, *The Boy's Book of Ships*. Vividly they came before him; he could have reached up and touched them, could feel the weight and slow slide with which *The Mammoth Book for Boys* would come out and slither down... (112; ellipsis Golding's)

"Everything was all right," Golding concludes in a narrative voice filtered through Ralph's point of view. "Everything was good-humored and friendly" (112). It is all very sad as well, poignantly highlighting the way the boy's once-happy childhood has been lost. Yet it also is difficult to imagine, even in the time of writing of 1954, a twelve-year-old being so terrified of an illustration in a children's book that he has to skip that page. It is as if Golding is doing everything he can to make even his most potentially promising character more childish and less capable.

Reinforcing this undermining of the stature of Ralph and the other biguns are the final descriptions of the boys at the very end of Chapter 12, filtered this time through the apparently objective viewpoint of the immaculately uniformed British naval officer who has come ashore from his "trim cruiser" (202). While the littluns are mere "tiny tots" (201), Ralph himself seems only a "little scarecrow" (201); Jack, who in Chapter 1 is "tall" (20) and possessed of "offhand authority" in his voice (21), is simply a "little boy" wearing "the remains of an extraordinary black cap upon his red hair" (201); and Jack's followers are "little boys" as well (200). Yes, youths of twelve or thirteen would be smaller than this self-satisfied exemplar of martial might with the revolver at his hip, and perhaps—just perhaps—the "little" in Ralph's case, combined with the scarecrow reference, might denote only thinness rather than shortness. The descriptions even of Jack and all his troops as "little," however, clearly refers to their height, as, of course, it likely does with Ralph as well. The officer "should have thought that a pack of British boys...would have been able to put up a better show than that..." (201-202), but one might as well expect six-year-olds to govern themselves alone.[4] Despite their chronological

---

ages, Golding's characters seem closer to six than to eighteen in the capabilities that truly matter.

Heinlein's *Tunnel in the Sky*

Although Robert A. Heinlein's *Tunnel in the Sky* begins without the grim backdrop of nuclear war to remind us of the supposedly irredeemable nature of humanity, this young adult novel is no utopia of universal happiness and plenty. While Heinlein in Chapter 2 implies that World War III and "[t]the hydrogen, germ, and nerve gas horrors that followed" (20) are merely a page from history, the nation-state still exists rather than being replaced by some science-fictional world government, and Chapter 1 shows the international friction that occurs when swarms of forced emigrants from the "Australasian Republic" of "His Serene Majesty Chairman Fung Chee Mu" are chivvied with casual "brutality" by "brawny Mongol policemen" while their North American counterparts can only look on helplessly (10-12). Despite high-tech gadgets like automatic food preparers (26), virtual reality windows for underground dwellings (23-24), and transdimensional gates that flick commuters instantaneously between points thousands of miles apart (18), population pressure that never decreases keeps Earth "slightly hungry" (18). In fact, in a world where, as Chapter 2 mentions nonchalantly, the crowded "Greater New York" has spread such that its subterranean apartments reach even to the Grand Canyon (23), it is only transdimensional portals—ones reaching not just halfway across a continent but instead to the stars—that keep Earth from descending once more into war. Here we are told that the galaxy "contains in excess of one hundred thousand Earth-type planets, each as warm and motherly to men as sweet Terra" (20), and now they are, essentially, "no farther away than the other side of the street" (22), although at the cost of a huge expenditure of energy.

Warm and motherly these worlds may be, and yet, just as Earth once did, they also contain "[v]irgin continents, raw wildernesses, fecund jungles, killing deserts, frozen tundras, and implacable mountains" (22). Humanity is a "biped omnivore" in Heinlein's description, metaphorically "ha[ving] need of his biting, tearing, animal teeth" in the literal struggle on the planets of far-flung stars "to kill or be killed, eat or be eaten" (23). Such phraseology at first might seem to suggest a pessimism about human nature, but Heinlein is a realist rather than a pessimist, and when he writes that Earth is "train[ing] its best children, its potential leaders, in primitive pioneer survival—man naked against nature" (23), it should be taken not as a reduction of the human to animal but as a fulfillment of the entirety of what it means to be human. Little children first are trained not to touch the stove, for example, but as they grow older and more capable they are trained in how to cook with this potentially dangerous implement; both are age-appropriate lessons of survival. Yet just as there is a difference between the lessons of, say, age six and age sixteen, even that older child would not be truly ready without careful guidance all along the way.

In this novel, parents and society work to provide the necessary guidance and opportunities for learning along the road to adulthood. Protagonist Rod Walker and his classmates at Patrick Henry High School, for example, are offered an "elective senior seminar" in Advanced Survival (1) taught by a wryly no-nonsense veteran of several dangerous expeditions to new worlds. While not required for graduation, this course would be needed for anyone intending to major in any of "the Outlands professions" in college (5) and then work in deep space. For a "final examination in Solo Survival" made possible by transdimensional gate, the following conditions are set:

(a) ANY planet, ANY climate, ANY terrain;
(b) NO rules, ALL weapons, ANY equipment;
(c) TEAMING IS PERMITTED but teams will not be allowed to pass through the gate in company;
(d) TEST DURATION is not less than forty-eight hours, not more than ten days. (2)

Even after all of his lessons, Rod still cannot help feeling a "quiver in his nerves" (2), and a very understandable one, for despite the benefit of a 24-hour notice, the survival challenge he will face is far more alien and potentially deadly than that of Golding's schoolboys.

Yet is not merely a matter of not knowing "whether to take a space suit, or a canoe" (6), as another student complains, or even the uncertainty of whether "you might be facing a polar bear at forty below—or wrestling an octopus deep in warm salt water," let alone "fac[ing] up to some three-headed horror on a planet you had never heard of" (2). Indeed, when asked if they will "run into dangerous animals," the instructor says, "You surely will! The most dangerous animal known" (4). Someone starts quoting from a book of exobiology, but the one-eyed old man explains that he is "talking about the *real* King of the Beasts, the only animal that is always dangerous, even when not hungry. The two-legged brute" (5). In some exasperation he continues,

> "I've said this nineteen-dozen times but you still don't believe it. Man is the one animal that can't be tamed. He goes along for years as peaceful as a cow, when it suits him. Then when it suits him not to be, he makes a leopard look like a tabby cat. Which goes double for the female of the species. Take another look around you. All friends. We've been on group-survival field tests together; we can depend on each other. So? Read about the Donner Party, or the First Venusian Expedition. Anyhow, the test area will have several other classes in it, all strangers to you." (5)

The reminder here is sobering, though, rather than appalling, as is the outlook in *Lord of the Flies*. Whereas humans in Golding's novel seem to have an actual propensity for pointless cruelty and evil when freed from societal restraint, Heinlein suggests evil to be only a possibility rather than a probability. In fact, since the antisocial force may stem from the individual survival instinct, it thus can be understood and even managed.

As if to highlight the danger posed by the unscrupulous, once Rod has gone through the gate to an unidentified world, Heinlein in Chapter 3 has him jumped by an assailant presumably from one of the other schools, and robbed of every piece of gear—even his clothing—except for one knife hidden under a bandage (60). Rod, who in a beautifully contrasting display of humanity just the night before almost had been moved to leave his safe perch in a tree by an animal's call that at first seemed "the terrible sound of a grown man crying with heartbreak" (51), is lucky to be alive after a blow to the head he is certain was "intended to kill" (60). Even this occasional predation is not the only danger, however, for a supernova disrupts the transdimensional gate that was to bring the students home, leaving them stranded for what ends up being more than two Earth years.[5] Yet despite some initial suspicions, trouble with a group of freeloading toughs, and minor political rivalries, more than two dozen strangers from several schools all over Earth come together on this alien planet to create a true community.

As leader of the band of three that first summons other survivors—with smoke rather than a conch—Rod naturally becomes de facto leader of the wider group as well. Soon, however, it becomes apparent that a more thought-out arrangement would be preferable. "The greatest invention of mankind is government," explains the other candidate for mayor in Chapter 8, a college boy a year or so older than Rod and significantly more eloquent, for it allows a species "[m]ore individualist than cats...to cooperate more efficiently than ants or bees or termites" (108). Echoing the sentiments of Rod's teacher, he reminds them all that while humans are "[w]ilder, bloodier, and more deadly than sharks, [they] have learned to live together more peacefully than lambs" (108). Voting here, obviously, will be more than just the "toy" it is in *Lord of the Flies*.

The rhetoric of the mayor-to-be, with its evocation of the survivors' imagined "descendants far into the womb of time" (108), of course is stagey, and his administration starts out being a bit pompous and yet do-nothing, but the motivations are light-years away—literally—from the childish fun-seeking to which Golding's schoolboys cling. When he asserts that their goal should be "not to elect a survival-team captain, but to found a new nation" (107), it cannot help but seem a stirring and noble thing. Unsurprisingly, Heinlein's characters eventually do not just survive but thrive. The group at last is rescued, but not before, as is shown in Chapter 14, they realize that they could "never [be] happier" (180) than on their unnamed world, in the town they have built with their own hands

---

and yet governed with the accumulated wisdom of millennia of human history.

Golding and Heinlein Juxtaposed

Although Ralph in Chapter 12 of *Lord of the Flies*, sobbing aloud, inwardly bemoans "the darkness of man's heart" (212), I would argue that had Golding not ginned up the inevitable-seeming plunge into murder and beheading, then mere self-centeredness and neglect, along with the occasional fight, would have been the extent of the "darkness" seen. Robert A. Heinlein's *Tunnel in the Sky* may not be as complex as William Golding's famous work, and certainly is not as grim, but Heinlein's use of characters who are older and more socially and politically accultured than Golding's allows his protagonists to benefit from the careful preparation they have been given on the path to full personhood; this, after all, reflects the way children in the real world learn to take, and to make, their places in society. In using characters so young and underprepared, *Lord of the Flies* has rigged the variables to miss the true potentials of a species that the deeply pragmatic but doggedly optimistic Heinlein elsewhere celebrated as an "animal barely up from the apes" that nevertheless possesses an "honesty and insatiable curiosity, [an] unlimited courage and [a] noble essential decency" ("This I Believe" 141). Had Golding's shortchanged schoolboys instead been older and more acclimatized to the world of adulthood, as Heinlein's are, perhaps they might have been able to learn not only about the darkness of the human heart but also, even more fundamentally, something of its goodness as well.

Notes

1. Ralph's reminder in Chapter 5 of needing to keep human waste to a specific area, for example, brings "sniggers," while his reference to being "taken short" with diarrhea causes "roar[s]" of laughter (80). And regarding names, the boy set apart by his lower-class accent, corpulence, asthma, and glasses (65) is never known as anything but "Piggy," except the few times Jack calls him "Fatty"; still, "Better Piggy than Fatty," Ralph advises him in Chapter 1 (25). Jack's idea of parliamentary persuasion, of course, is shown in Chapter 5, when

he tells the younger children that they are merely "a lot of cry-babies and sissies" (82).

2. We may point to child soldiers in Africa or civil wars in the Middle East, but the terrible crimes committed by youngsters have occurred with, at the very least, adult encouragement. Golding's schoolboys know vaguely of the atom bomb and the enemy of the Communist Bloc, but actually, as may be indicated by their evacuation from Britain, they probably have had little exposure to war at all.

3. Jack in particular in Chapter 1 swaggers with his familiar mention of exotic locales like "Gib." and "Addis" (20), and at first scorns the use of "[k]ids' names" rather than adult-sounding last names (21).

4. William F. Nolan picks the age of six in his classic science fiction story, "The Underdweller" (first published in 1957), wherein aliens attempt to kill off all humans older than this, knowing that without adult guidance, "survivors would revert to savagery" (28).

5. In Chapter 14, the child of the first couple married after it becomes apparent that the group is truly lost from Earth is described as being "sixteen months" (174). A young adult novel of the mid 1950s would not have had conception occur before marriage, so they were stranded at least nine or ten months earlier than the birth.

Works Cited

Golding, William. *Lord of the Flies*. Penguin, 2016.

Heinlein, Robert A. "This I Believe." Host Edward R. Murrow. Dec. 1, 1952. *Grumbles from the Grave*. Ed. Virginia Heinlein. Del Rey, 1989. pp. 140-41.

_____. *Tunnel in the Sky*. 1955. Dey Rey, 1978.

Nolan, William F. "The Underdweller." *The Last Man on Earth*. Edited by Isaac Asimov, Martin Harry Greenberg, and Charles G. Waugh. Fawcett, 1982. pp.17-28.

CRITICAL
READINGS

Critical Essays on *Lord of the Flies*, 1954-1969

Robert C. Evans

In the first decade and a half after its initial publication in 1954, William Golding's *Lord of the Flies* (hereafter *Lord*) went from being a relatively unknown novel to being one of the most widely read fictional works of its era. By the early 1960s it had become required reading in many schools and colleges, both in Britain and America, and by 1963 it had been turned into a big-budget film overseen by one of England's leading directors. Why had the book taken off in such a stunning fashion? Why had it helped turn Golding from an unknown schoolteacher into one of the most highly regarded novelists of his time? Why is the book still so often read and taught today? By examining the book's critical reception—especially in the crucial period from 1954 to 1969, we can begin to answer these kinds of questions. Arguments about *Lord* in the 1950s and 60s raised important issues that have been discussed and debated ever since.[1]

The 1950s

Walter Allen in 1954 praised *Lord* for resembling a "lightly told ... fragment of a nightmare." He admired its credibly dark depiction of human nature but faulted its too-obvious allegory, ultimately calling it "only a rather unpleasant and too-easily affecting story" (3). In that same year, Douglas Hewitt commended *Lord* for being "completely convincing and often very frightening" but faulted its sometimes "too explicit" insistence on obvious meanings, as when depicting the boys as "archetypal savages" (4). Hewitt, like many later critics, found *Lord* insufficiently subtle and too clearly allegorical, but he called its plot development "magnificent" (4).

In 1955, Louis J. Halle, although commending *Lord* for powerfully exploring "the irony and tragedy of man's fate" and "the eternal moral conflict," nevertheless felt that Golding "could not quite find his meaning in his material." The book's "commotion" ended with a playwright's contrivance for bringing down the curtain," making readers ask, "What was the point?" (5). Halle considered *Lord* less successful than Richard Hughes' 1929 novel *The Innocent Voyage* (also titled *A High Wind in Jamaica*). Halle praised Hughes for achieving thematic consistency but faulted Golding for trying to combine his own perspective with the conflicting vision of "the textbook anthropologist" (6). Halle considered *Lord* only briefly brilliant and illuminating.

James Stern, in 1955, reacted enthusiastically to *Lord*, noting its theme that civilization is only "skin deep," calling the novel convincingly realistic and well written, and suggesting that anyone willing to accept its basic premises would "surely be carried away" by its "plausibility and power," its "skillfully worked-out progress," and by its perfections of "characterization, dialogue, and prose" (7). Stern also noted various ironies associated with Piggy, whose near-blindness "finally saves the lives of the surviving boys while failing to save his own." Stern called Piggy "the hero of a triumphant literary effort" (7).

Dan Wickenden, also in 1955, although bothered by "nagging questions" about some details of plot (8), nonetheless found the novel compelling, "exciting," and "powerful." He found the boys "altogether convincing," the style "vivid and crystalline," and the "sense of mounting terror … brilliantly conveyed." Wickenden (like Halle) compared and contrasted *Lord* to Hughes's *A High Wind in Jamaica*," finding *Lord* more ambitious but perhaps a bit less successful (9).

Philip Drew, in 1956, was one of many critics who would compare Golding's book with R. M. Ballantyne's 1858 novel *The Coral Island*. Drew noted that Golding had deliberately given some of his characters the same names as Ballantyne's characters while "reconceive[ing] Ballantyne's story in remorselessly unromantic terms" (9). Drew argued that Golding, using "skill and discretion," as well as "subtlety and fidelity," conveyed the boys' "progressive degeneration" both individually and as a group (10). He compared *Lord* to Orwell's *1984* as both "allegory and satire" but found *Lord* actually closer in form to Orwell's *Animal Farm*. Drew thought the conch symbolized "the right of free speech in a free society" and thought the fire symbolized "a duty which must be done" not for immediate profit but in "hope of ultimate salvation" (11). He also discussed individual characters' significance (12-13), found the ending problematic, and wondered whether the boys symbolized different kinds of persons or different aspects of human nature (13). He considered the book's "dominant tone ... unsavoury and depressing" and emphasized its "grim" and "macabre" aspects (14). He highlighted the importance of superstition as a key theme, stressed the novel's repeated tone of "despair" and "disappointment," and commented on its depiction of "the superficiality of our civilization and the impotence of good will and the forms of democracy against the instinctive savagery of man" (14-15). Drew faulted Golding's Romantic emphasis on the primitive, found the novel lacking in imaginative breadth and inventiveness, noted the basic plainness of its phrasing, and praised the book's occasionally rich metaphors (15). He commended Golding's decision to limit his point of view "to that of the uncomprehending eyes of the boys," commented on the themes of communication and community, and ended by emphasizing the optimistic implications of Ralph's gradual maturation (16-7). Ralph, according to Drew, "grows by discovering more about himself and his fellows, but especially about himself" (17).

In 1957, Wayland Young suggested that the book's "specifically Christian element ... is always subordinate to a generalized sense of natural religion" (18), contending more broadly that Simon's death "is handled with a success as resounding, as complex, and as profoundly beautiful as anything in Western literature" (19). William Peters, also in 1957, defended *Lord*'s conclusion against charges of seeming contrived; Peters instead called it "a deliberate device ... to throw the story into focus" (26). He saw the mysterious beast as a symbol of "Man himself, the boys' own natures, the something that all humans have in common" (27). But he faulted Golding for making this meaning too obvious, calling such "over-explicitness" his main general criticism of *Lord* (27).

V. S. Pritchett, in 1958, argued that although *Lord* emphasized pain, Golding's imagination was also "heroic," juxtaposing the grotesque with "adventure, the love of natural life, [and] the curiosity of the eye" (37). Like other critics, Pritchett noted resemblances between Golding's book and *The Coral Island* and *High Wind in Jamaica*, suggesting that the children in *Lord* symbolize flaws in adults as well and calling *Lord* Golding's "most accomplished" work (38). Also in 1958, Frank Kermode likewise compared *Lord* with *The Coral Island* (39-42), while Ralph Freedman discussed *Lord* within the context of Golding's other books, comparing it to certain eighteenth-century novels (such as *Robinson Crusoe*). Freedman argued that *Lord*, like other novels by Golding, "begins with a significant change"—a "traumatic break from one reality into another of distorted experience from which his protagonists expect to be 'rescued'" (44-5). Abrupt changes force previous complacent protagonists to define themselves; Golding's books suggest that people must control conditions "by imposing order" (45). *Lord* explores issues of "order" vs. "moral decay" (46), and shows order being imposed partly by giving names to things (47). Freedman set *Lord* fully within the contexts of Golding's other writings, as did John Bowen in 1959. Bowen praised Golding's imaginative and stylistic originality but faulted him for ending *Lord* with a "gimmick" (56). He saw *Lord* as an allegory of "how sin destroys the garden of innocence and kills the saints," such as Simon (56). Like many later critics, Bowen discussed *Lord* as part of Golding's developing career.

1960-1963

Sam Hynes, in 1960, called Golding "unusual, perhaps unique, among English novelists" in his strong emphasis on religiousness. Hynes thought Golding was especially concerned with such issues as "the nature of good and evil, guilt and responsibility, the meaning of death, and free will" (70). He noted Golding's tendency to isolate characters (71) and claimed that *Lord* dealt with humans' "dual nature" of both good and evil (72). The fact that the book's "beast" is actually human symbolizes that "what the boys fear is in fact in themselves." Noting that Golding himself had also described the beast as symbolizing history, Hynes found this claim less than obvious (72).

Also in 1960, Martin Green dissented from recent praise of Golding and of *Lord*. Green found Golding "not importantly original in thought or feeling" and argued that Golding's latest book (*Free Fall*) showed that he was not even "a significant artist" (77). Although he considered *Lord* more successful than *Free Fall*, Green thought its success did not, "after all, transcend the limitations of Golding's talent." *Lord* merely shows "how brutal twelve-year-old boys can be to each other," and it then, through a kind of "trick," offers that fact as a "specious" insight into human nature (78). *Lord* shows Golding "loading the dice, prejudicing the issue, [and] insuring the triumph of greed, savagery, slyness and panic" (81). "In other words," Green continued,

> Golding is a belated recruit to the ranks of those writers who have rediscovered for this century man's essential savagery; who have triumphantly rejected science and hygiene, liberalism and progress; who have, in any account of contemporary conditions, alternated between effects of commonplaces and effects of nightmare. He is so belated as to inherit these themes in their decrepitude. (81)

Green considered Golding just the latest acclaimed writer who was essentially hostile to modern life and modern science (82).

Far more enthusiastic was a 1960 article by C. B. Cox. Like many others, Cox compared and contrasted *Lord* with *The Coral Island*. "On one level," he claimed, "the story shows how intelligence (Piggy) and common sense (Ralph) will always be overthrown in society by sadism (Roger) and the lure of totalitarianism (Jack). On another, the growth of savagery in the boys demonstrates the power of original sin" (82). Cox called *Lord* "probably the most important [English] novel" of the 1950s (82-3), seeing its "success [as] due in part to the quality of Golding's Christianity. He is neither puritan nor transcendentalist, and his religious faith is based upon his interpretation of experience, rather than upon an unquestioning acceptance of revelation" (83). Golding (Cox said) "explores actual life to prove dramatically the authenticity of his religious viewpoint" (83). *Lord* achieves an "exceptional force" deriving that "from Golding's faith that every detail of human life has a religious significance" (84).

Golding's faith in worldly experience, Cox claimed, is reflected in his "vivid, imaginative style," particularly his descriptions of "the mystery of Nature, with its weird beauty and fantastic variety." The novel shows a "passionate interest in both physical and moral life" (84). Interestingly, Cox noted that the "island itself is boat-shaped, and the children typify all mankind on their journey through life" (85). Golding thus explores ancient themes in new ways (86), shows his (and Ralph's) admiration for Piggy's intelligence, and makes Piggy's death symbolize the ways society often mistreats the good (87). But Cox considered Simon perhaps the book's "one weakness," finding Simon less convincingly real than deliberately symbolic, even though the "whole story moves towards Simon's view of reality" (87). Cox did, however, defend the sudden appearance of the naval officer," calling it a "highly original device to force upon us a new viewpoint" that is rich in irony at the expense of the officer himself, who resembles the warring boys more than he would want to admit (88).

Again emphasizing Ballantyne's *The Coral Island*, Carl Niemeyer in 1961 noted that Golding "refers obliquely to Ballantyne many times" throughout *Lord* (89). According to Niemeyer, Ballantyne himself sometimes implied "some darker aspects of boyish nature" while mainly emphasizing "the paradisiacal life" of his "happy castaways" (90). In contrast, Golding's view is far darker and more realistic. Ironically, however, the naval officer in *Lord* turns away from this chaotic darker view, preferring instead to see his "trim" warship as "something manufactured, manageable, and solidly useful" (91). Citing another example of Golding's grim vision, Niemeyer notes that the "dead parachutist [is] ironically stifled in the elaborate clothing worn to guarantee survival" (92). Simon's death is likewise ironic ("he is killed for being precisely what he is not"), while Jack, the mature boy, unironically personifies "absolute evil." Although an experienced leader as head of the choir, ultimately he "is a villain" and his "red hair and ugliness" may suggest he is "a devil" (93). Niemeyer consistently offers intriguing comments about particular details, as when he notes that when the choirboys take off their robes, they remove their Christian crosses (94).

Margaret Walters, in 1961, compared and contrasted Golding and Albert Camus, calling Golding a writer of fables in which every detail illustrates an overarching idea, although she cautioned that fables can sometimes seem too formulaic, abstract, schematic, and explicit (96-7). She thought *Lord* better than Golding's later works, noting that the warfare *on* the island reflects the larger state of war beyond (97). "Even as a realistic narrative" she found the story "both convincing and absorbing" calling it "a rigorous inversion of *Coral Island*" whose "main interest" lies in its forceful "embodiment of a controlling idea" (97-8). She admired how the parachutist's appearance ironically answers Ralph's call for "a sign from the adult world," calling this event "tremendously effective in dramatic terms" even as it illustrates the book's often "tremendous range of suggestion" (99). "The Beast," we discover, is "a human victim," just as the officer at the end "represents a more sophisticated form of the impulses that appall him in the boys" (99). Yet despite such praise, Walters did sometimes find *Lord* too explicit, too formulaic, and too blatantly symbolic, particularly in depicting Simon, whom Walters found "neither plausible nor representative." She considered the book flawed when it failed to seem sufficiently realistic (100).

Frank Kermode, also in 1961, began by noting that although no other book by Golding had been as well received as *Lord*, Golding was nevertheless generally considered "the most important practising novelist in English" (107). Mostly Kermode commented on *Lord*'s links with *The Coral Island*, but he did argue that Simon's goodness signifies God's existence. "Piggy, the dull practical intelligence, is reduced to blindness and futility," and then "Simon, the visionary, is murdered before he can communicate his comfortable knowledge" (112-13). Kermode emphasized Golding's programmatic intentions, sometimes finding those intentions (such as calling the parachutist a symbol of history) unsupported by the text (113).

Claire Rosenfield, in 1961, published an often-reprinted article arguing that *Lord* illustrated Sigmund Freud's assumption that "no child is innocent" (122). She thought Piggy resembled an archetypal wise old man (122-23) and thought the game-playing boys resembled precivilized humans, just as their superstitions resembled those of primitive peoples (124-25). Jack increasingly resembles a demon associated with irrationality (126), and Piggy's gradual demise suggests that the "dominance of reason is over; the voice of the old world is stilled" (127). When the boys become preoccupied with hunting, "every kill [symbolically] becomes a sexual act" and is "a metaphor for childhood sexuality." Through their rituals, the boys symbolically share dreams and free repressions (127), and Simon's temporary loss of consciousness symbolizes "annihilation of the ego, an internal journey necessary for self-understanding, a return to the timelessness of the unconscious" (128). Simon, according to Rosenfield, functions both as redeemer and scapegoat, while the smashing of Piggy's head, like the smashing of the conch, symbolizes the destruction of order (129). But Rosenfield also offers a larger argument:

> Having populated the outside world with demons and spirits which are projections of their instinctual nature, these children—and primitive men—must then unconsciously evolve new forms of worship and laws, which manifest themselves in taboos, the oldest form of social repression. (129)

All the kills except the first, she argued, are ritualistic and illustrate Freud's ideas about totems and taboos. Simon's death symbolizes a break from old authority, while Piggy's death may symbolize the boys' sharing of "responsibility for their crime" (130). Rosenfield cautioned against reading the novel as "an imaginative recreation of Freud's theory that children are little savages" (130-31); the book, she thought, implies much about the adult world, and the parachutist, as scapegoat, resembles Simon (131). "Paradoxically," Rosenfield concludes, "the children not only return to a primitive and infantile morality, but they also degenerate into adults" (132).

Golding himself, in 1962, described *Lord* as a fable, called it intentionally moralistic and didactic, emphasized its focus on humans as fallen creatures "gripped by original sin," disclosed that it had been inspired by the evils of World War II (especially the Holocaust), emphasized that all people, everywhere and always, are capable of evil, even civilized Britons (40-1). Golding made the boys young to prevent sex from being an issue, made the island fruitful to prevent Marxist explanations of the rise of evil, and wanted to show the boys yearning for the adult wisdom that sometimes tempers evil (42). He called Simon a deliberate Christ figure who prays in the jungle (44) and said he himself agreed with Simon's message (45).

James Gindin, also in 1962, alleged that Golding's novels tended to end with "gimmicks" (133), so that the officer's arrival in *Lord* tends to soften the book's conclusion (134). A 1962 article in *Time* magazine noted the novel's popularity on US college campuses and quoted Golding's own view of the book as implying an evil inherent in human nature as well as his claim that he had never read Freud (141-42). Edmund Fuller, also in 1962, was heartened by college students' growing interest in *Lord* rather than J. D. Salinger's *The Catcher in the Rye* (a book Fuller found "soft," partly for blaming society, rather than individuals, for the world's ills). In contrast, young readers thought that *Lord* "terrifies, fascinates, shocks, [and] depresses," and Fuller argued that Golding implies "that the young are no better than the old" (143-44).

John M. Egan, in 1963, disagreeing with many other commentators, called *Lord* essentially non-Christian and even nonsupernatural. Instead, Egan thought the book emphasized chaos resulting in a materialistic worldview (146). He noted Golding's emphasis on human excrement, even asserting that "beelzebub" ("lord of the flies") also meant "lord of dung"—a detail relevant to the novel's dark view of human nature (147). The fact that Simon, the airman, and Piggy are all swept out to sea suggested, to Egan, the book's emphasis on a cruel, meaningless, chaotic universe (147). Similarly, in 1963 Francis E. Kearns also stressed Golding's distance from traditional Christian views, although Kearns did contrast Golding's emphasis on humanity's innate evil with the liberal humanist values found in Salinger's *Catcher* (154). Kearns claimed that "Golding is content to picture evil and then stand back," failing to emphasize any "sense of personal desperation in the face of evil" and failing, too, to stress free will as an alternative to the darkness it depicts (155). Peter Green in 1963 surveyed Golding's "world," emphasized the novelist's interest in human self-knowledge, his use of theological symbolism, his concern with man's innate evil, and the ways his ideas were compatible with traditional Christian views (172-73). Green saw Piggy as symbolizing sanity and individualism and as a victim of totalitarianism (176): "Man, Golding seems to be saying, cherishes his guilt, his fears, his taboos, and will crucify any saint or redeemer who offers to relieve him of his burden by telling the simple truth," as Simon does (177).

Luke M. Grande in 1963 argued that in "a world that tends to equate evil with unfavorable environment, Golding sees instead man's inner responsibility for choosing between good and evil" (157). Although conceding that *Lord* could be read in part by seeing "Jack-Ralph-Piggy" as "id-ego-superego" and also by emphasizing conflicts between democracy and totalitarianism, Grande thought the novel's real appeal to young readers lay in taking them seriously as combatants in the age-old "spiritual struggle" of good versus evil (158). He saw Ralph as a kind of "philosopher-king," Piggy as a personification of "right reason," and Jack as a symbolic hunter. Evil, he claimed, is first alluded to as a "snake-thing" and "then, in ascendingly concrete images, as a 'beastie,' an 'animal,' a 'pig,' and finally as Simon/Ralph." By worshiping the pig's head, the boys "satanically enthrone their own power of blackness" (158). In a subsequent published debate (in 1963), Francis Kearns challenged Grande's praise of Golding's symbolism, claimed that *Lord*'s symbols were often unclear, and objected to Golding's view that humans are inherently evil (161). Grande responded by finding Kearns's interpretations too simplistic, pointing to Simon as a character who suggested Golding's capacity to see not only evil in people but also potential good (163-64). Kearns, however, returned to the fray, disputing Grande's efforts to find some evidence of goodness and optimism in *Lord*. Kearns found Ralph's survival (and the book's ending) ironic, challenged Grande's hopeful view of Simon (especially since Simon is murdered), and suggested that any optimism in the book's final scene is contrived, unprepared for, and too abrupt (166-68). Kearns argued that *Lord*'s appeal lay largely in its implied view that social progress was impossible and therefore not worth any effort to achieve (169).

Peter Green in 1963 argued that *Lord* showed Golding's interest in lost innocence, theological symbolism, and human responsibility for evil (173). He saw *Lord* as a parody of *The Coral Island* (174), viewed Piggy as a "voice of sanity," a "Promethean symbol," and a stubborn individualist. For Green, the novel was a relevant reflection on totalitarianism (176), and he not only traced the history of the term "Lord of the Flies" but saw this symbolic beast as inherent in human nature—a significance he thought many early critics had missed (174-75). The rest of his article related themes in *Lord* to ideas also found in Golding's later novels (176-89). A 1963 article by Venita Colby was mainly biographical (189-91), although it did report critics' views of alleged flaws in *Lord* (191).

Bern Oldsey and Stanley Weintraub in 1963 began by noting that *Lord* had as yet received relatively little attention as literature. They noted its debts to such genres as the "boy's book," the "survival narrative," works in which a culture is examined by transplanting it, "anti-science writing," and works assuming humanity's "fall from grace" (91). They particularly compared it to *Gulliver's Travels*, noted its "Swiftian obsession with physical ugliness, meanness, and nastiness (sometimes bordering on the scatological)," and thought it also resembled Swift's writing in its "sense of how tenuous is the hold of intelligence, reason, and humaneness as a brake upon man's regression into barbarism" (91). They praised the book's "exceedingly fine style," lamented its "admittedly tricky plot methods," noted its "scenic qualities," but commented that Golding often relies on his readers to "pull narrative and descriptive elements into focus" (92). Oldsey and Weintraub observed that the island is shaped "roughly like an outrigged boat," described its various physical features, noted that its precise location "is kept deliberately vague," and commented on inconsistencies in Golding's account of events in the larger world (92-93).

According to Oldsey and Weintraub, the "very tension between realistic novel and allegorical fable" gave the book "some of its unique power," and they saw this tension not only in the whole narrative but also in particular characters (93). They called the book, in part, Ralph's "rites-of-passage" novel of development; commented that Ralph is as close to a hero as *Lord* offers; and praised Ralph's concern with "individual responsibility" (93-4). They called Jack "the text's Esau," termed him "a compelled being," and argued that he "does not symbolize chaos, as sometimes claimed, but rather a stronger, more primitive order than Ralph provides" (94). They considered Roger "not so subtly or complexly characterized"; called Simon "the lonely visionary, the clear-sighted realist, logical, sensitive, and mature beyond his years"; and argued that Simon's "murder becomes the martyrdom of a saint and prophet, a point in human degeneration next to which the wanton killing of Piggy is but an anticlimax" (94-5).

Piggy himself (according to Oldsey and Weintraub) "has all the good and bad attributes of the weaker sort of intellectual." His obsession with eating made him, in their opinion, a poor symbol of the Freudian superego, and they called him "physically incapable and emotionally immature" (95). They noted that eighteen boys are mentioned by name (95), praised Golding's "ability to characterize memorably with a few deft lines," commented that only two boys are given surnames, and regretted that so much criticism had "forced the book into a neat allegorical mold" (96). They observed that none of the boys ever prays or seeks God's help, resisted views of the island as especially attractive, and disputed common opinions of the book as simply a fable or parable (97). "It *is*," they claimed, "allegoristic, rich in variant suggestions, and best taken at the level of suggestive analysis" (98).

Because three main characters exhibit some strong moral sense, Oldsey and Weintraub resisted overly pessimistic interpretations of *Lord*'s meaning. Calling this book Golding's "simplest novel," they nevertheless disputed charges that its meanings are too obvious, and they defended the navel officer's sudden arrival as necessary to the book's final "change of focus" (98). The novel's ultimate emphasis, they argued, was not on hope, charity, or contrition but on the need for recognition (99).

1964-1969

In 1964, Bernard F. Dick emphasized similarities between Golding's novel and Euripides's *The Bacchae*, especially since (1) characters in both works "revert to savagery and murder during a frenzied ritual," (2) both works end with somewhat artificial conclusions involving the sudden appearance of a figure of authority, and (3) both drama and novel "contain three interrelated ritual themes: the cult of a beast-god, a hunt as prefiguration of the death of a scapegoat-figure, and *sparagmos* or dismemberment of the scapegoat" (145-46). Also in 1964, Richard H. Lederer transcribed comments about *Lord* written by high school students, many of them offering various original insights and all of them indicating why the book was popular with students. They were intrigued by the book's "omnipresent reminders of global warfare, the interplay of group antagonisms, and the breakdowns of diplomatic relations," although a recent poll showed the books being taught in only 13 percent of private schools and a mere 5 percent of public schools (575). Quoting observations from his tenth-graders, Lederer reported that one had observed that the "abundance of water, fruit, and wild animals eliminates the man vs. nature conflict and means the boys are safe from any danger except themselves," while another noted that as "the representative of civilization, Piggy was most tied to it, especially for his ability to see (his specs), to breathe (shots for his 'assmar')." Another student noted that as the other "boys moved farther away from civilization, their hair grew longer" but not Piggy's (576). Lederer's students commented on Piggy and Simon as outcasts, on Simon's sympathy for Piggy, on Roger's growing sadism, and on the similar advisory relationships of Roger to Jack and of Piggy to Ralph (577). They also discussed the boys' initial preference for rules they later rejected, their attitudes towards shelter and fire, the ways violent chants replaced earlier singing, and the boys' fears of their own fearfulness

(578). The most important conflicts, the students commented, were not so much between the boys as within them (including Ralph). Lederer remarked that at the end of the novel, the boys "will be loaded onto a ship and will no longer destroy each other. Instead, they will watch the grownups" (579).

A 1964 note by Jacob Leed suggested that in Chapter 7, Ralph touches the dead body of the first slain boy. Also in 1964, R. C. Townsend radically questioned both the artistic and philosophical value of Golding's novel, claiming that it offered both "false profundity and false art" (153) and contrasting it very unfavorably with Richard Hughes's *High Wind*. Townsend claimed that only Piggy had a distinctive voice, but he more generally faulted Golding for pushing interpretations the book itself did not support. Golding, he claimed, "forces children into moral positions and attitudes they could never take," ones he could never "make explicit in the novel itself." He accused Golding of exploiting both his characters and his young readers with his "easy cynicism" (156). Townsend argued that whereas "Golding continually intrudes into the child's world in order to extract his own moral," Hughes in *High Wind* continually presents "a gap between their world and ours," so that "it is all but impossible to translate their thoughts into adult terms" (158). Ultimately, Townsend accused Golding, in depicting evil, either of self-contradiction, a failure of nerve, or of both at once (160).

In contrast, Gladys Veidemanis in 1964 argued strongly for *Lord*'s artistic merits, contending that its exciting plot gave it appeal to many students (569). She quoted her own students, who commended *Lord* for raising intriguing issues, for being easy to relate to, for reflecting young people's concerns with growing up in the atomic age, and for appealing to their yearning for autonomy. Golding's novel, they said, dealt with the dangers of uncontrolled desires and explored widely shared but rarely admitted common fears. Since its characters were young boys, high-school-aged readers could simultaneously relate to them and feel more mature than the boys were. High schoolers were not threatened by the book in ways their often self-defensive parents were. Veidemanis's students admired *Lord* for being "compact, yet rich in sense impression, characterization, and imaginative appeal," and they valued its "fusion of realism and allegory" (570). She concluded by offering much practical advice about teaching the book effectively.

Kenneth Watson, in 1964, praised *Lord* for its "close-knit texture and significant pattern" and its "immediate vividness and force," but he questioned religious interpretations of the novel (2). He extolled the book's "shock of its impact even on non-literary students, precisely because it is not 'literary' but unfalteringly tough-minded." First-time readers found it frightening in its emphasis on the uncanny and even "supernatural evil" (3). Watson admired its immediacy, vivid imagery, poetic qualities, and tendency to embed metaphors in verbs. He noted the ways Golding created claustrophobia, praised the book's "firmness and clarity" of symbolism, and argued that it could be read in broadly moral (rather than specifically religious) terms (3). He discussed Piggy and Simon as literal and symbolic torchbearers, compared Ralph to a typical politician, called Piggy a thoughtful realist, and emphasized Piggy's mature mind and atypically middle-class background (4). Watson found both Ralph and Jack somewhat vain, saw Samneric as "ordinary good-hearted nonentities," and viewed the first murder victim as symbolizing typical citizens who can neither understand nor control their fates. Watson noted that many readers overlook or forget about this first victim, focusing instead on the deaths of Simon and Piggy (5-6). According to Watson, the boys deteriorate not because of original sin but "through a failure of imagination and therefore a neglect of thought" (6). Their boyhood means that they aren't affected by the sexual desires that might make them seem individuals rather than members of society. Cruelty creeps into their thoughts and behavior at first in small ways and then hardens, and Golding (Watson claimed) structures the book around a series of similar "repetitions with a difference." For example, the pig hunting foreshadows the later hunting of Ralph, and just as the first victim, Simon, and Piggy all exhibit physical defects, so all three die. Yet Simon's morality implies that the book's vision is not completely pessimistic (7).

Robert White, also in 1964, praised *Lord*'s phrasing and argued that it traces defects in politics and society back to defects in human nature—defects apparent even in children (163-64), so that even Ralph helps kill Simon. White was especially interested in how Golding used butterfly imagery to symbolize the human soul and to contrast with the titular flies (166-68). Ultimately (White argued) the book suggests that any "attempt to rid society of evil is clearly impossible" (170).

In 1965, E. C. Bufkin argued that *Lord* deals with evil, the quest for order, the fall of man, and the myth of desert islands. He emphasized its irony, saw it as inverting *The Coral Island*, and also stressed its similarities to *Paradise Lost*, with the island resembling both paradise and hell. The boys (Bufkin thought) resemble fallen angels, who, like Milton's angels, fall during warfare, hold assemblies, and find in Jack a leader resembling Milton's Satan (41-43). Bufkin stressed how Golding's use of dialogue, dramatization, and an omniscient point of view contributed to the novel's irony (43-44), but he also argued that the book's two-part structure (Chapters 1-9 and 10-12) involves repetitions-with-a-difference (in the final chapters) of incidents already dealt with in the first part (44). Bufkin also commented on Golding's frequent use of words suggesting downward movement, his strong storm imagery, his allusions to the four traditional elements, and his stress on imagery involving heads (45-49). Robert Gordon in 1965 explored Golding's echoes of Homer and Euripides, saw the conch episodes as similar to council scenes in the *Iliad* and the *Odyssey,* interpreted the parachutist as a parody of Zeus, and interpreted the dispute between Ralph and Jack as resembling the argument between Agamemnon and Achilles (424-25). According to Gordon, Euripides's influence appears in Golding's emphasis on irrational violence overcoming rational control, in the abrupt and deliberately contrived intervention of the naval officer, and in the novel's final pessimistic implications.

In 1966, Suzanne Gulbin compared and contrasted Golding's book with Orwell's *Animal Farm*, while Charles Mitchell looked at *Lord* from various philosophical perspectives, calling it a book in which "human beings react to their primal confrontation with existence" (27). Mitchell noted how Ralph transforms "his aloneness into individuality"; cited the work of Erich Fromm to support this point; drew on Nikolai Berdyaev's idea that humans consist of masters, slaves, and free persons; and called Ralph an example of the latter (27-28). Mitchell interpreted *Lord* by employing Kierkegaard's concept of "dread" (28); argued that "the destructive circle is closed when Percival, the youngest boy, tries to destroy Ralph, the oldest"; and contended that the novel "develops through three stages in which opposing forces first relate, then divide, and finally clash" (30). Each section, Mitchell claimed, "ends in a killing," first of the piglet, then of the sow, then of Simon, Piggy, and (almost) Ralph (31). Mitchell saw Simon as representing "the pure truth, the acceptance of freedom" and argued that while "Ralph unifies society through himself, Jack separates it for himself" (31). He saw Simon, Piggy, and Jack as symbolizing, respectively, the "heart, reason, and will" (32) and he associated the hunt with irrationality and the fire with reason, civilization, and morality (33). Jack's followers surrender their chances of achieving true freedom; he gives them license so he can control them more effectively (35). Mitchell concluded by seeing Jack as symbolizing the threat of "atomic holocaust" (39).

J. D. O'Hara, in 1966, called *Lord* a fable about the impossibility of Utopia, one that deals "largely in psychological rather than political, economic, or social ideas" (411). O'Hara saw Ralph's leadership as "essentially religious," equated his desire to get home with a desire to attain heaven, and likened the signal fire to "an altar tended by priests" (411-12). The book shows that God and Mammon cannot both be served, demonstrates that even choirboys can be "lured away from piety," and implies that physical traits of the three main characters (Ralph, Piggy, and Jack) determine their outlooks on life (412-13). O'Hara suggested that the boys find morality boring, that the book provides little hint of religious hope or consolation, that the "rescuing naval officer" is "no more than a grown-up Jack," and that although Jack's values seem exciting, they seem to give his followers little real pleasure (414). O'Hara argued that Golding tends (like eighteenth-century novelists) to describe characters in terms of dominant passions reflected in physical appearance, that he finds most people ethically defective, that he pushes his moral lessons too obviously and overtly, that the pig's head on a stick is an "emblem of man's sadistic cruelty to natural things and of his ignorant attempts to placate a falsely externalized evil," and that the "flies preying on the head and on Simon are the boys, worshipers of a revolting demon and devourers of innocence" (416). O'Hara argued that *Lord* emphasizes fear as a motivating force; rarely mentions love, friendship, or family attachments; and exaggerates the power of evil (417-18). He faulted the book for treating imaginary problems as relevant to realistic adult dilemmas, for underestimating the age-old and demonstrable power of good, for doing insufficient justice to the beneficial effects of society, and for viewing children as "worse than adults" and then implying that adults act like children (419-20). O'Hara concluded that "Golding's images of society are erroneous. Our society, though bad, is not as corrupt as Jack's; our society's morality is not as impotent as that of Ralph's society" (420). *Lord*, in other words, is naïvely pessimistic.

Mark Kinkead-Weekes and Ian McGregor in 1967 noted *Lord*'s exceptional popularity, stressed its power and excitement, and praised its vivid narrative effectiveness (37). They commended its complex meanings, "high polish," and skillful design, and although they noted that some readers found the book *too* clear, they thought its "thematic clarity" and "narrative momentum" helped explain its "popular success" (38). They closely analyzed various passages, explored Golding's subtlety, stressed his concern with realistic description, and emphasized *Lord*'s rich symbolism and effective ambiguity—richness and ambiguity critics had often missed (39-42). Kinkead-Weekes and McGregor noted that Jack gradually acquires useful knowledge (49), questioned the view of Simon as savior, stressed instead his breadth of sensibility, and emphasized the importance of his eventual realizations (50). The book, they thought, treated children as symbolic adults rather than as children per se (57), and they stressed significant parallels between Chapters 3 and 8 (60). Calling Simon's death the novel's crucial event (65), they sought to show its plausibility by discussing prior events that make it credible, particularly the pervasive emphasis on hunting (65-76).

They defended the novel's ending, viewed the naval officer ironically, and stressed the maturity implied by Ralph's final weeping (78-79). Bruce A. Rosenberg argued in 1967 that Golding himself was responsible for critics' tendencies to stress *Lord*'s ideas rather than its craft, including its symbolism and design. Rosenberg stressed the book's emphasis on fire (128), calling it the work's key symbol, especially because of its traditional religious significance (129). He suggested that Simon, like Christ, faced temptation but defied it (131); that Simon, like Moses, brought revelation down from a mountain (132); that Simon's epilepsy was a traditional symbol of holiness (133); and that Simon the prophet is abused by those he wants to help (133-34). Rosenberg saw fire as symbolizing both potential purity and potential destruction (134), noted that Ralph calls out to God when the fire dies (136), suggested that Golding treated fire as simultaneously sacred and profane (137), and contended that although the boys think they are rescued at the end, Golding's readers should know better (138).

Sanford Sternlicht, in 1968, drawing on Golding's novel *The Inheritors*, argued that the boys in *Lord* are evil simply by being humans and by having been even briefly exposed to human adults (386-87), and he saw hints of homosexual sadism in the killing of the sow (389). Also in 1968, Samuel Hynes linked *Lord* to science fiction, contrasted it with *The Coral Island*, noted its openness to varied interpretations, and sketched the traits of its key characters, seeing Ralph as responsible, likening Jack and Ralph to Cain and Abel, calling Piggy fat, inadequate, and naïvely trustful of adult wisdom, and emphasizing Roger's lust for the power to destroy life (58-60). Hynes noted the movement from pretend violence to real violence, the ritual nature of Simon's death, the absence of innocence in Ralph from the very beginning, the way the naval officer seems as naïve as a *Coral Island* character, the way the book can be read as (but not only as) a parable of original sin, the limited effect of Simon on others, and the novel's silence on the subject of salvation (60-64). Finally, it was also in 1968 that Henri Talon emphasized play as a source of evil, regression, and disaster in *Lord*, stressed the irony of the boys' degenerative games, meditated philosophically on the nature of play, noted the boys' lack of Christian virtue, and commented on the lack of salvation in the book (including salvation for the island). Talon focused on Ralph's growing perception of irony and ended by observing, ironically, that the fire meant to destroy Ralph actually leads to his rescue (296-309).

Leighton Hodson, in 1969, stressed Golding's concern in *Lord* with evil (83), argued that Golding tries to be realistic rather than pessimistic (84), contrasted *Lord* with *Coral Island* (84), and stressed the early appearance of discord on the island (85). Hodson saw Simon as Golding's ideal human (85), argued that Simon is depicted both realistically and symbolically (86), cautioned against dividing the characters into groups of the good and the bad (86), and defended Simon against a critic who viewed him as superfluous (88). Hodson disputed simplistic Freudian and political interpretations (89), suggested that Simon was a richer character than such interpretations implied (89-90), rejected the view that Golding implies that power always corrupts, and in general rejected tendencies to reduce the novel to simple meanings (90). Hodson argued that Golding emphasizes the potential and reality of evil, not its inevitability (90-91), and he also contended that Golding is often subtle, wants his readers to respond to subtleties, and designed the book so that its details continually enrich one another (93-4).

Towards the 1970s and Beyond

By the end of the 1960s, *Lord of the Flies* had become one of the most widely discussed novels of its time. It was read, taught, and debated throughout the English-speaking world and even beyond. The issues raised by commentators in the 1950s and 60s continued to reverberate in discussions during the 1970s and beyond. *Lord* had quickly aroused the interest of readers and critics and continued to do so for decades to come.

Note

1. Almost all the early commentary on *Lord*, from 1954 to 1962, is reprinted in full in the extremely helpful *Sourcebook* edited by William Nelson. Therefore, and to save space, I have cited page

numbers from that book when discussing all the material beginning with the Walter Allen article in 1954 and ending with the article by Oldsey and Weintraub in 1963.

Works Cited

Bufkin, E. C. "*Lord of the Flies*: An Analysis." *Georgia Review*, vol. 19, 1965, pp. 40-57.

Gordon, Robert C. "Classical Themes in *Lord of the Flies*."*Modern Fiction Studies*, vol. 11, 1966, pp. 424-27.

Gulbin, Suzanne. "Parallels and Contrasts in *Lord of the Flies* and *Animal Farm*." *English Journal*, vol. 55, 1966, pp. 86-8.

Hodson, Leighton. "The Metaphor of Darkness *Lord of the Flies*." 1969. *William Golding's Lord of the Flies.* Edited by Harold Bloom. Chelsea House, 1999, pp. 81-94.

Hynes, Samuel. "Several Interpretations of *Lord of the Flies*." 1968. *Readings on Lord of the Flies*. Edited by Clarice Swisher. Greenhaven, 1997, pp. 56-64.

Lederer, Richard H. "Student Reactions to *Lord of the Flies*." *English Journal*, vol. 53, 1964, pp. 575-79.

Nelson, William. *William Golding's Lord of the Flies: A Sourcebook.* Odyssey, 1963.

O'Hara, J. D. "Mute Choirboys and Angelic Pigs: The Fable in *Lord of the Flies*." *Texas Studies in Literature and Language*, vol. 7, 1966, pp. 411-20.

Oldsey, Bern, and Stanley Weintraub. "*Lord of the Flies*: Beezlebub Revisited." *College English*, vol. 25, no. 2, 1963, pp. 90-9.

Rosenberg, Bruce A. "Lord of the Fire-Flies." *Centennial Review*, vol. 11, 1967, pp. 128-39.

Sternlicht, Sanford. "Songs of Innocence and Songs of Experience in *Lord of the Flies* and *The Inheritors*." *Midwest Quarterly*, vol. 9, 1968, pp. 383-90.

Talon, Henri. "Irony in *Lord of the Flies*." *Essays in Criticism*, vol.18, 1968, pp. 296-309.

Townsend, R. C."Lord of the Flies: Fool's Gold?" *JGE: The Journal of General Education*, vol. 16, 1964, pp. 153-60.

Veidemanis, Gladys. "*Lord of the Flies* in the Classroom—No Passing Fad." *English Journal*, 53, 1964, pp. 569-74.

Watson, Kenneth. "A Reading of *Lord of the Flies*." *English*, vol. 15, 1964, pp. 2-7.

White, Robert J. "Butterfly and Beast in *Lord of the Flies*." *Modern Fiction Studies*, 10, 1964, pp. 163-70.

Critical Essays on *Lord of the Flies*, 1970-1989

Sarah Fredericks

If the first decade and a half after its publication saw the meteoric rise of *Lord of the Flies* (hereafter *Lord*) as a modern classic, then the next twenty years, 1970-1989, witnessed its decline, especially inside college classrooms in the United States. Yet even as numerous instructors and students turned their attention to the works of other writers, some continued reading and thinking about *Lord*. Many of these scholars challenged previously established critical interpretations—especially simple allegorical readings—offering instead new ways to think about Golding's novel, particularly as a work of literature.

1970-1975

In 1970, Howard S. Babb argued that the characters in *Lord* "develop according to much the same principle as the narrative itself" and that *Lord* can be outlined according to the formation, splintering, and ultimate degeneration of "society" on the island. "Golding's fundamental narrative method," Babb explained, is "the recurrence of some event, situation, or fact in slightly varying form, the variations so managed that the sequence generates an ever-increasing emotional intensity" (99). Elaborating, Babb asserted that "Golding's narrative power derives not only from the carefully graded variations in any particular sequence, but from the number of these sequences that move in parallel, as it were, towards a single destination" (99). Numerous parallel sequences or motifs (Babb believed) illustrate "some kind of regression from innocence to savagery": setting huge fires (99), dropping rocks (99), fighting (99), dancing (100), dying (100), and identifying and hunting the beast (100).

Babb thought that the meanings evident in the narrative structure are also tied to character development. Taking a somewhat unpopular position, Babb asserted that "Golding seems ... for the most part successful in preventing his figures from becoming simplified allegorical types, and extraordinarily successful in sustaining the representation of children as children" (102). Although Babb criticized the omniscient narrator's explicit comments on the significance of individual boys (102), he praised Golding's realistic depiction of the "contradictory impulses which complicate [children] as individuals" and the boys' natural childishness (103). Babb particularly applauded the sharp juxtaposition between Jack— who "lawlessly thrusts aside the restraints of civilization, makes a principle of fear, and relentlessly pursues power"—and Piggy—who "is devoted to the orderly processes of civilization, constantly brings to bear what rationality he can muster, and proves woefully weak" (104). Babb also highlighted Ralph's inadequacies, including his "inch-by-inch regression ... to savagery," his "lapses in logic," his betrayal "again and again [of] his fundamental emotional kinship with the others," and his instinctual rather than rational knowledge at the end of *Lord* "when he is becoming an animal himself" (105). Unlike Ralph, who is guided by instinct, Simon (Babb claimed) is guided by intuition and "constantly reveals a kindness that no other child possesses, and ... is gifted with suprarational insight" (106).

Next, Babb closely analyzed Simon's first encounter with the Lord of the Flies, asserting that it illustrates "how Golding's style creates a magnificently substantial world in which the symbolic values emerge almost of themselves"—what Babb identifies as "the essential method of the novel" (106). Babb emphasized "how delicately Golding roots the symbolic values in physical details" (108) and praised how this scene is "superbly poised between realism and symbolism," claiming that "this is the mode of the entire novel, whose statement about man is anchored in the substantial world of the island and children" (109). Babb concluded his article by addressing the seemingly unexpected arrival of the naval officer at the end of *Lord*—a contrivance frequently criticized by other commentators. Babb asserted that the unexpectedness of this ending, which is consistent with the endings of Golding's subsequent three novels, serves to "dislocate us by altering in one fashion or another the perspective through which we have viewed the characters during most of the books" (109) and thus "bring[s] home the meanings of the stories" (110).

During the same year, 1970, James R. Baker addressed the decline of *Lord*, arguing that its waning popularity was due not just to academic "boredom with the familiar," but to a prevailing sense that *Lord* "no longer suits the temper of the times" (448). Baker asserted that people at both ends of the political spectrum— the Radical Right and the New Left—shared a common belief that changing the economic and social environment could solve human problems; *Lord*, however, undermines this "naïve faith in the moral progress we like to read into modern social history" (454). According to Baker, *Lord* urges readers to "recognize that 'human nature' is dynamic and capable of extraordinary transformations which may result in social good or ill" (454). Several factors (according to Baker) also contribute to misinterpretations of *Lord*: reductive interpretations of Golding's philosophy of "original sin" (454), suspicion of classical tragedy's indictment of "rationalism as expressed in personal and national pride" (455), and the "decline of literary modernism" (455). Baker argued that *Lord* effectively forces readers to examine the "genesis of crisis and violence," confront the "likelihood of apocalyptic war" and the "wanton abuse and destruction of environmental resources" necessary for survival, and acknowledge that "all humanity is involved in explosive crisis and is on the edge of disastrous violence" (447-48).

Also in 1970, Eugene Hollahan addressed the prominence of circles as a motif in *Lord*, arguing that the language and imagery of a circle are frequently used to describe the novel's physical settings, individual characters, groups of boys, opposing factions, and important artifacts and objects, such as Piggy's spectacles and the pig's head. This imagery culminates in Simon's murder within the concentric rings of boys. Hollahan argued that *Lord* features two kinds of circles: (1) "the socio-political circle where the assembled boys engage in rational discussion in order to plan their way out of their difficulties"—a circle that dominates the first half of the novel—and (2) "the tribal circle where the regressive boys dance ritually and kill savagely"—which dominates the last half (26). Even the plot structure, Hollahan asserted, can be described as the "disintegration of the rational circle" and the "formation of the irrational primitive circle" (28).

In 1970, David Spitz challenged Golding's claim that *Lord* illustrates the inherent evil in human nature. Spitz argued that *Lord* instead depicts a "quest for authority," with the main characters each representing a different (failed) means of legitimizing power: Simon is a "Christ-figure, the voice of revelation" (25); Piggy, "Socrates, the voice of reason" (26); Ralph, "democratic man, the symbol of consent" (26); Jack, "authoritarian man" (27); and the Lord of the Flies, "Beelzebub .... the beast that is part of man" (28). Spitz further explained that "the boys are the flies and the beast, the evil, the senseless passion that is in man; in each and every man—in Jack, in Roger, even (under special circumstances) in Ralph and Piggy, even in you and me—is the Lord" (28). The ending, Spitz asserted, is ironic because, although the children think the naval officer will return them to the safety of English civilization, in fact while they are on the battle cruiser they will be part of another pack of hunters on a larger scale than that of Jack's ragtag band. Thus, "the boys move not from one evil to another evil, but from one aspect or level to another of the same evil; they go from the Lord of the flies writ small to the Lord of the flies writ large" (28).

Returning to Golding's original claim, Spitz asserted that *Lord* doesn't actually show human nature in its most essential, raw state (as Golding suggested) because "a state of nature is not necessarily a state of political and moral innocence" (29). As products of middle-class, twentieth-century British civilization, the boys bring to the island values, cultural norms, and systems of governance and authority all associated with the West (30). Additionally, literature is incapable of depicting raw human nature, Spitz explained, because

> the individual apart from society is an inconceivable thing—he is always, no matter how peculiar or unique a person, still a social animal. And if it be said, despite this, that all societies are evil, or that there is evil in all societies, which means that men however created or evolved are necessarily the source of that evil, it is still not shown

what in man or in his circumstances produces that evil, or why, and whether this is irredeemable. (30)

Furthermore, Spitz argued, societies are not homogenous; their horrors are of differing degrees and orders, and good emerges despite evil (31). Thus, Spitz believed that Golding's claim about the root of social ills was too simplistic: "The evil that is common to them all cannot causally account for that which distinguishes them from each other" (33).

Again in 1970, Stephen Wall asserted that *Lord* is valuable as "literature" not because of its narrative appeal (which attracts adolescent readers) or its moral and theological doctrines (which appeal to pedagogues). Rather, it is valuable as literature because it offers a variation on the myth originating in *Robinson Crusoe* and echoed in the Victorian novel *The Coral Island,* to which the ending of *Lord* refers. Golding (Wall argued) "uses his children as the presenters of the 'end of innocence, the darkness of man's heart' and one of the larger questions his novel provokes is how far it is satisfactory, or simply fair, to use the potential savagery of boys as an indication of the innate depravity of man" (137). Instead of focusing solely on allegorical significance, Wall praised the novel's vivid descriptions of the island, the boys, and their "physical sensations." Wall points to Simon's burial at sea as an example of how "physical descriptions yield metaphysical implications" (138).

In 1971, A. D. Fleck compared *Lord* to James George Frazer's *The Golden Bough* (1890), asserting that *Lord* is a "myth" (rather than a "fable") which demonstrates that every human being is "a morally flawed creature" (190). "Both books," Fleck believed, "are concerned … with the passing of power and authority from one leader to another" (191). Fleck especially focused on contrasting Ralph and Jack and analyzing the gradual erosion of Ralph's power and its shift to Jack. Analyzing other characters, Fleck concluded that, like Frazer at the end of *The Golden Bough*, Piggy represents "the voice of reason" (195) while Simon is the "most complex character" (197), a "Christ figure in the classic mould of the dying

God" (199). Fleck noted that the "dying God" is often ambiguously associated with pigs and boars in myths (200).

In 1972, Frederick R. Karl reevaluated *Lord*; although he praised Golding's originality, especially as a "metaphysical writer interested in states of being and aspects of survival," Karl nevertheless criticized Golding's "crucial avoidance of subtlety," "didactic intrusions," and "eccentric themes" (154-55). Comparing *Lord* to Joseph Conrad's *Heart of Darkness*, Karl asserted that both novels share an ideological focus on "situations that offer no other restraint except what the self may provide" (157). However, Karl argued that *Lord*'s gimmicky ending suggests that civilization and the adult world combat innate savagery whereas *Heart* implies that they are simply plagued by their own forms of savagery (158). Because of its "complacent Christian morality," Karl concluded that the "secular fall from grace" in *Lord* "never approaches the intensity of [that in] *Heart of Darkness*" (158).

A. C. Capey also assessed the literary worth of *Lord* in 1972, arguing that the novel's acclaim results from its "teachability" rather than its intrinsic merit (146). Teachers, he argued, appreciate the fact that *Lord* can support numerous interpretations; for example, he felt that the question of "who is the lord of the flies?" can be plausibly answered as the pig's head, Jack, Ralph, the parachutist, Simon, and the naval officer (140-41). This array of interpretations, Capey claimed, was not "imaginative development of a theme but intellectually imposed alterations or alternatives of 'significance'; the ideas sit on the narrative, unassimilated" (141). Capey criticized Golding for failing to develop thematic ideas (143), tarnishing his depiction of the boys with his cynicism (144), and denigrating Piggy (145). Golding's art, he concluded, is "incoherently conscious" (146).

Finally in 1972, Torben Ditlevsen challenged what he saw as misinterpretations of *Lord* based on "reductionist" allegorical readings. He claimed the "ethical-cultural 'constitution of the novel's universe … is characterized by the crossing (not the coupling) of ethical ('good/evil') and cultural ('culture/nature') taxonomies in one system" and that attached to this system is a "religious taxonomy ('sacred/profane')" (20-21). These two systems create a "confessional culture" in the novel (21). In the beginning, Ditlevsen explained, many of the boys equate "civilization" with "supervision" and "non-civilization" with "freedom" (21), and the novel is characterized by competing, "progressive-regressive" movements to either reaffirm or disintegrate civilization on the island (23). Pitted between Jack and Piggy, Ralph's mind is divided between "duty" and "inclination" (25). *Lord*'s message, however, is neither the "naïve optimism of civilization" nor the "naïve pessimism of civilization" (29); rather (Ditlevsen argued), "Good and Evil are powers within both nature and culture" (30). Ditlevsen observed "five different attitudes to life" in *Lord* that are "distinguished by their attitudes to good and evil, profane and sacred, and by the distribution of dominance within the latter taxonomy" (35).

1976-1985

Ildiko de Papp Carrington in 1976 took an inductive approach to analyzing *Lord*, arguing that the novel's language, especially its imagery and metaphors, "sharpens our awareness of the novel's organic unity and deepens and expands our interpretation of the novel's themes" (66). Golding (Carrington claimed) depicts the boys' degeneration by blurring (1) "the distinction between motile organisms, both animal and human, and the sessile [i.e., growing directly from the stem] world of plants," (2) "the distinction between individual human faces, living or dead," and (3) the distinction between human and animal faces and buttocks (66-67). This blurring occurs both when external environmental conditions and internal psychosomatic conditions impede the characters' ability to see and perceive and when boys' faces undergo physical transformations that mirror their shifting moral perceptions (68-69).

In 1977, W. K. Thomas analyzed *Lord*'s numerous literary allusions. First, like many critics before and since, Thomas compared *Lord* to R. M. Ballantyne's *The Coral Island*, arguing that Golding modified his parallels to Ballantyne's novel to "elaborate on certain themes" such as sexuality and death (34) and to "reinforce the regression that occurs in *Lord of the Flies*" (35). Next, Thomas connected the character Percival in *Lord* to the figure Sir Percival from Mallory's and Tennyson's legends of the Holy Grail. Thomas noted twelve similarities, including parallels between the castle of the "life cult" in the Grail legend and Castle Rock in *Lord* (36), the Fisher King and the naval officer (36), the dance of the life cult and the boys dancing and chanting "kill the pig!" (37), the life cult's ritual feast and the sharing of roasted meat (37), and the Grail itself and the conch (38). Thomas believed these similarities "emphasize the perversity by which his juvenile society, and by implication the adult society of which it is a microcosm, consistently takes whatever has the potential for life and twists it so as to produce death" (38).

Thomas argued that Piggy's death shares elements with both an ancient Greek religious festival, Attic Thesmophoria, in which pigs were thrown into a chasm, and an ancient Scandinavian Christmas custom in which a boar is sacrificed as part of a fertility ritual (39). These allusions underscore the boys' "descent into savagery," Thomas asserted, revealing that "at every opportunity, offering progress towards life or regression towards death, the boys choose regression" (39). Thomas contended that another significant literary connection to Greek myth in *Lord* is through Percy Bysshe Shelley's *Prometheus Unbound*. Thomas claimed that not only are the events in *Lord* a backwards regression through Prometheus's gifts (41), but Prometheus allowing the "wrong god to reign" calls into question Golding's own claim that Simon is "a Christ figure" (42). This assertion, in turn, led Thomas to analyze similarities between the character Simon and biblical figures such as Jesus Christ, various saints, and Simon of Cyrene (who carried Christ's cross).

Two other important sources for *Lord*'s allusions (according to Thomas) are John Milton's *Paradise Lost* and the Bible. Thomas connected the pig's head, or "the Lord of the Flies," to Beelzebub—who is both a prominent character in Milton's *Paradise Lost* and the figure also known as Satan in the Bible—(44); the pagan god Baal (44) and his persona as Hadad-Rimmon (46); and Baal's father, Dagon (44). Thomas argued that these parallels signify how the boys "lost touch with moral values and the sense of a transcendental reality" (47). Thomas also noted that, in their dismissal of God, the boys break all of the Ten Commandments (47). Thomas also explored the theme of "perverted sexuality" in *Lord* (49), connecting Simon's bower (where he presumably masturbates) with both settings and symbols in the legend of the Grail, Shelley's *Prometheus*, and Mosaic Law. Thomas took *Lord*'s condemnation of masturbation as an indictment of the twentieth-century turn "from morality and metaphysics of old to an eager embracing of a worship of naturalism," which resulted in a "perversion of the power of love" (51). Finally, Thomas analyzed *Lord*'s closing allusion to Conrad's *Heart of Darkness*. Thomas concluded his essay by explaining how Golding's own comments on *Lord* relate to and ultimately support the conclusions Thomas makes.

Jeanne Delbaere-Garant in 1978 argued that "contrastive and repetitive patterns govern the structure of [*Lord*], which is built on a contrapuntal balance of opposites and on repetitions, echoes, parallels, which blend and culminate in the last chapter" (112). *Lord*'s setting, Delbaere-Garant observed, is characterized by a "basic opposition between sea and island, liquidity and hardness, flux and fixity, roundness and angularity" (111). Delbaere-Garant asserted that the opposition between water and reef parallels the opposition between Ralph's group of boys, which is "democratic" and "characterized from the start by its heterogeneity," and Jack's group, which is "authoritarian" and characterized by "its organization" (113). Similar to the lagoon on the island and the reef in the sea, neither Piggy nor Simon (claimed Delbaere-Garant) "really belong to their groups" because of their physical differences, their roles as "outsiders," and their "significant deaths" (113). The "correspondences between setting and characters," Delbaere-Garant argued, "intimates that the same law governs the geophysical world and the world of man. Human nature is an aspect of nature at large" and "each living creature is victim to a force larger that itself" (114).

In addition to perceiving this rhythm, Delbaere-Garant observed a corresponding pattern of "expansion" in which "the same act recurs with an amplification similar to that of waves spreading in larger and larger circles around a stone thrown in the water" (117). The "throwing of stones and the killing of pigs," Delbaere-Garant explained, "develop in similar ways: pursuits are initiated out of necessity, repeated for fun, turned against a human being ... and finally [against] Ralph" (119). Delbaere-Garant argued that "through a rhythmical balance of opposites," *Lord* illustrates that "all things, animate and inanimate, are governed by the same law, that evil does not spare man any more than it does nature....[and] that there is no stopping evil" (119). Delbaere-Garant concluded that *Lord*'s ending (which has been much criticized) is actually consistent with the contraction-expansion pattern of the rest of the novel since it offers "a further duplication of the whole story," indicating that "the events witnessed in *Lord of the Flies* do not end when the book does" (120).

In 1980, Arnold Johnston criticized Golding's "authorial presence" in *Lord* as "overly obtrusive" in his "didactic interpositions" and in his "unconvincing manipulation of his characters" (10). Johnston believed Simon's overtly didactic imaginary conversation with the Lord of the Flies in Chapter 8 was "a nagging flaw" in a novel committed to realism (13). Johnston also challenged Golding's insistence that Simon is a Christ figure, arguing instead that Simon is "the first of Golding's 'portraits of the artists'" (15). Piggy's death, Johnston asserted, reveals Golding's "antirationalist bias" (16) and reinforces a dichotomy between Piggy as a "misguided rationalist" and Simon as an "artist-mystic" (17). On the other hand, although Johnston briefly entertained the popular critique that "Golding oversimplifies complex truth through manipulation of his microcosmic world" (18), he ultimately concluded that "Golding's world exists compellingly on its primary level: Its strained moments seem more like surface blemishes than structural defects, blemishes that catch the eye because of their dissimilarity to the skillfully woven fabric of the whole" (19). Johnston conceded that Golding is "a maker of myth" (19) and compared him to a "puppet master who has wrought his marionettes meticulously and beautifully and led them skillfully through a captivating and frightening drama, while only occasionally distracting the audience by the movement of his strings" (20).

In 1981, Leah Hadomi asserted that irony is a "major principle of structure" in *Lord* (126). Hadomi claimed that *Lord*'s "ironic

---

playground" functions on two levels: "Circumstantial Irony," which is "based on the tension between outward cultural presumptions and the rhetorical effect of the novel," and "Internal Irony," which is "mediated mainly by metaphor" (126). The metaphors in *Lord*, Hadomi contended, form three interrelated "figurative clusters" that express central themes with ironic undertones: (1) "the clothing-nakedness cluster," which comments on the "validity of cultural coverage" and "carries the truth-appearance theme," (2) "the cluster centered around fire-sight," which "reflects man's attempt to comprehend the covert and concealed truth under the coverage," and (3) "the dominant man-animal cluster," which "relates to the problem of human nature fluctuating between animality and spirituality" (128-29).

Although each cluster contains "a covert thematic meaning," the structural arrangement of the clusters within the novel (Hadomi asserted) destabilizes these meanings, producing an "ironic effect" (129). The clothing-nakedness cluster, for instance, "points at the moral paradox whereby naked truth asks for covering by cultural robes because human existence is impossible in a state of total exposure" (129). In the second cluster, Hadomi claimed, *Lord*'s "three 'seeing' heroes" have "complementary" but "incomplete" abilities to see: "Piggy possesses mainly knowledge, Simon understanding, and Ralph wisdom" (132). Associated with the sight image is the fire image, which is, paradoxically, pragmatic, spiritual, and poetic (135). According to Hadomi, the third and final cluster is the most thematically significant because it probes the essence of human nature (136); while *Lord* seems to equate man and beast, implying that "man's nature is subject to violation and apparently conquerable by chaos," it also suggests that man's nature is "ultimately able to understand and reassert itself" (137). Hadomi concluded that "in spite of its epistemological skepticism and its powerful realization of human depravity," *Lord* "seems nevertheless to offer an affirmation of values" (138).

Kathleen Woodward in 1983 challenged the prevailing classification of *Lord* as a "dystopian novel" and argued against formalist, or New Critical, readings of the book. Woodward praised both "the care with which *Lord of the Flies* was constructed" and its "formal and structural elements"—including "the imagery of beasts, the recurring fires, [and] the increasing tempo of violence," which are "artfully articulated" (200). However, Woodward asserted that criticism focusing on aesthetic elements and symbolism is "inappropriate to the [novel's] texture and scope" (201) and "[falsifies] the character of *Lord of the Flies* by imputing interpretations to it whose weighty significance the straightforward text cannot support" (201). The text, Woodward claimed, "is literally small in scope: It is in reality a long short story rather than a short novel" (201). Because "there is a one-to-one correspondence between each literary sign and the political system to which it refers," *Lord* (Woodward asserted) "simply does not invite multiple and meaningful symbolic interpretations" (202). Comparing *Lord* to utopian and dystopian novels such as B. F. Skinner's *Walden Two* (1948) and Aldous Huxley's *Brave New World* (1931), Woodward concluded that *Lord* is not similarly "a vehicle for social criticism" because it operates on the premise that "human nature is fixed" and thus social change is not possible (203). Nevertheless, if readers "suspend [focus on] its literary nature" (204), *Lord* offers "a programmatic view of the relationship between human nature and the shape of society" (203).

According to Woodward, Golding's "model of the origins of human politics" is "completely unrealistic," and rather than depicting "how a state of peace under a rational form of government breaks down," Golding illustrates "how the conceivably pleasant condition of anarchy disintegrates under the pressure of aggression" (207). Woodward criticized Golding for "[dismissing] the basic problem of scarcity"; selecting a "homogeneous group of middle-class white children, all of whom are boys, as a representative cross-section of society"; and omitting the "fundamental adhesive of society—the family" (208). By claiming that society is shaped by the ethical nature of each individual, Golding has (Woodward claimed) "misread the moral of his own fiction" (209). Furthermore, Woodward believed Golding's understanding of "a democratic form of government" is "naïve and innocent" (210), his "vision of human nature implicitly sets a limit to political possibilities" (212), and his depiction of aggression using a "superstitious metaphor" serves to mystify rather than illuminate the phenomenon of violence" (216). In the end, Woodward concluded that *Lord*'s emphasis on the primal, animal nature of humans masks an underlying modern "fear of the child as a violent other" (220).

Norman Macleod in 1985 analyzed *Lord* using stylistics, a process he defined as "a way of telling us how language is put to work in literary texts, and of showing how the organization of such a text is a matter of language, and how our conception of—and response to—that text involves our apprehension of its linguistic details in relation to our understanding of the language as a whole" (119). Macleod closely read the scene in Chapter 10 in which Ralph and his small band are ostensibly attacked in their shelter by Jack's group. Macleod pointed out numerous key stylistic features: "unity of perspective and event" (121), five sections exhibiting different viewpoints (122), subject-predicate constructions in which the subject is either indefinite or existential (124), insistent "identification of a source or responsible agent even when one is not identifiable ... or when activity in unintentional ... or when it is instinctive" (126), "emphasis on the interrelatedness ... of several entities, rather than seeing these entities as isolated or separated" (127), conjunctions that indicate "temporal sequence" and seem to imply "causal connection ... a cause-and-effect predication" (131), lack of "fully-functional subordinate clauses" (133), a subtext of "sexual excitement" in Ralph's fight (134), and language that often implies rather than states (137).

1986-1989

In 1986, Philip Redpath countered what he considered reductive interpretations of *Lord*—those that concluded somewhat tritely that human nature is evil—arguing instead that the structural patterns of six assemblies and six trips to the mountain complicate the simple binary of good and evil. Redpath observed that the action in *Lord* occurs in three areas: (1) the beach, which is "a site of light and space," (2) the jungle, which is "an area of darkness," and (3) the mountain, "an area in which reason and unreason confront each other" (134).

"It is a law of the text," Redpath asserted, "that whatever force dominates the mountain dominates the novel" (134). In the first half of the novel, assemblies precede trips to the mountain; in the second, the trips precede assemblies (135). This reversal is significant, Redpath argued, because "reason loses control on the mountain ... [and] from then on, the darkness and fear on the mountain has precedence over the rationalism of the assemblies as the beast sits in dominance over the island" (135). *Lord*'s "overall structure," then, is "based around the antithesis reason/unreason"(136)—but, Redpath cautioned, the "simple division and the labeling of one side as good and the other evil" means ignoring "the complexity created through the novel's structure" (138). Comparing *Lord* to Golding's *The Inheritors*, Redpath noted that "both novels overturn their own structures, break down the antithesis, and replace a too simple dismissal of themselves as about the evil of man with an ambiguous mixing of darkness and light" (146). In *Lord*, Simon is a key agent of this breakdown (146). The result of *Lord*'s structural antithesis, Redpath explained, is the "conclusion that man is somehow good and evil, that his nature endlessly contradicts itself" (149).

Also in 1986, Ian McEwan praised the accuracy of Golding's depiction of boys. Both the difficulty of "talking something through in a group to a useful resolution" (103) and the cruelty and irrationality of schoolboys (105) resonated with McEwan's own boarding school experiences. Taking such realistic portrayals of boys personally, McEwan explained that as a boy reading *Lord*, he "felt indicted by it" (105) and "felt ashamed in a rather luxurious way" (106).

In 1988, S. J. Boyd analyzed *Lord* in conjunction with numerous other works, including *King Lear*, *Gulliver's Travels*, *The Coral Island*, and Golding's own subsequent novels. Boyd asserted that Ralph's tears over the loss of innocence at the end of *Lord* is "not a matter of transformation from childish goodness to adolescent depravity," but rather "the coming of an awareness of darkness, of evil in man's heart that was present in the children all along" (191). Boyd explained that setting *Lord* on a confined island is "a long-established literary method of examining human nature and human polity in microcosm" which depicts "human nature at an extreme" (194). Noting Golding's frequent references to human excrement, Boyd asserted that "Man seems to be a natural producer of filth as well as evil, and the one is a symbol of the other" (196). "While civilized values are endorsed by the novel," Boyd argued, "actual civilizations are condemned as barbaric and monstrously destructive" (198). Like other critics, Boyd emphasized the social hierarchy in *Lord*, contending that "Piggy is isolated … by being lower-class" and that Jack's "privileged choir-school background … taught him much about the necessity of hierarchies" (199). Boyd further explained that *Lord* demonstrates that "a person may be treated not on the merits of his complex make-up as an individual but merely in accordance with his being recognized as a component of a mass class-group" (200). Boyd also asserted that although Piggy and Simon are both "outsider[s], scapegoat[s] and victim[s] of murder," Piggy exhibits "faith in science and rationality, with a marked disbelief in anything supernatural," while Simon is "intuitive, introspective, otherworldly" and "represents and has access to a dimension of experience it is proper to call religious" (202). Simon also exhibits traits characteristic of a prophet: "his central insight is gained in a vision or trance" (202), he "awaken[s] men to the truth of their own sinfulness" (203), he "foretell[s] the future" (203), and he ascends a consecrated mountain and returns to bring a truth to the people (which they, in turn, reject) (204). Boyd concluded that "what desperate hope the book offers is simply the example of Simon, the acknowledgement of our guilt, of the 'thing of darkness' within us, and the overcoming of this guilt and darkness in generous, if unsuccessful, self-sacrifice for the sake of others" (208).

Also in 1988, James Gindin explored how *Lord*'s allusions to *The Coral Island* target "the naïveté of Victorian confidence in English boys and in public schools, as well as on the whole Enlightenment doctrine about the progress and perfectibility of the human species" (12). Despite *Lord*'s ideological decimation of such naïve ideology, the tone of *Lord*, Gindin affirmed, is suffused with "grief, sheer grief"—something Golding himself claimed was the text's theme (12). Gindin compared and contrasted similarly named characters in *Lord* and *The Coral Island*, noting that of the characters in *Lord*, Ralph "comes closest to following the Ballantyne model" (12) while Jack is changed "more immediately and markedly" (13). Unlike other characters, Piggy—who (Gindin argued) represents "rationalism and confidence in social organization" (13) and is wise because he "[knows] what to fear" (14)—is entirely Golding's creation. Gindin explained that *Lord*'s other "scapegoat," Simon, is similar to the character Peterkin in *The Coral Island* (14). However, Gindin rejected Golding's overt symbolism in depicting Simon as a sort of Christ figure, arguing that "Simon is his own sort of visionary religious martyr, sometimes seen as more Cassandra-like than Christian" (14).

Gindin believed that the complexity of the "cluster of symbolic meanings" associated with "The Lord of the Flies" or Beelzebub "make it difficult to push the novel into the total narrative and legendary coherence of parable" (15), and that "the way in which Golding handles time, space and location" further complicates parabolic readings (15). Gindin suggested that *Lord*'s "directed perspective, moving through narrative time, and its symbolically conveyed ... implications" misled critics and readers to see *Lord* as a parable, but a more apt though still not entirely accurate term, he asserted, is "fable," especially since *Lord* alludes to a number of Greek myths. Nevertheless, the false rescue of *Lord*'s ending "violates the structural expectation" that a parable "should be able to carry all of the novel's meaning," so that "the term 'fable' cannot account for the extraordinarily strong feeling of coherence" in *Lord* (19). Gindin praised *Lord*'s prose for its "strength, immediacy and suggestiveness" (15) as well as its "remarkable blend of the abstract and the concrete" (16) and applauded Golding as "a strikingly visual writer, evoking physical sensation" (15). *Lord*'s overt reaction to *The Coral Island*, however, limited the novel's ability to function as a fable (19).

Finally, Patrick Reilly in 1988 challenged prevailing critical understandings of *Lord*'s relationship to *The Coral Island*. Reilly argued that *Lord*'s "real triumph" is "the innovative skill" demonstrated by the original creation of Piggy, Simon, and Roger—a skill that "makes it an original work of art, the authentic expression of its age, and not simply a spoof deriving its second-hand force from the work of another era" (172). Reilly praised Piggy as a "complex character" who "has a monopoly of commonsense and practical intelligence" (173) and a "liberal-democratic outlook and sense of fair play" (176). According to Reilly, Piggy "supports a polyphonic society" (176) and "introduces the reality principle" (177). Even his physical handicaps lead to "insights" (175). Nevertheless, Reilly identified a number of Piggy's flaws: His "sense of inferiority" makes him foolish, "to some extent [he] bring[s] his troubles upon himself" (174), he is "depressingly literalist, totally lacking in a sense of humor," his "intelligence is seriously limited," he is "handicapped by an unfounded trust in a rational universe administered by rational man" (178), he "clings to the delusion of legitimacy" (183), and his "abysmal English reveals him as unmistakably working class" (173). Reilly believed "the language barrier is the crucial thing," arguing that "Golding employs the prejudices of the English class system to support his allegorical intention … [which] requires that the boys should undervalue, ignore, and even despise common sense" (174). Piggy's shortcomings, Reilly explained, are emphasized by Simon, whose "mystical speculations are beyond Piggy's limitedly sensible mind" (178). Simon produces numerous paradoxes in *Lord*, "confounds all simplistic interpretations of the novel" (181), and "transcends" the "culture versus nature debate" (181). Turning his attention to Roger, Reilly argued that "Roger is simply the most frightening instance of the emptiness of civilization" (187). He is "a much more frightening figure than Jack … [because] Roger's sadism is the pure, unadulterated thing, with pleasure as its motive" (188).

Towards Twenty-First-Century Interpretations

Although critical praise of *Lord* diminished in the 1970s, some scholars continued to read and analyze Golding's most famous novel. Their criticism—which often featured close readings; structural, linguistic, and stylistic analysis; explication of *Lord*'s literary allusions; and discussions of *Lord* as a myth or fable—

quietly sustained academic interest in *Lord* as the twentieth century moved towards its conclusion.

Works Cited

Babb, Howard S. *"Lord of the Flies."* In Bloom, 1999, pp. 95-110.

Baker, James R. "The Decline of *Lord of the Flies.*" *The South Atlantic Quarterly*, vol. 69, 1970, pp. 446-60.

Bloom, Harold, editor. *Bloom's Modern Critical Interpretations: William Golding's Lord of the Flies*. Infobase Publishing, 2008.

_____. *Modern Critical Interpretations: William Golding's Lord of the Flies*. Chelsea House, 1999.

Boyd, S. J. "The Nature of the Beast: *Lord of the Flies.*" In Bloom, 2008, pp. 27-44.

Capey, A. C. "Questioning the Literary Merit of *Lord of the Flies.*" In Swisher, pp. 140-46.

Carrington, Ildiko de Papp. "What is a Face? Imagery and Metaphor in *Lord of the Flies.*" *Modern British Literature*, vol. 1, no. 1, 1976, pp. 66-73.

Delbaere-Garant, Jeanne. "Rhythm and Expansion in *Lord of the Flies.*" In Bloom, 1999, pp.111-20.

Ditlevsen, Torben. "Civilization and Culture; or, Pro Civitate Dei: William Golding's *Lord of the Flies.*" *Language and Literature*, vol. 1, no. 3, 1972, pp. 20-38.

Fleck, A. D. "The Golding Bough: Aspects of Myth and Ritual in *The Lord of the Flies.*" In *On the Novel*. Dent, 1971, pp. 189-205.

Gindin, James. "The Fictional Explosion: *Lord of the Flies* and *The Inheritors.*" In Bloom, 2008, pp. 11-25.

Hadomi, Leah. "Imagery as a Source of Irony in Golding's *Lord of the Flies.*" *Hebrew University Studies in Literature and the Arts*, vol. 9, no. 1, 1981, pp. 126-38.

Hollahan, Eugene. "Running in Circles: A Major Motif in *Lord of the Flies.*" *Studies in the Novel*, vol. 2, no. 1, 1970, pp. 22-30.

Johnston, Arnold. *"Lord of the Flies*: Fable, Myth, and Fiction." In *Of Earth and Darkness: The Novels of William Golding*. U of Missouri P, 1980, pp. 8-20.

Karl, Frederick R. "Assessing *Lord of the Flies*." In Swisher, pp. 153-58.

McEwan, Ian. "Golding Portrays Young Boys Accurately." In Swisher, pp. 102-06.

Mcleod, Norman. "How to Talk about Prose Style: an Example from Golding's *Lord of the Flies*." *Revista Canaria De Estudios Ingleses*, vol. 10, 1985, pp.119-40.

Redpath, Philip. "Doorways through Walls: *Lord of the Flies* and *The Inheritors*." In Bloom, 1999, pp.133-52.

Reilly, Patrick. "*Lord of the Flies*: Beelzebub's Boys." In Bloom, 1999, pp.169-90.

Spitz, David. "Power and Authority: An Interpretation of Golding's *Lord of the Flies*." *The Antioch Review*, vol. 30, no. 1, 1970, pp. 21-33.

Swisher, Clarice, editor. *Readings on Lord of the Flies*. Greenhaven Press, 1997.

Thomas, W. K. "The Lessons of Myth in Lord of the Flies." *Cithara*, vol. 16, 1977, pp. 33-58.

Wall, Stephen. "Ranking *Lord of the Flies* as Literature." In Swisher, pp. 134-39.

Woodward, Kathleen. "On Aggression: William Golding's *Lord of the Flies*." In *No Place Else: Explorations in Utopian and Dystopian Fiction*. Edited by Eric S. Rankin, Martin H. Greenberg, and Joseph D. Olander. Southern Illinois UP, 1983, pp. 199-223.

Critical Essays on *Lord of the Flies*, 1990-2010_____

Kelley Jeans

By the final decade of the twentieth century and the first decade of the twenty-first, critical interest in William Golding's *Lord of the Flies* had diminished. Although *Lord* had been immensely intriguing to critics of the 1950s and '60s, by the end of the century the book was still widely taught (at least in Britain) but had lost much of its appeal among college-level academics. Why this was so is not entirely clear, but the fact can easily be demonstrated by comparing and contrasting the number of articles written about the book during the first twenty years of its existence and the number written during the past two decades. Nevertheless, worthwhile work on *Lord* continued to be published.

1990-1999
In 1991, Paulette Michel-Michot focused on the myth of innocence as presented in Golding's *Lord of the Flies,* Ballantyne's *The Coral Island,* and Defoe's *Robinson Crusoe.* Michel-Michot argued that in each of the works, the author's main strategy "is to isolate his protagonist(s) on an island" in support of the idea that "the characters, what they are, what they undertake and their approach and relation to their natural and human environment can be viewed as reflecting the ethos of the age in which these works were written" (35). Michel-Michot argued that Ballantyne's boys in *Coral Island* clearly reflect what British boys in the nineteenth century were meant to be. They were bred to be civilized, brave, never impatient, and steadfast in their belief that "practical difficulties are easily overcome" (35). They are fine, upstanding Britons to the end. Golding's boys in *Lord of the Flies*, on the other hand, are a clear antithesis to Ballantyne's characters. Having been raised in an environment similar the still-healing Europe facing the dangers of the Cold War, the boys on Golding's island initially survive in a democratic society but quickly

devolve into little more than beasts, revealing that the evil they experience on the island "is in the children themselves" (37). The title character of Defoe's *Robinson Crusoe*, the only main character who starts out alone on his own island, is, according to Michel-Michot, "the glorification of man's capacity to do things, of the individual who is never beaten down: his energy, common sense and practical intelligence are all he needs to conquer his environment" (42). Still, Michel-Michot argued that the characters in both *Robinson Crusoe* and *Lord of the Flies* stand in stark contrast to those in *Coral Island* because Ballantyne's characters are inherently good whereas Defoe's and Golding's characters "are or become aware that evil is in themselves" (43). Michel-Michot concludes that innocence is a myth because man's soul is fundamentally dark, an idea that "undermines the ethos of the Christian British Empire and nineteenth-century faith in a progress that would also lead to man's moral improvement" (44). This darkness is something that Ballantyne credited only to the cannibals or "the other" in his tale while Defoe "read the way of the world as a manifestation of God's will, a way of absolving man from his moral responsibility towards himself and towards others" (44).

In 1992, John F. Fitzgerald and John R. Kayser addressed the role of pride as original sin in *Lord of the Flies* and how the myth of Osiris could be seen within the story as an Egyptian influence. Fitzgerald and Kayser argued that instead of the now standard interpretation of *Lord* by James R. Baker and Bernard F. Dick that the fundamental takeaway from Golding's story is that "mankind's essential illness is irrational fear," an "Osirian interpretation ... illuminates man's fallen nature" (79). According to Fitzgerald and Kayser, the myth of Osiris "accounts for the emergence of discord and, hence, war. It thereby demonstrates the precariousness of civilization" (80). In Egyptian mythology, Osiris is the god who established civilization by "introducing laws, worship of the gods, marriage, and agriculture" (80). Prior to Osiris's reign, Egyptian culture was savage. Osiris's brother, Set-Typhon, envied his brother and made repeated attempts on his brother's life until he was at last successful and Osiris lay dead. Fitzgerald and Kayser related Osiris to the good in the universe and saw Set-Typhon as a representative of evil. They noted that when Jack turned red in the face because he had been outwitted by Ralph in the second vote on the island, his reaction resembled the standard description of Set-Typhon as "envious, proud, and red" (81). Ralph, on the other hand, manifesting the qualities of Osiris, "insists that the boys must have and follow rules" (81). According to Fitzgerald and Kayser, the depictions of Simon and Piggy also seem to support an Osirian interpretation, for these characters serve alongside the democratically minded Ralph, and both boys, like Osiris before them, end up dead and awash in the sea. Finally, Henry, the child in *Lord* who, after seeing his sandcastles destroyed, realized his ability to control the fate of the tiny sea life in the eddy pools before him, is the picture of original sin. Fitzgerald and Kayser argued that "Henry may be distinguished from Jack, or Typhon, but only in power and magnitude. This is the terrible, dark truth that resides at the heart of *Lord of the Flies*" (85).

In 1995, Stefan Hawlin noted how frequently *Lord* was taught in schools and how often it was assumed to reflect a liberal point of view. Hawlin challenged this assumption by instead seeing the book as profoundly conservative, especially when viewed in relation to the process of British withdrawal from its African colonies in the 1950s. Hawlin thought the book implied imperial and even racist ideas and amounted to an implicit defense of colonialism (125). Instead of being grounded in eternal, universal concerns about some inherent human temptation to do evil (the standard reading, and a reading encouraged by Golding himself), *Lord* is, in Hawlin's view, rooted instead in Golding's assumption that white people in general, and Britons in particular, enjoyed more ethical governments than people elsewhere in the world (126). *Lord*, according to Hawlin, relies on racist, anti-African stereotypes to depict the "savage" boys, thus resembling Joseph Conrad's *Heart of Darkness* (126). As some of the boys descend into barbarism, they behave more and more like stereotypically uncivilized Africans, abandoning the sophisticated British constitutionalism that originally prevailed in their island republic. In particular (Hawlin assumed), *Lord* reflects fear of the violent African Mau Mau uprisings of the 1950s, which

---

Britain vigorously opposed through military intervention (131-33). Golding's backsliding children resemble Africans supposedly descending into alleged tribal chaos as Britain withdrew from its colonies. According to Hawlin, the "ending is a kind of fantasy. The white 'grown-ups' come back to take care of the African 'children'; the savages are cowed—they see themselves for what they are—and order is restored," much as the US Cavalry stereotypically restored order by suppressing revolts by Native Americans (133). Ultimately, for Hawlin, *Lord* reflected an often violent nostalgia for imperialism common in Britain in the 1950s.

Minnie Singh approached Golding's *Lord of the Flies* and Ballantyne's *Coral Island* in 1997 by comparing how strongly ingrained civility and the effects of maturation are in the minds and actions of the characters in both stories. Singh argued that as Golding's story opens we see Roger throwing rocks at Henry while purposefully missing him. This behavior, Singh maintained, results from what he has learned from a civil society, those "restraints taught by parents, school, policeman, and the law" (205). The willingness to abide by the rules of civilization is what sets the boys in each story apart; in Ballantyne's story, the "boys' forced sojourn on the island is both the occasion and the means for their education" (207). The boys in Golding's work, however, "forget more than they learn and unresistingly fall prey to their irrational terrors," and by the story's end, it is Roger who seems to have shown the greatest loss of civility (207). The boys of *Coral Island,* Singh argued, share an existence on their island that combines work with pleasure, but in *Lord,* work and play "are absolutely and irrevocably divorced; work is conservative and constructive; play, liberating but destructive" (208). Though Singh considered both stories remarkably similar in theme, she asserted that *Lord* has made such an enormous cultural impact because it "represents the transformation from the civilized to the savage as simultaneously regression and maturation. To become savage is to regress to the anthropological infancy of mankind, but to recognize one's essential savagery is to be psychologically mature" (212).

Also in 1997, Mark Roncace observed, like others before him, connections between Golding's *Lord of the Flies* and Euripides's *The Bacchae*. Roncace included Golding's comments on E. R. Dodds's edition of *The Bacchae*; these comments indicated the clear and obvious connection between the two works: "Of course I know the play (*The Bacchae*), and at the time (of the writing of [*Lord of the Flies*]) knew Dodds's magnificent edition better than my own hand" (37). Unlike other critics of *Lord*, Roncace argued that Ralph actually shares some similarities with Pentheus in *The Bacchae* in that both characters "clearly reveal the Dionysian urge, the desire for the irrational and chaotic, but both feel the need to repress these longings" because they are fundamentally Apollonian in nature (38). According to Roncace, Jack, who is normally cast as the Dionysian in critics' eyes, "still retains attributes of the orderly, rational, and elitist tendencies inherent in him," the same tendencies an Apollonian would possess (38). Roncace argued that Golding captured a theme that permeates *The Bacchae*: "the Apollonian and the Dionysian must both be part of the human experience" (38). Perhaps most significantly, Roncace argued his main point: "Apollonian and Dionysian forces are beyond good and evil. They simply exist as part of the natural order" (39). Jack never completely morphs into a Dionysian character any more than Ralph ever fully becomes an Apollonian character. Roncace posited that both Euripides and Golding warned their audience of the dangers of denying the forces of Dionysus. He further argued that there is "no need to try to expunge the Dionysian element; one must find an appropriate place for it…. Dionysus is part of what it is to be human" (50).

2000-2010

An article by James R. Baker published in 2000 began by recounting how *Lord*, once hailed as an instant classic, had soon come to seem naïve and politically retrograde by the 1970s. The book was increasingly dismissed as old-fashioned, especially in its implicitly religious concerns with human evil (312-13). Baker, quoting from his own correspondence with Golding, reported the latter's growing interest in science, which had been depicted fairly negatively in *Lord* (313-15). Discussing Golding's early interest in the writings of Aldous Huxley, Baker saw in them (for instance) a model for the presentation of Simon in *Lord* (317) as well as a foreshadowing of Golding's somewhat satirical presentation of Piggy in that book (318). Baker blamed E. M. Forster's early praise of Piggy for later uncritical views of Piggy as the novel's hero, noting that Golding himself had expressed real misgivings about some of Piggy's views and attitudes (318-19). Piggy, according to Baker, is the sort of rationalist Golding himself mistrusted—a boy who dismisses the possibility of evil and is therefore (like some scientists) likely to produce it himself (319). Baker also saw Jack as a kind of character foreshadowed by Huxley, only this time as an evil ape rather than a martyred saint (319). Huxley's 1948 novel *Ape and Essence*, according to Baker, strongly resembled *Lord*, which was published in 1954 and which may have been influenced by Huxley's book. In the second half of his essay, Baker discussed many parallels between the two works.

In 2001, Peter Hollindale lamented the lackluster response *Lord of the Flies* had received over the years and argued for a new perspective on the novel. Hollindale noticed that many in the literary world (and the reading world in general) dismissed Golding's story because it did not fit the polite and civil reality they wanted to see and had seen in Ballantyne's *Coral Island*. In that regard, Hollindale felt that regardless of one's personal view of the story, *Lord* is inarguably one of the most influential novels of the twentieth century. He called it "enormously influential, but never quite influential enough" (2). Hollindale pointed out that because the story "exacted recognition and provoked recoil in countless readers, [it] has incited literary professionals such as teachers to find literary and technical pretexts for refusing classic status to a work they find, for ideological reasons, unendurable" (4). Hollindale, then, offered up another view of *Lord*. Rather than labeling the story as an unsuccessful attempt to portray a skewed and unrealistic reality, he invited readers to see Golding's work as an "'idea', or 'thesis', or 'vision'—with no intention that any one of these words should be thought denigrating" (5). He called the novel a fable but contended that to dismiss it out of hand simply because one is squeamish about its method of presentation does nothing to enrich students' minds, especially in the twenty-first century when every day brings fresh news reports of horrors around the world. Hollindale asserted that it is "Golding's doctrinal assurance and his claim to universality that cause offence, but these are the very things we must all 'endure knowing' in a century where all of us, like the boys [in the book], can so easily burn each other, and our 'island'" (12).

Paula Alida Roy, in 2003, noted the glaring absence of any female presence in *Lord of the Flies*. Roy argued that though there is limited mention of females within the story (only Piggy's aunt is mentioned with any regularity), the "very absence of girls or women underscores how *feminine* or *female* stands in sharp contrast to *masculine* or *male* in Golding's island world" (175). According to Roy, two of the major characters, Jack and Ralph, are presented as the chief "men" on the island. Each holds a leadership position and dictates to subordinates the tasks they should perform. Piggy, on the other hand, symbolizes the feminine in the story. Like the stereotypical female archetype, Piggy gives advice that is quickly disregarded; he is heeded only in conversations he has alone with Ralph. Their dialogue resembles a nonsexual version of pillow talk. Piggy is soft and round and, as Roy argued, his "weakness and whining seem to be the result of the feminizing influence of his 'auntie'" (176). Roy further suggested "the rape/murder of the sow and the final murder of Piggy suggest that the final movement into savagery involves the killing and defiling of the maternal female" (177). The boys, removing all traces of the female by killing both the pig and Piggy himself, have thus eradicated all feminine presence and influence. They have devolved to the basest of mankind, thereby demonstrating what Roy called the "perils of ultramasculinity" (177).

Marijke van Vuuren, in 2004, opted to consider *Lord* a postwar rewriting of salvation history instead of focusing on the theme of original sin. She argued that Golding "draws heavily on imagery from Genesis and the Apocalypse, together with prophetic eschatological imagery" (4). Likening the boys' island to Eden in Genesis, van Vuuren called the island both a paradise and a prison. The boys, she maintained, have everything they need to sustain life but succumb to violence in order to have a leader who seeks knowledge and power rather than living as an equal and democratic society. With obvious parallels to the fall of man and the Apocalypse, the boys "pollute, violate and finally destroy [the island] by fire, blackening the sky in a conflagration reminiscent both of nuclear destruction and of Biblical prophecies of the end" (9). Just as Adam and Eve were ousted from the Garden of Eden, so it is impossible for the boys to return to their "Eden" because "human nature, even in children, is no longer sinless" (9). Van Vuuren further argued that Golding's story resembles salvation history because the beast on the island and in the sea is a biblical symbol of the anti-Christ. When the beast appears in the Apocalypse, it is the "symbol of demonically-inspired human power" that represents the "'man of lawlessness'" (10). Van Vuuren admitted, however, that *Lord* departs from traditional biblical salvation history because in Golding's novel "demonic rule is not overcome. The messianic Simon is destroyed, but the children, with the exception of Ralph, are no better off for his death" (12). Likewise, readers are left to conclude that Jack, the physical manifestation of the anti-Christ, returns to civilization forever contaminated by his savage sins.

Adding to the biblical parallels already cited by *Lord*, van Vuuren also focused on the imagery and meaning of the fire on the island. She noted that Judaic law commanded priests to "keep a fire of burnt offering burning continuously 'before the Lord'" and that "only with the coming of the Messiah ... could there be an end to offerings" (16). According to van Vuuren, the fire initially symbolized the removal of guilt and also "hope for a new order" (16). Van Vuuren ironically noted that while the final fire means rescue and life, its "demonic form means death, as the children create their own destruction" (17). Still, Ralph, the last and most vocal of those who wanted to keep the signal fire ablaze, "represents the faithful who escape, 'as the Lord has said'" (18). Ralph doesn't escape unscathed, however. Lamenting the "end of innocence,"

Ralph, according to van Vuuren, realizes that "the adult world can offer no salvation, but only further destruction on a larger scale" (20).

In 2008, Mohit K. Ray suggested that Golding "introduces several motifs which invite us to recall ancient myths" (364). He argued that Golding evokes biblical myths of the Fall of Adam and Eve as well as the sibling rivalry between Cain and Abel. Ray also saw the myth involving the Greek gods Apollo and Dionysus as relevant to the novel, since those gods traditionally represent the rational versus the irrational. Like many before him, Ray also argued that Golding shatters the myth of the good British boys depicted in Ballantyne's *Coral Island*. Ray argued that "man comes to his real self only when the trappings of society are removed and there is no external control" (366). He related this idea to the beliefs of the largely orgiastic Dionysian cult, whose representative god, Dionysus, became the god of revelry and wine. In a parallel similar to a Dionysian orgy, as the boys of Jack's group in *Lord* hunt and kill the sow, they "become wedded to her in lust": As Golding puts it, the sow "collapsed under them, and they were heavy and fulfilled upon her" (368). According to Ray, the boys have now lost all sense of civilization and revel in their baser natures. Ray argues that the "history of human 'civilization' [sic] gives iron confirmation ... [of] the fact that the removal of civilized restraints does not lead to a better society; on the contrary it results in a complete regression to brutality whose seeds are embedded in the 'darkness of man's heart'" (370). Ray significantly added, "What is true about man is also true about the child. What is manifest in man lies in potential in the child" (370).

In that same year, 2008, Kevin McCarron stepped outside of the role of critic and discussed Golding's own perceptions and intentions in his early writings. McCarron noted that Golding, having served with the Royal Navy during World War II, had come home "angry with writers, all male, and the texts that he believed misrepresented the actuality of human experience" (290). Golding was known to have been a staunch believer in the worthwhileness of society prior to war, but his wartime experiences, McCarron contended, changed his perception of the world. McCarron argued that *Lord* "could not have been written, or perhaps even published, without the historical actuality of Auschwitz, Bergen-Belsen—and Dresden" (290). Because of his experiences, Golding could not write without considering the concept of masculinity as only a cultural construction and nothing more. Other male writers of the time associated masculinity and strong and successful male characters with "conflict, aggression, possession, attainment, and, particularly, material success" (290). Golding, on the other hand (according to McCarron), peopled his novels with characters whose success was presented as a moment of revelation or an epiphany, "never as a material acquisition or as a favorable advance in society" (290). Unlike other writers, Golding also rejected the dichotomy of good and evil. McCarron argued that instead of focusing on the two opposites, Golding illustrated the "ways in which [the good and evil] concepts are interwoven rather than in opposition" (291). In this way, according to McCarron, we see that "Golding's was an art of essences; he strove to depict what lay beneath, or above, the observable surface of life" (291).

Zeynep Z. Atayurt, in 2010, argued that Golding was not only interested in showing how violence is socially produced but also in using *Lord of the Flies* to critique the stigma of obesity. According to Atayurt, people who are fat or obese have been stigmatized since the early twentieth century, while previous centuries often saw fatness as a mark of prosperity. As wars began to proliferate in the twentieth century, a concern was born that fat and obese recruits would weaken the military. According to Atayurt, those "who do not conform to a narrow norm" were now "seen as political, social, and even moral threats" (44). Atayurt argued that Golding uses Piggy to flip the fatphobic stereotypes on their heads: "Piggy represents the voice of reason, wisdom, and democratic order, as against the savage anarchy and even fascism of the hunting gang of boys. Far from being the lazy and indolent figure that the fatphobic stereotype would assume him to be, Piggy is intellectual, orderly, and energetic" (48). Atayurt further argued that because Piggy is fat and always considered an outsider, Golding uses his character to "explore the way in which violence" results from "social and cultural conditioning that is acquired at an exceptionally young age" (48). Atayurt contended that Golding constructed Piggy to challenge prejudices against obese people by "choosing to make Piggy the very antithesis of what we assume the fat child must be" (51). Unlike those supposedly troublesome recruits who could endanger national security, here is a fat child who has the "courage to oppose the boys in matters of central importance to the democratic government of the island" (51). Recognizing Golding's theory that violence is a social construct, Atayurt added: "Even though [the boys] are marooned on an uninhabited island in the Pacific and thus have no adult supervision, their mistreatment of Piggy suggests their allegiance [to] social codes that consider anti-fat bias as justifiable" (52). Atayurt concluded by arguing that by depicting the climactic killing of Piggy, "Golding makes us interrogate society's prejudices against fat individuals. Ralph offers us an example of the potential for reform in the reader" because we realize "that Ralph has learned to question prejudices that have made the boys devalue the friend he has come to admire" (61).

The fact that Atayurt is a Turkish scholar suggests that *Lord* continues to attract interest among scholars beyond the English-speaking world, even if their interest, and interest in general, has recently been on the decline.

Works Cited

Atayurt, Zeynep Z. "'Kill the Pig!' *Lord of the Flies*, 'Piggy,' and Anti-Fat Discourse." *Historicizing Fat in Anglo-American Culture*, edited by Elena Levy-Navarro, Ohio State UP, 2010, pp. 43-65.

Baker, James R.. "Golding and Huxley: The Fables of Demonic Possession." *Twentieth Century Literature*, vol. 46, no. 3, 2000, pp. 311-27.

Delbaere, Jeanne. "Rhythm and Expansion in *Lord of the Flies*." *William Golding, the Sound of Silence: A Belgian Tribute on his Eightieth Birthday*, 1991, pp. 25-34.

Fitzgerald, John F., and John R. Kayser. "Golding's *Lord of the Flies*: Pride as Original Sin." *Studies in the Novel*, vol. 24, no. 1, 1992, pp. 78-88.

Hawlin, Stefan. The Savages in the Forest: Decolonizing William Golding." *Critical Survey*, vol. 7, no. 2, 1995, pp.125-35.

Hollindale, Peter. "*Lord of the Flies* in the Twenty-First Century." *The Use of English*, vol. 53, 2001, pp. 1-12.

McCarron, Kevin. "William Golding's *Lord of the Flies* and Other Early Novels." *A Companion to the British and Irish Novel 1945-2000*, Blackwell, 2005, pp. 289-301.

Michel-Michot, Paulette. "The Myth of Innocence: *Robinson Crusoe, The Coral Island,* and *Lord of the Flies.*" *William Golding, the Sound of Silence: A Belgian Tribute on his Eightieth Birthday,* 1991, pp. 35-44.

Ray, Mohit K. "Golding's Use of Myths in *Lord of the Flies.*" *Interlitteraria*, vol. 13, no. 2, 2008, pp. 364-73.

Roncace, Mark. "*The Bacchae* and *Lord of the Flies*: A Few Observations with the Help of E. R. Dodds." *Classical and Modern Literature*, vol. 18, no.1, 1997, pp. 37-51.

Roy, Paula Alida. "Boys' Club—No Girls Allowed: Absence as Presence in William Golding's *Lord of the Flies.*" *Women in Literature: Reading through the Lens of Gender.* Edited by Jerilyn Fisher and Ellen S. Silber. Greenwood, 2003, pp. 175-77.

Singh, Minnie. "The Government of Boys: Golding's *Lord of the Flies* and Ballantyne's *Coral Island.*" *Children's Literature*, vol. 25, 1997, pp. 205-13.

Van Vuuren, Marijke. "Good Grief: *Lord of the Flies* as a Post-War Rewriting of Salvation History." *Literator*, vol. 25, no. 2, 2004, pp. 1-25.

International Reactions to Golding's *Lord of the Flies*

Grace Chen

By the early 1960s, William Golding's novel *Lord of the Flies* had become one of the most popular works of fiction both in England and in the United States. The book was routinely taught at American colleges and even seemed, for a time, to have become more popular than its closest rival, J. D. Salinger's *The Catcher in the Rye*. Golding's book was also widely read and taught throughout the English-speaking world, but it soon also began to attract sustained attention in non-English-speaking countries, especially in Western Europe. That attention continues to this day, and in fact some especially valuable commentary on *Lord* has appeared in foreign languages. Unfortunately, much of this work is largely inaccessible, for various reasons, to Anglophone readers. My purpose in this essay, then, will be to survey representative examples of foreign reactions to *Lord*. The international reputation of this book, combined with growing international acclaim for Golding's work as a whole, eventually led to the decision to award him the 1983 Nobel Prize for Literature, perhaps the most important of all international literary honors.

Early International Reactions

One of the earliest foreign responses to *Lord* was an article by Arno Esch, published in German in 1965. Esch began by praising the novel's stirring narrative and intriguing phrasing, and he also noted the novel's thematic focus on fundamental issues of being human. Like many critics then and since, he saw *Lord* as an inversion of R. M. Ballantyne's highly popular 1858 novel *The Coral Island*, in which plucky British boys, stranded in the South Pacific, overcome all obstacles by adhering to the ideals of Victorian England. Esch saw these youngsters as deliberate symbols of the virtues of white British imperialism and of sincere Christian belief. He saw Golding's novel, in contrast, as a much darker version of the same basic story of boys left to their own devices.

Right from the start (Esch suggested) the island in *Lord* is full of foreboding darkness and shadows, with ominous forces becoming especially strong in chapters 4-7. Esch devoted much attention to comparing and contrasting the various main characters as well as central developments of the plot. Part of his article's value would have been to introduce the book to German readers who had heard about it and wondered why it was so popular.

Perhaps the most interesting of Esch's comments on the major characters involved his emphasis on Piggy's reaction to Simon's murder. Although Piggy denies that Simon was indeed murdered, Esch saw this very need to deny that obvious fact as indicating Piggy's troubled conscience—a conscience present also in Ralph but utterly lacking in Jack. Esch saw Jack as a kind of manipulative dictator who uses fear of the "beast" to dominate the other boys. Piggy, in contrast, symbolizes logic, practical rationality, and reasonable consistency. Simon is more mysterious, more distanced from the other boys; he symbolizes truth and is eventually martyred.

More interesting, perhaps, than Esch's comments on *Lord*'s characters are his observations about its structure, which he regarded as unusually lucid and straightforward (especially for a modern novel). He praised Golding's ability to link an apparently simple plot to resonant symbolism, and he also noted the ways Golding used similar but contrasting episodes with real effectiveness. He commented, for instance, that the rolling of huge rocks is at first a game but later becomes shockingly deadly, and in general he observed how innocent games eventually turn evil. Esch stressed Golding's skillful use of imagery, whether involving fire, the conch, Piggy's glasses, the rotting pig's head, or even butterflies. He also noted the novel's effective use of foreshadowing and its symbolic descriptions of the island's physical features. Ultimately, Esch saw Golding's book as a warning suggesting that evil could easily become pervasive if humans did not resist it. The novel (he thought) should inspire readers to examine their own consciences.

Another German article about *Lord*, by Peter Freese, was published in 1972. In his article, Freese referred to Esch's work and examined many of the same themes. However, he focused specifically on how Piggy and Jack are characterized as antithetical to each other. His analysis was also unusual because of his wide variety of cross-references, ranging from Freud to pop culture examples such as *Swiss Family Robinson*. At the start of his essay, Freese briefly overviewed a history of theories about childhood innocence. He observed the historical shift from the concept of the romantic child to the idea that even children are afflicted with original sin. Freese stated that after the Romantic movement, led by such writers as William Blake, William Wordsworth, and the American transcendentalists, the concept of original sin began to take hold, partly as a reaction against the alleged naïvety and sentimentalism of the Romantics. Instead, in a throwback to Puritanical thinking, the Calvinist idea of children being undeveloped adults now became more prominent. When the romantic idea of childhood innocence was denounced in Freud's *Three Treatises on Sexuality*, the concept of original sin was not only theological but was apparently supported by the findings of anthropology and psychology as well.

Discussing Golding's characterization of Piggy and Jack, Freese noted numerous symbolic elements. For instance, he correlated Jack with other famous literary redheads, such as Christopher Marlowe's Jew of Malta, and Fagin in Dickens's *Oliver Twist*. Red hair has often traditionally been associated with Judas or the devil. Likewise, Jack's knife may also (Freese contended) allude to Jack the Ripper. Freese also contrasted Piggy's glasses, a symbol of visual and mental clarity, with Jack's mask, which aims to obscure. Similarly, he saw the conch shell as a symbol of the common good and the knife as a sign of individual power. Lastly, Freese discussed how the conclusion of the novel resembles the conclusion of Joseph Conrad's *Heart of Darkness*. Ralph has experienced a harsh initiation into adulthood. Crying bitterly about "the end of innocence, the darkness of man's heart," Ralph is like the character Kurtz, who can only utter "The horror! The horror!" as his last words (183). Throughout his analysis, Freese supplemented his reading of *Lord* with historical research and his knowledge of other literary texts.

Simon's Character and Biblical Interpretations of Evil

Two other early articles focused on interpreting *Lord* by using Christian scripture and the spiritual concept of evil. Gisela Pira's 1969 article in German used Genesis Chapter 3 as a starting point for her discussion on the problem of evil. She noted the serpentlike imagery of the phrase "snake-thing," which the boys used to describe the beast on the island (36). She also compared Simon to an enlightened Old Testament prophet: He is aware of the evil, but he seems to be immune to its power. She then elaborated on possible interpretations of the name "Lord of the Flies." Aside from discussing the name's obvious allusion to Beelzebub, she also connected the name to animistic worship of forest spirits as well as to Mephistopheles in Goethe's *Faust*. In Goethe's story, the demon Mephistopheles is traditionally only visible to the protagonist Faust, and acts as a tempter. Similarly, the Lord of the Flies is a demonic figure who is only visible to Simon. As a result, the Lord of the Flies monster, she stated, is possibly inspired by this well-known German legend.

In addition to assessing Simon, Pira also wrote briefly about the other boys. For example, she commented on Ralph's and Piggy's faith in systems emphasizing reason and good will. She also discussed whether Jack was fundamentally evil. Overall, she concluded that he was not. Instead, she argued that Jack is depicted as a good companion at times, as when he says, "I could not let you do it on your own" (106). However, he is susceptible to evil's influence because his machismo destroys his inhibitions. Additionally, Pira analyzed how the boys' school clothes symbolize their previous values. While the clothes are treated with care at the beginning, they become worn out over time and deteriorate. Finally, the clothes are torn and removed altogether. Pira also explored the symbolism of Jack's mask and its connection to losing a sense of civilization. The deus ex machina ending, Pira suggested, is a commentary on the ways evil is shrouded by the mundane in everyday life. Although the boys are saved, the rescue appears to be an imperfect resolution. The naval officer demonstrates society's false sense of security regarding the existence of evil in the world.

André Raphael's 1972 article, published in French, also discussed the issue of evil, this time through the lens of Simone Weil's *Gravity and Grace* (first published in 1947). Weil was a Jewish contemporary of Golding's. According to Weil, gravity and grace work as opposing forces. She defined gravity as a negative force "which above all others draws us from God" (xxi). Raphael saw this gravity as the source of tension between the boys on the island. Likewise, Weil described worshiping the beast as thinking and acting in conformity with the reflexes of a crowd. Raphael used this passage to analyze the boys' indulgence in groupthink.

Raphael began with Golding's claim that the inspiration for *Lord* came from (1) his war service, (2) learning about the Nazis, and (3) his experience teaching young boys. Golding himself resisted the idea of critics overanalyzing his book. He attempted to dissuade readers from looking for additional sources to explain his novel. While Raphael acknowledged that there was no clear evidence that Weil influenced Golding's work, he drew attention to their use of similar religious imagery. He combined biblical references and quotations from Weil's work to support his interpretation. He also paid specific attention to the character of Simon and the Christlike nature of his death.

Raphael analyzed Simon's interaction with the Lord of the Flies in Chapter 8 and the description of his dead body moving out to sea in Chapter 9. He saw the Lord of the Flies as a manifestation of human evil. Raphael considered Simon unique because he is the first boy who can acknowledge such evil. This threatening knowledge isolates him from the others. As the Lord of the Flies notes, Simon worries that he will appear "batty" before the other boys. Unfortunately, his attempts to warn them of the evil within them result in his death. Raphael cited Matthew 15:16-20, where Jesus states that it is not what enters the mouth that defiles humans, but what comes out of the heart. Raphael compared Golding's and Weil's understandings of evil, which he described as a trait inherent in every human being. Raphael also noted Golding's use of light imagery after Simon's death, including the references to "inquisitive bright creatures" forming a "silver shape" around his body. Grace, represented by the light, constantly struggles with the gravity that threatens to tear the boys apart. Raphael ended by emphasizing thematic parallels between Weil's writing and Golding's work.

Thinking about Historical Context

In the 1980s, critics continued thinking about *Lord of the Flies* and its historical contexts, but in new ways. For example, Jacqueline Bardolph's article, published in 1982 in French, examined how the Mau Mau revolts, which occurred in Africa between 1952 and 1960, may have influenced Golding's work. She described how the revolts were widely sensationalized in the media; the Mau Mau were depicted as vicious savages consumed by bloodlust. These media images of the Mau Mau, Bardolph claimed, had numerous parallels with Golding's portrayal of the boys on the island. She argued that the interest in the Mau Mau was fueled by anxiety about the possible social/evolutionary regression of humankind. She pointed out how Golding's pessimistic vision of humanity potentially and problematically validates the need for authority for the sake of maintaining order. However, she argued that this logic was also used as a justification for colonial activity in Africa. Since the Mau Mau were often compared to unruly children, this disciplinary mindset perpetuated already well-established colonial attitudes towards supposedly uncivilized people.

For instance, Bardolph explained how the Mau Mau were supposedly driven by a sadistic, bestial sexuality. She then paid close attention to the hunting imagery in *Lord*. For example, she cited how in Chapter 3 the "promise of meat" was described as "seductive" and "maddening" (49). In the same way, in Chapter 8, Jack's tribe is described as following their prey—a female pig—because they are "wedded to her in lust" (135). These examples demonstrate (according to Bardolph) how Golding uses sexual imagery to depict the boys' pursuit as deeply instinctual, a confusing mix of powerful emotions. She also cited the boys' expressions of pleasure as they kill and, in a sense, rape the pig. Bardolph noted that in Chapter 4,

Golding writes how the boys "seemed to share one wide ecstatic grin" (69). This imagery, she argued, is particularly significant, especially since she also elaborated on the eventual dissolution of the boys' individual identities. Bardolph noted how they become "anonymous savages" (140). By sharing the very same facial expression, the boys become a singular "organism," a transformation that eventually leads to Simon's murder in Chapter 9 (152). According to Bardolph, Golding's novel was very likely influenced by common narratives at the time about the Mau Mau rebels.

Some scholars, however, warned about the problems of reading literature purely within historical contexts. For example, Juan José Coy Girón's article, published in 1986 in Spanish, discussed two particular methods of examining texts: a sociohistorical approach and a formal one (focusing primarily on the text.) Coy Girón stated that there are weaknesses to exclusively using either approach. As an example, he stated that thinking from just a historical perspective can reduce the work of art to a mere effect of a historical moment. Thinking this way can also severely limit a text's meanings. To demonstrate his point, he began by outlining the similarities and differences between Golding's work and that of the so-called Angry Young Men movement, a group of British authors who published in the 1950s, such as John Osborne and John Wain, who were disillusioned by British society. Coy Girón states that while Golding is often lumped into the same category as these men, he still differs significantly from these other authors. For instance, simply in terms of time, Golding was active in World War II, while the other men were too young to be heavily involved. Overall, the movement was fueled by an attitude of discontent and jadedness. Girón argued that Golding's work seems to have stronger connections with absurdist literature. For these reasons, Girón maintained that while studying Golding's time period may be essential to understanding *Lord*, looking at just history itself is insufficient.

Reading Form and Genre in *Lord of the Flies*

Other writers chose to focus more on the text itself. For example, J. F. Galván Reula's article, published in 1981 in Spanish, elaborated on the symbolism of the novel, as well as on the relationship between form and content in *Lord*. Like Raphael, he also discussed Simon's character in depth. His article began with a general overview of the story and a discussion of the deus ex machina ending. He stated that while some critics viewed the ending as a gimmick, Golding's novel, on a formal level, was very carefully crafted to suit the story's thematic needs. All of the novel's elements, Galván argued, are deliberately placed to create a sense of mystery and convey the children's sense of fear. Galván paid attention to three sets of symbolism: (1) the natural vegetation, (2) the dark, and (3) depictions of silence and noises. The imagery related to the lush vegetation of the island, he stated, created a sense of the island's hidden hostility. The world thus feels threatening and uncertain because of the island's mysterious landscape. On a related note, overwhelming plant growth also results (according to Galván) in an ominously dark atmosphere. Golding also describes the choirboys as wearing black, imagery that possibly creates a sense of foreboding in the reader. Last but not least, Galván noted that in Chapter 3, Golding wrote that "the silence of the forest was more oppressive than the heat" (49). In the same way, the absence of noise also contributes (he argued) to the sinister ambiance. All of these elements together contribute, in Galván's view, to the children's fear of the unknown.

Like other international critics, Galván also discussed Simon's death. Citing Simon's observation that maybe the source of evil is "only us," Galván examined the quote in conjunction with Golding's words about the murderous nature of humans—an innate evil that Golding considered "mankind's essential illness" (89). Galván noted that Simon himself is referred to as a beast three times within the same paragraph in Chapter 9. By describing Simon in the same way as he is perceived by the boys, the narrator becomes, according to Galván, an accomplice to the murder. At the end of his article, Galván also discussed the pacing of the novel and how the end of each chapter increases the sense of mystery, thus propelling the reader further along the plot. All in all, Galván's piece illuminates how Golding used formal elements of the mystery genre to compose his own mysterious novel.

An article by French critic Frédéric Regard, published in 1992, also considered the issue of genre, analyzing *Lord* as a fable. Over the course of the article, he noted the various similarities and differences between Golding's novel and the fable genre. He began by quoting English writer Anthony Burgess, who strikingly claimed that the novel form was closely linked to comedy because "it shows men trying to cope with problems, and not succeeding very well. It's like Charlie Chaplin trying to cope and not succeeding. That's the novel" (qtd. in Ingersoll 141). Burgess found *Lord* disappointing because it lacked this comic dimension. While Regard disagreed with Burgess's assessment of Golding, he did agree that novels blend various generic categories. According to Regard, although *Lord* begins as a grim fable, it ultimately transcends the bounds of traditional genres. As previous critics have noted, *Lord* appears to communicate a specific moral or lesson, just like a fable. However, the direction of a fable is generally predictable and controlled, something the novel is not. Although Golding may have intended the story to be a fable at the beginning, it appears that he loses control of the story in the process of writing—something that happens in most good fiction. In any case, the novel loses its resemblance to a fable over time. In a strange way, Regard asserts, the author's loss of agency parallels the loss of order that occurs in the plot itself. Golding's authority is undermined and his role becomes more that of an unwilling spectator.

To demonstrate his point, Regard observed how the beast, the dead parachutist, appears like a puppet on a string. At this point, although the parachutist terrifies the boys, the audience and Golding are aware that the beast, in fact, does not actually pose an immediate physical threat. This knowledge also prevents the reader from feeling any deep sense of foreboding. However, the pig perceived as the Lord of the Flies does begin to appear to speak for himself. The lines between fantasy and reality thus become horrifically blurred; this monster appears to take over the novel, almost in place of the narrator. Regard even interpreted the pig's statement that "You are a silly little boy" as possibly referring to the novel's narrator (143). Likewise, the Lord of the Flies' dialogue replicates specific words and phrases previously used by the narrator, and the dead pig's head even speaks "in the voice of a school-master," the job Golding held in real life. In this way, real horrors emerge from the story, and the novel surpasses the bounds of a traditional fable.

Aside from exploring issues of genre, other scholars paid attention to Golding's writing techniques. For instance, María Nadal's article from 1991, published in Spanish, focused on analyzing the novel's structure and its use of point of view. While specifically centering on the characters of Ralph and the naval officer, she acknowledged that the novel's point of view is quite complex. Additionally, she argued that although readers sometimes perceive third person narrators as omniscient, the narrator of Golding's story provides only partial information. This technique, she claimed, creates a sense of mystery, a topic Galván also touched on in his own publication.

Nadal observed how the narrator's focus works like a camera: Sometimes the perspective seems distant, and sometimes it ends with a comment about a character's inner thoughts. This method, she claimed, is used when the characters are individually introduced. Although readers first receive descriptions of the protagonists' physical appearance, we never receive really critical information until later. For instance, we do not learn the names of the boys until their conversations with each other after we first meet them. Such important information is deliberately delayed. Nadal referred to this strategy as progressive revelation, a narrative approach that creates a constant sense of suspense.

Discussing Ralph, Nadal stated that while he is not perfect, his growing ability to engage in self-reflection allows him to develop more maturity. She contrasted him with Piggy, who refuses to acknowledge Simon's death as a murder. Similarly, the naval officer in the last chapter also suffers from limited vision. The officer's remarks about the boys' "fun and games" are woefully ignorant and undercut the horrors Ralph has experienced. Nadal argued that Ralph's crying resulted not just from his sense of lost innocence, but also from the officer's inability to comprehend the true situation. Golding (Nadal asserted) sharply contrasted Ralph's point of view with the officer's. Through her emphasis on point of view, Nadal was able to examine the intricate design behind *Lord*'s narration.

Theoretical Approaches to *Lord of the Flies*
Last, but not least, a number of critics examined the novel through various theoretical methods. An article by Jens-Peter Green and Doris Veith, published in 1984 in German, took an interesting new approach to the novel. Green considered *Lord* from a pedagogical perspective and explored strategies to teach the book to ESL students. Green suggested that students oftentimes ignore or overlook the descriptions of the island in favor of more action-packed scenes. In order to emphasize the importance of these descriptions, he suggested that teachers should have students actually draw their perceptions of the island. This activity would lead students to pay closer attention to the book's descriptions of nature and would also give them a diagram to refer back to when reading the rest of the book. He also proposed that having this kind of detailed image would furthermore allow the students to visualize the fact that the island physically resembles a boat, thereby making this important symbolism more apparent and meaningful. To support his claim and provide some examples, he actually included a number of very helpful illustrations.

Within his own analysis of the text, Green observed that much of the natural imagery was still connected to civilization in some way. For instance, in Chapter 1, Ralph compares the sea birds resting on the island to "icing . . . on a pink cake" (25). In the same way, the curve of the beach is compared to a bow-stave in Chapter 10 (168). Likewise, Simon's hiding place in Chapter 3 is described as a "little cabin" (57). Green also noted how the island presents a mixture of utopian and life-threatening elements. While one side of the island features a sandy beach and waterfall, the other side is filled with rocky terrain. Moreover, despite some images of peace and harmony, there are other moments when nature is presented as a harbinger of death. In Chapter 8, for instance, the heat is depicted as oppressive. Similarly, the swarming flies around the Lord of the Flies are unpleasant and ominous, a far cry from the dancing butterflies in previous scenes. These images of the flies, in conjunction with the surrounding darkness, convey a sense of rottenness as well as death and destruction. In the end, Green offered a new perspective on the novel, drawing primarily on his experiences in the classroom.

Gilles Mathis's article, published in 1989 in French, also used a specific theoretical approach to *Lord*. Quoting from Jacques Derrida, Julia Kristeva, and Roland Barthes, Mathis used ideas from French theorists to develop his analysis of the book. Mathis elaborated on the concept of the foreigner, or stranger, and the development of Jack's character. While admitting that the terms *foreigner* and *stranger* are not always interchangeable, Mathis discussed overlaps in their definitions and how the experience of encountering something strange is conveyed in the novel through both form and content. He states that the ground between the strange and the familiar is constantly being crossed in literature; for instance, Romantic poets describe everyday things in ways that make them appear new. They make the familiar seem strange and the strange appear familiar. In fact, Mathis argues that for literature even to exist, there fundamentally must be something familiar, or the audience will reject the work.

In *Lord*, specifically, Mathis argued that in the beginning, Jack was depicted as an unusual or aberrant figure who eventually becomes the norm in the boys' colony. Similarly, Ralph is the one who eventually becomes the outsider in the midst of all the boys. Like Green, Mathis describes how the events on the island can be split into two parts, some of them dreamlike, some of them nightmarish. For example, Mathis focused on the transition between the two and closely analyzed a passage from Chapter 4. In this passage, Jack becomes more animal-like as his laugh is described as a "bloodthirsty snarling" (64). This passage, according to Mathis, is also creepy; Mathis noted that before Jack loses his soul, he figuratively loses his body, as the mask becomes animated and seems to operate independently, "a thing on its own" (64). As Jack is reduced to a swirling face, Golding creates a sense of vertigo in the boy's movements. The episode resembles Alice's encounter with the Cheshire cat in its strangeness and dream-logic narrative. With his head detached from his body, Jack has metaphorically died, and order is replaced by chaos.

Mathis also paid attention to the narrator's description of the water in the coconut husk. Jack uses it to look at his reflection. After looking at himself, he throws the husk away. Mathis argued that Jack's act of discarding the husk symbolized the way the meaning of the conch is lost thanks to the rise of a new symbol of authority: the mask. According to Mathis, Jack's look into his makeshift mirror is also significant because it recalls the myth of Narcissus. In the way that Narcissus's look triggered his transformation, Jack's view of himself in the water also shifts to make him an "awesome stranger" through his own gaze (63). Mathis interpreted this scene in the novel by relying on psychoanalytic theory and Greek mythology.

Overview

International reactions to *Lord of the Flies* have varied significantly over time, and from country to country. Many foreign writers were interested in Golding's personal background and considered his involvement in World War II a significant influence on his writing. Over time, scholars began to branch out and investigate other possible historical connections. Additionally, some critics examined the novel through the lens of genre, comparing the form of Golding's work to other literary forms such as mystery novels and fables. On a practical level, some writers considered the novel from a pedagogical perspective and thought about the best methods of bringing the novel alive in a classroom. Clearly, Golding's novel, although published sixty-three years ago, still appeals to a wide audience, including historians, theorists, students, and general readers. Golding's striking examination of human nature will continue to leave a mark on literary criticism and classroom conversations.

Works Cited

Bardolph, Jacqueline. "Le Mythe 'Mau Mau' et Lord of the Flies." *Société des Anglicistes de l'Enseignement Supérieur*, Echanges: Actes du Congrès de Strasbourg, 1982, pp. 335-44.

Conrad, Joseph. *Heart of Darkness and the Secret Sharer*. Pocket Books, 2004.

Coy Girón, Juan José. "El terror del hombre moderno: *Lord of the Flies*." *Atlantis: Revista de la Asociación Española de Estudios Ingleses y Norteamericanos,* vol. 8, no. 1-2, 1986, pp. 109-14.

Freese, Peter. "Verweisende Zeichen in William Goldings *Lord of the Flies*." *Die Neueren Sprachen*, vol. 21, 1972, pp. 160-72.

Galván Reula, J. F. "El misterio en la estructura de *Lord of the Flies*." *Revista Canaria de Estudios Ingleses*, vol. 3, 1981, pp. 66-73.

Golding, William. *Lord of the Flies*. Penguin, 2016.

Green, Jens-Peter, and Doris Veith. "Kartenskizzen als Hilfsmittel bei der Erarbeitung von Goldings *Lord of the Flies*." *Neusprachliche Mitteilungen aus Wissenschaft und Praxis*, vol. 37, no. 2, 1984, pp. 87-94.

Ingersoll, Earl G., and Mary C. Ingersoll, editors. *Conversations with Anthony Burgess*. UP of Mississippi, 2008.

Mathis, Gilles. "En tête à tête avec l'étrange: La métamorphose de Jack dans *Lord of the Flies*." *L'Etranger dans la littérature et la pensée anglaises*, Univ. de Provence, 1989, pp. 247-78.

Nadal, María. "El punto de vista en *Lord of the Flies*." *Revista Canaria de Estudios Ingleses*, vol. 22-23, 1991, pp. 69-82.

Pira, Gisela. "Die Macht des Bösen in Goldings Roman *Lord of the Flies*." Die Neueren Sprachen, vol. 18, 1969, pp. 67-73.

Regard, Frédéric. "Fabula fabulans: *Lord of the Flies* de William Golding (1954)." *Licorne Poitiers*, vol. 22, 1992, pp. 69-76.

Weil, Simone. *Gravity and Grace*. Routledge Classics, 2002.

Prejudice against Obesity in *Lord of the Flies*___

Robert C. Evans

One especially striking—and uncomfortable—aspect of reading and teaching Golding's *Lord of the Flies* involves the novel's repeatedly demeaning references to obesity. The idea that all children contain the possibility of evil somehow seems less disturbing than the idea of singling out particular children for special abuse because they are overweight. The claim that all children are potential moral monsters somehow raises fewer ethical qualms than attacks on young "fatties." Most readers would be willing to admit the strong possibility that everyone is capable of evil and that civilization may be only a thin veneer over a much darker human nature. Most would be willing to concede their own potential for dark thoughts and dark deeds. After all, a flaw involving everyone involves no one in particular. In contrast, the constant mockery of Piggy's obesity in *Lord of the Flies* makes for uncomfortable reading, especially for any teacher who must present the novel to young people in an era when increasing numbers of the young are indeed overweight. For obese young persons, and for anyone who cares about their feelings, reading *Lord of the Flies* and teaching it to them can be a painful experience.[1]

The Narrator and Piggy

References to Piggy's obesity appear almost immediately. Most come from the objective narrator himself. In fact, far more references to Piggy as *fat* occur in the early chapters than anywhere else. Piggy is quickly described as "shorter than the fair boy [Ralph] and very fat" (1). Not just "fat," but "very fat." Piggy also immediately seems less physically fit, and less confident and competent, than Ralph: "He came forward, *searching out safe lodgments* for his feet, and then looked up through *thick spectacles*" (2; my italics). Piggy could easily have been presented as overweight but highly self-confident and indeed intimidating. His weight could have been depicted as a source of strength. Instead, Piggy is presented as a fat child with bad vision who seems both literally and symbolically unsure of his footing. Many readers might initially want to identify with the happy-go-lucky, physically fit, and enormously energetic Ralph; few would want to identify with this kind of "Piggy." This is especially true since the narrator continually refers to Piggy as if his weight is the only thing that matters about him:

- "The fat boy looked startled" (2)—a statement that again equates obesity with nervousness and insecurity.
- "'All them other kids,' the fat boy went on" (2)—a statement that now associates "the fat boy" with bad grammar and presumably a poor education.
- ". . . the fat boy hurried after him [i.e., Ralph]"—a statement that again makes "the fat boy" seem insecure and dependent.
- Ralph stands on his head and grins "at the reversed fat boy" (2)—a statement implying Ralph's self-confidence, both physically and psychologically, in contrast to the often needy, insecure Piggy.
- "The fat boy thought for a moment" (2) and "The fat boy shook his head" (2)—just two of many comments emphasizing the narrator's obsession with Piggy's weight. Piggy's fatness is not an incidental characteristic, to be mentioned once and then dropped; it is a trait the narrator stresses repeatedly.
- "The fat boy waited to be asked his name in turn but this proffer of acquaintance was not made" (3). Piggy shows proper etiquette, but Ralph seems strangely, immediately disdainful. Perhaps he sees this other child as fat, nervous, incompetent, and therefore not his equal. If Piggy had only taken the chance here to reveal his "real" name, that is how he might have been known throughout the book ("My name's Fred!"). By holding back, Piggy is named and defined by others.
- References to Piggy merely as "the fat boy" continue to pile up: "The fat boy hung steadily at [Ralph's] shoulder (3)";

"The fat boy stood by [Ralph], breathing hard" (3); "'I was the only boy in our school what had asthma,' said the fat boy with a touch of pride" (3); "And I've been wearing specs since I was three" (3). All four examples reinforce our sense that Piggy is not only fat but is also dependent, weak, somewhat ridiculous, and physically impaired in more ways than one.

- Later we hear about "the fat boy's grunts" as he tries to keep up with Ralph (4), and later still we are told that the "fat boy lowered himself over the terrace and sat down carefully" (5). In both cases the narrator implies that the "fat boy" is weak, nervous, and even somewhat undignified (especially because of his grunting).

- Three more times in the next few sentences Piggy is identified as "The fat boy" whom Ralph basically ignores (5-6). When Piggy finally takes off his clothes, we are told that "he was palely and fatly naked" (8).

Ralph shows Piggy little respect, and neither—it must be said—does the narrator. The narrator repeatedly both constructs and reinforces standard prejudices against fat people in the early pages of the book. This is why I cannot wholly agree with the arguments by Zeynep Z. Atayurt (one of the few scholars who have examined the book's treatment of obesity) that "Golding uses the novel to critique the weight stigma of his day" (43), that the book offers a "critique of fatphobia and weight stigma" (44), and that *Lord of the Flies* "challenges" an "emerging dislike of fat" in the midtwentieth century (47). According to Atayurt, the novel shows how this contempt for fat people leads to "violent exclusion of individuals like Piggy" (47). She again claims that Golding depicts Piggy, "and the mistreatment of him by his peers, to represent and critique the common social attitudes to fatness in his contemporary society" (49). She makes such claims repeatedly throughout her essay (51, 58, 60, 61, 62).

Unfortunately, I think things may be less clear-cut than Atayurt contends. After all, of the first seventeen references to Piggy's fatness, all come from the narrator, not from Ralph. In total, it is the narrator who calls Piggy "fat" eighteen times out of grand total of twenty-seven throughout the book. (Ralph uses that term two times, Jack three times, and the other boys once; and it is Ralph, of course, who mercilessly makes fun of Piggy's nickname). When Mark Twain uses the *n* word repeatedly in *Huckleberry Finn*, it is always Huck (as narrator) or some other character who continually uses that term. It is never Twain himself. Golding could easily have solved his own problem similarly: He could have made Ralph or another boy the book's narrator, or he could have made Ralph or other boys the ones obsessively concerned with Piggy's weight. Or he could have had his objective narrator indicate some discomfort with the habit of continually defining Piggy as fat. Instead, in no instance cited so far does the narrator indicate any discomfort with the abusive adjective. If we sensed that the narrator was continually inviting us to disagree with this repeated focus on Piggy's weight, the book would be far easier to read and teach than it now is. Instead, it is the narrator's own repeated and casual use of the word *fat* that gives the book much of its power to sting any reader who is overweight, or any reader who cares about the feelings of obese people.

Atayurt is right, I think, in suggesting that the novel does partially help undermine fatphobia by eventually associating Piggy with many good traits, and also by associating the slim, fit Jack with many bad ones. Whether the book offers a strong, sustained, obvious critique of fatphobia is another question. Any reader can see that Piggy is unfairly picked on *because* of his weight, and in that sense the novel *does* critique prejudice. But the critique would be more obvious, more powerful, and less open to dispute if readers were not simply left to draw their own conclusions. For example, if another character in the book—someone like Simon or even Ralph—(a) spoke out on Piggy's behalf, (b) insisted on knowing his real name, and/or (c) defended him from attacks for being fat, it would be more obvious that Golding was challenging prejudice. Instead, by putting most of the *fat* references into the opening pages, and by having *all* those *fat* references come from the narrator himself, Golding created great potential for misunderstanding. When the *n* word is used in *Huckleberry Finn*, we cannot attribute even one usage to Twain. Despite this fact, the novel is routinely attacked—wrongly, I emphatically believe—for reflecting and endorsing racial prejudice. Thus, even though Twain carefully distanced himself from the word, its use in his novel (on over two hundred occasions) demonstrably causes pain to many readers and demonstrably makes the novel difficult to teach, especially in high schools. This, I would argue, is also true of Golding's novel, partly because Golding made *no* effort to separate his narrator from fatphobia. *Lord of the Flies*, unfortunately, does not condemn prejudice against obese people as clearly as one might have hoped or as Atayurt suggests.

Piggy and Ralph

One particularly important moment in the novel, especially for anyone interested in issues of obesity, occurs when a naïvely trusting Piggy reveals his nickname:

> The fat boy glanced over his shoulder, then leaned toward Ralph. He whispered. "They used to call me Piggy."
>
> Ralph shrieked with laughter. He jumped up. "Piggy! Piggy!"
>
> "Ralph—please!" Piggy clasped his hands in apprehension. "I said I didn't want—"
>
> "Piggy! Piggy!" Ralph danced out into the hot air of the beach and then returned as a fighter-plane, with wings swept back, and machine-gunned Piggy. "Sche-aa-ow!" He dived in the sand at Piggy's feet and lay there laughing. "Piggy!"
>
> Piggy grinned reluctantly, pleased despite himself at even this much recognition. "So long as you don't tell the others—"
>
> Ralph giggled into the sand. The expression of pain and concentration returned to Piggy's face. (6)

Ralph's behavior here probably makes most right-minded readers think less of him. Clearly we are meant to sympathize with Piggy: His trust has been violated, and the prejudice he had hoped to avoid now risks being revived all over again. The fact that Ralph's first impulse is to pretend to shoot Piggy is significant. Violence against this obese person is already being foreshadowed. (He will be murdered by the end of the book.) Already the human tendency to pick on the weak is being suggested here, and later, of course, Ralph himself will be victimized by that very tendency (but not before he indulges in it himself, especially when he participates in murdering Simon). Rather than feeling any compassion for Piggy, Ralph reflects and restates the prejudices he has probably grown up hearing. Or, perhaps more sinisterly, Golding may be implying that the potential for prejudice against fat people is just part of a fundamentally dark human nature.

In a different (perhaps less effective) kind of novel, this would have been a moment for Piggy to plead for compassion or at least toleration. Ralph might have rejected or ignored that plea, but in either case he would have had to respond. Instead, Piggy merely accepts his fate, perhaps because he is so used to being treated as an inferior. Even worse, he continues inadvertently to reinforce common prejudices about fat people. At one point, for instance, the narrator lets Piggy say this: "I used to live with my auntie. She kept a candy store. I used to get ever so many candies" (8). Piggy's repeated references to his "auntie" (3, 5, 8, 11, 12, 101) make him sound both immature and a bit of a momma's boy, thus reinforcing our sense that he is needy. Meanwhile, his repeated use of "ever so" makes him sound somewhat effeminate; it is easier to imagine a little girl of this period using that phrase than a little boy. Finally, Piggy's satisfaction in getting "ever so many candies" implies that he is partly responsible for his excessive weight. Rather than presenting Piggy's obesity as simply a natural fact, over which he has no control, the narrator instead suggests that Piggy cannot control his appetite. Apparently he gives in too easily to a taste for sweets and (as a corollary) has not engaged in enough boyish activity to burn off the extra calories. Once again, then, it is the narrator even more than any boy on the island who goes out of his way to emphasize Piggy's obesity and even make Piggy sound responsible for his own condition.

The narrator often makes Piggy sound both emotionally and physically weak. For instance, Piggy almost begins to cry when he realizes that he and Ralph are alone on a desert island and are unlikely to be rescued: "His lips quivered and the spectacles were dimmed with mist" (9). Besides making Piggy obese, the narrator also makes him nearsighted, asthmatic, and emotional. When Piggy speaks, he often sounds needy: "We got to find the others. We got to do something" (10). Ralph, in contrast, seems far more self-confident: "Protected from the sun, ignoring Piggy's ill-omened talk, he dreamed pleasantly" (10). Of course, as many commentators have pointed out, ultimately it is Piggy who thinks rationally, offers intelligent advice, and in that sense seems the most adult of the boys. But we are rarely allowed to forget that he is also fat, asthmatic, and emotionally immature. He willingly plays second fiddle to Ralph, as if he knows that there is no point in trying to assert himself. Thus, after the conch is discovered, Piggy reports that when he himself once had access to a conch, "My auntie wouldn't let me blow on account of my asthma." Piggy explains that a man he met who knew about shells "'said you blew from down here.' Piggy laid a hand on his jutting abdomen. 'You try, Ralph. You'll call the others'" (12). The narrator reminds us that Piggy not only has an abdomen but that it is "jutting." Yet Piggy, whatever his weight, would be easier to take if he dropped all his "ever so many" references to his "auntie." The obese boy often sounds almost infantile. (Many readers will be inclined to sympathize with Ralph when he tells Piggy, "Sucks to your auntie!" [8]).

The narrator's negative presentation of Piggy continues. Piggy can't swim because of his asthma (8); he doesn't simply move upward but "haul[s] himself up" (10); he doesn't simply speak but instead "babble[s]" (11); and when he and Ralph walk, Piggy "pause[s] for breath" (11). When Ralph and Piggy encounter Jack Merridew and his gang, Piggy quickly feels "intimidated by [their] uniformed superiority and the offhand authority in Merridew's voice" (17). In no time at all, the following painful moment occurs (Jack is addressing Piggy):

"Shut up, fatty."
Laughter arose.
"He's not fatty," cried Ralph, "his real name's Piggy!"
"Piggy!"

"Piggy!"

"Oh, Piggy!"

A storm of laughter arose and even the tiniest child joined in. For the moment the boys were a closed circuit of sympathy with Piggy outside: he went very pink, bowed his head and cleaned his glasses again. (17-18)

Piggy doesn't even try to defend himself, reinforcing our sense both that he is not only weak but accustomed to being ridiculed. No one defends him, and in fact it is Ralph who throws him to the wolves (perhaps reinforcing Golding's point that even the best boys can be insensitive and potentially evil).

Interestingly, when the boys vote for a leader, with Jack and Ralph as the leading candidates, Piggy votes for Ralph only at the last minute. Ralph asks the boys, "'Who wants me?' Every hand outside the choir except Piggy's was raised immediately. Then Piggy, too, raised his hand grudgingly" (19). Perhaps Piggy is understandably annoyed with Ralph for exposing his nickname. Or perhaps Piggy simply lacks courage. In any case, the narrator continues to depict him unflatteringly. As Ralph, Jack, and Simon walk, Piggy comes "bumbling" behind them (21). Not only Jack but also the saintly Simon pretend as though Piggy isn't even there but someone (Ralph?) eventually tells him "You can't come" (21). Now, however, for the very first time, Ralph begins so show some sensitivity towards Piggy's feelings. Piggy speaks:

"You told 'em. After what I said."

His face flushed, his mouth trembled.

"After I said I didn't want—"

"What on earth are you talking about?" [Ralph replies].

"About being called Piggy. I said I didn't care as long as they didn't call me Piggy; an' I said not to tell and then you went an' said straight out—"

Stillness descended on them. Ralph, looking with more understanding at Piggy, saw that he was hurt and crushed. He hovered between the two courses of apology or further insult. "Better Piggy than fatty," he said at last, with the directness of genuine leadership,

---

"and anyway, I'm sorry if you feel like that. Now go back, Piggy, and take names. That's your job. So long." (21-22)

Ralph makes *some* moral progress here, but it never occurs to him to ask for Piggy's real name and begin using it. It's either *fatty* or *Piggy;* those are the obese boy's only two options. Nor does Piggy himself reveal his real name, let alone insist on others using it. One of the best characters in the book (Ralph) thus persists in calling Piggy *Piggy*, and he does so right until the very end. Piggy is presented as a fat boy who remains a fat boy from start to finish.

Meanwhile, the narrator continues to reinforce negative stereotypes of fat persons. Thus, while the other boys collect wood, Piggy sits nearby but "giv[es] no help" (30). Later, during a meeting, the silence is so "complete that [the other boys] could hear the unevenness of Piggy's breathing" (32). Even later, when the boys again collect wood, "everyone but Piggy [is] busy" (38). Only after all the collecting is done does Piggy become involved: "My! You've made a big heap, haven't you?" (41). The narrator presents Piggy as both fat and lazy, as well as unassertive: when Jack tells him to "shut up," Piggy simply "wilt[s]" (42). Shortly thereafter, we are told that "Piggy opened his mouth to speak, caught Jack's eye and shut it again" (42). Of course, it is hard to blame Piggy for feeling intimidated. He has already learned that his mere size makes him subject to mockery and that no one—not even Ralph—will defend him. The other boys tend to look at him "with eyes that lacked interest in what they saw," partly because he behaves so "nervously" (45). In fact, Jack quickly mocks him for this reason: "'You're always scared. Yah–Fatty!'" (45). This insult makes the other boys begin "shrieking with laughter" (45), and no one—not even Ralph or Simon—tries to defend him. Later, the narrator describes Piggy in ways that make him sound somewhat rudderless and perpetually infantile:

> Piggy was mooning about, aimlessly picking up things and discarding them. . . . Presently, seeing Ralph under the palms, he came and sat by him.

Piggy wore the remainders of a pair of shorts, his fat body was golden brown, and the glasses still flashed when he looked at anything. He was the only boy on the island whose hair never seemed to grow. The rest were shock-headed, but Piggy's hair still lay in wisps over his head as though baldness were his natural state and this imperfect covering would soon go, like the velvet on a young stag's antlers. (67)

Even in a moment as nondescript as this, the narrator feels compelled to remind us of Piggy's "fat body" (67). Even Ralph, the closest thing to a friend Piggy has, views him with contempt, despite the obvious (if somewhat self-protecting) loyalty Piggy shows him:

Piggy was a bore; his fat, his ass-mar and his matter-of-fact ideas were dull, but there was always a little pleasure to be got out of pulling his leg, even if one did it by accident. Piggy saw [Ralph's] smile and misinterpreted it as friendliness. There had grown up tacitly among the biguns the opinion that Piggy was an outsider, not only by accent, which did not matter, but by fat, and ass-mar, and specs, and a certain disinclination for manual labor. (68)

Again, the narrator does little to counter this perception. In fact, in the matter of Piggy's fatness, the narrator seems to have as little sympathy for him as anyone. Instead, the narrator tells us that Piggy is "always clumsy" (68), that he speaks "anxiously" (70), that his efforts to run involve "stumbling" (71), and that even his efforts to walk can best be described as "bumbling" (71). He arrives at places "out of breath and whimpering like a littlun" (71). When Piggy "snivel[s]," even the saintly Simon "shush[es] him quickly" (72). Occasionally Piggy forgets his customary "timidity," but Ralph easily "push[es him] to one side" (74). Aside from Simon (who is eventually beaten to death), Piggy is the most physically abused character in the book. At one point, Jack sticks "his fist into Piggy's stomach. Piggy sat down with a grunt. Jack stood over him. His voice was vicious with humiliation. 'You would, would you? fatty!' Ralph made a step forward and Jack smacked Piggy's head" (75). No one else is treated with so much psychological and physical contempt. Having knocked Piggy down, Jack now begins to mock and parody him. And, once again, even Ralph can barely stop from laughing: "Piggy and the parody were so funny that the hunters began to laugh. Jack felt encouraged. He went on scrambling and the laughter rose to a gale of hysteria. Unwillingly Ralph felt his lips twitch; he was angry with himself for giving way" (76).

Piggy is usually, both figuratively and literally, just "outside the triangle" (84) of the other boys. Occasionally he "tiptoe[s] to the triangle" to make an "ineffectual protest" (85), but even the youngest children frequently pay him little respect: "You shut up, you littluns!" (89). When Piggy speaks, his voice is sometimes said to have "shrilled" or "cried" or emerged in "an appalled whisper" (100). Jack typically addresses him as follows: "Shut up, you fat slug!" (98). Even when Piggy tries to appear courageous, his actual behavior reveals his true feelings: "Piggy hung about near for all his brave words" (103). So frightened is Piggy of the possibility of a beast that Ralph says, "We can't leave the littluns alone with Piggy" (128). In fact, an especially effective insult Jack hurls at Ralph is to tell the other boys, "He's like Piggy. He says things like Piggy. He isn't a proper chief" (138).

One could easily go on and on, listing all the ways Piggy is disrespected not only by the boys but also by the narrator. No one, at first, seems to value the "fat boy." If the boys ultimately turn evil, that evil is strongly foreshadowed by the way Piggy is treated almost from the beginning. And the narrator often seems as hard as anyone on the "fatty."

Piggy's Strengths

Of course, Piggy is not depicted in uniformly negative terms, and by the very end of the novel Ralph has come to think of Piggy as a "true, wise friend" (225). Ironically, though, Ralph rarely treats Piggy as a true friend when he has the chance to do so, and a case can even be made that his final assessment of Piggy is a sentimental imposition by Golding rather than an assessment that grows organically out of the text itself. (The same kind of criticism has been leveled at the sudden appearance of a rescuing naval officer.)

Yet there *are* passages in which both the narrator and Ralph imply Piggy's positive traits. One of the earliest—Piggy's matter-of-fact if inaccurate conclusion that the world's adults are "all dead" (9)— can be read as a mature acceptance of reality (although it can also be read as evidence of the boy's basic pessimism). More definitely positive is the moment when Piggy is said to have "helped [Ralph] up" (13), and even more obviously positive is the way he behaves when he and Ralph first meet the "littluns": "Piggy moved among the crowd, asking names and frowning to remember them" (14). It is Piggy, of course, who thinks of using the conch to impose order on the boys' gatherings: Whoever holds the conch is allowed to speak. As the narrator notes, "what intelligence had been shown was traceable to Piggy" (18-19). And when Ralph is elected leader and needs assistance, Piggy becomes almost always his right-hand boy: "You're hindering Ralph," he tells the yammering youngsters. "You're not letting him get to the most important thing" (32). And it is Piggy who defends the right of a very shy littlun to speak: "'Let him have the conch!' shouted Piggy" (34). At last Ralph induces the little boy "to hold the shell but by then the blow of laughter had taken away the child's voice. Piggy knelt by him, one hand on the great shell, listening and interpreting to the assembly" (34). Piggy treats this frightened littlun with a compassion Piggy rarely if ever receives himself. In some ways, he is the most intellectually and ethically mature boy on the island. Sometimes (if rarely) he receives compassionate treatment in return. When Jack knocks off Piggy's glasses, "Ralph [stands] away from the pile and put[s] the glasses into Piggy's groping hands" (40).

Occasionally, Piggy *does* try to assert himself: "Daring, indignant, Piggy took the conch. 'That's what I said! I said about our meetings and things and then you said shut up—'" (43). But often the narrator immediately adds details that spoil the effect: "His voice lifted into the whine of virtuous recrimination. They stirred and began to shout him down. 'You said you wanted a small fire and you been [sic] and built a pile like a hayrick. If I say anything,' cried Piggy, with bitter realism, 'you say shut up; but if Jack or Maurice or Simon—'" (43). Even when Piggy tries to speak up for himself,

---

then, he is often shut down by the narrator, the other boys, or both. To his credit, however, it is Piggy who raises the possibility that one of the youngest boys may have been killed in the huge accidental blaze the boys initially create: "Something strange was happening to Piggy, for he was gasping for breath. 'That little 'un–' [sic] gasped Piggy– 'him with the mark on his face, I don't see him. Where is he now?'" (46). No one else seems to care.

When other boys think they see things, "Piggy discount[s] all this learnedly as a 'mirage'" (60). And when Jack mocks Piggy and knocks his glasses off, Ralph seems disgusted but speaks only quietly in Piggy's defense: "He muttered. 'That was a dirty trick'" (76). Later, though, the narrator begins to imply that the bond between Ralph and Piggy is strengthening. It has (almost) always been strong on Piggy's part, partly because Piggy sees Ralph as a potential protector. But now Ralph may be feeling a stronger, more genuine attachment to "the fat boy": "Not even Ralph knew how a link between him and Jack had been snapped and fastened elsewhere" (77). Eventually Ralph even admits to himself that he "can't think. Not like Piggy. Once more that evening Ralph had to adjust his values. Piggy could think. He could go step by step inside that fat head of his, only Piggy was no chief. But Piggy, for all his ludicrous body, had brains" (83). Thus, even admitting Piggy's real merits, Ralph still cannot stop himself from referring to the boy's "fat head" and "ludicrous body." Even, then, when Ralph seems to have crossed a kind of threshold of respect for Piggy, he still expresses prejudice against Piggy's physique. It is as if, both for Ralph and the narrator, Piggy can never be seen as simply a boy, let alone a real individual with a real given name. He always remains a "fat boy."

Yet as the novel develops, Piggy is given more and more credit for his legitimate strengths. At one point he is mentioned, along with Jack and Maurice, as one of the island's three "practised debaters" (84), and he deserves credit for trying (at least openly) to seem rational when the other boys, especially the littluns, are worried about a possible beast ("What I mean is that I don't agree about this here fear" [90]). He tries to sound like a wise man ("Life," said

Piggy expansively, "is scientific, that's what it is" [90]). Of course, it soon turns out that he is at least as frightened as anyone else, but he deserves credit for trying to calm the smallest children. And, as the novel proceeds, Ralph begins to identify more and more openly with Piggy. He also begins to realize more and more deeply how it feels to be treated as Piggy is treated: "Now it was Ralph's turn to flush but he spoke despairingly, out of the new understanding that Piggy had given him. 'Why,'" Ralph asks some of the other boys, 'do you hate me?'" (129). Earlier, only Piggy had felt actually "hated"; now, Ralph is beginning to relate. Eventually, and partly because Ralph himself now feels needy, he begins to treat Piggy with a new sense of kindness: "Softly, looking at Piggy and not seeing him, Ralph spoke to himself." Later, he "sought for help and sympathy and chose Piggy" (141). It might be argued that Ralph's new kindness towards Piggy results from his own sense of need, but at least he *does* begin to treat "the fat boy" with greater consideration. Piggy is now described as speaking with "more assurance" than before and even with a certain "pleasure" (141). He is credited with possessing "intellectual daring" (142), and at one point the narrator reports that "Piggy was so full of delight and expanding liberty in Jack's departure, so full of pride in his contribution to the good of society, that he helped to fetch wood" (142). At one point, Ralph even solicits Piggy's advice: "Piggy. What are we going to do?" (153). Ralph even begins "unburdening" himself, much to Piggy's genuine "astonishment": No one has treated Piggy with this much respect before. "Piggy, what's wrong?" Ralph asks. ". . . what makes things break up like they do?" (154).

Piggy, then, at least for Ralph, goes from being a despised "fat boy" to being a trusted confidant and source of wisdom—at least for a brief moment.

Piggy on the Death of Simon
Yet no sooner does the narrator suggest that Piggy deserves the fullest respect of both Ralph and the novel's readers than he complicates this impression in quite disturbing ways. By this point,

all the boys—including Ralph and Piggy—have participated in the ritualistic slaughter of Simon. This fact disturbs Ralph:

> "Piggy."
> "Uh?"
> "That was murder."
> "You stop it!" said Piggy, shrilly. "What good're you doing talking like that?. . . We was scared!"
> "I wasn't scared," said Ralph slowly, "I was—I don't know what I was."
> "We was scared!" said Piggy excitedly. "Anything might have happened. It wasn't—what you said." . . .
> "It was an accident," said Piggy suddenly, "that's what it was. An accident. . . . "It was an accident," said Piggy stubbornly, "and that's that. . . . And look, Ralph"—Piggy glanced round quickly, then leaned close—"don't let on we was in that dance. . . .We was on the outside. We never done nothing, we never seen nothing." (172-73)

Piggy, then—Ralph's "true, wise friend" (225)—becomes not so much an apologist for murder as a blatant denier that murder has ever taken place. Jack, capable of justifying anything, could readily concoct an explanation of the killing, but all Piggy can do is insist that a deliberate killing has never occurred. Piggy's reaction to Simon's murder makes him, once again, seem weak and (even more significantly) immoral and dishonest. The "fat boy's" brief experience as a valued friend and wise advisor to Ralph does not last very long. He now returns to seeming the kind of character the narrator had mocked at the beginning: frightened, self-concerned, and unwilling to accept responsibility.

Piggy's Death

Part of the irony of Piggy's hush-hush reaction to Simon's death results from the fact that Piggy is himself the next boy to die. Yet even as the book moves towards that tragic conclusion, the narrator never lets us forget that Piggy is fat. At one point, his "crouched" back is described as being "as shapeless as a sack" (194). Admittedly, Ralph does fight on Piggy's behalf to regain Piggy's glasses (196-

97), but when Piggy himself tries to speak he is met only with "steady booing" (199). When Roger (standing above on a ledge) looks down on Piggy, he sees only "a bag of fat" (199). To his great credit, Piggy (just before he is killed) speaks forcefully on behalf of democratic ideals. But before he can say more much, Roger loosens a huge boulder and lets it bound down towards Piggy:

> The rock struck Piggy a glancing blow from chin to knee; the conch exploded into a thousand white fragments and ceased to exist. Piggy, saying nothing, with no time *for even a grunt*, traveled through the air sideways from the rock, turning over as he went. The rock bounded twice and was lost in the forest. Piggy fell forty feet and landed on his back across the square red rock in the sea. *His head opened and stuff came out and turned red.* Piggy's arms and legs twitched a bit, *like a pig's after it has been killed.* (201; my italics)

Even in death, Piggy is treated without much dignity. Ralph tries to speak but can't produce a sound. And even the narrator, who might have used this moment to pay some sort of tribute to Piggy, remains silent. Piggy's death is over in a split second, and we hear little more about him for the rest of the novel. The quick grotesqueness of his death is emphasized, rather than, at this point, the admirable values he (usually) defended. The dead Piggy, at this point, merely resembles a dead pig. And then he is mostly forgotten.

Ralph, to be sure, *does* recall Piggy several times before the book's final pages (204, 207, 211, 213, 218, 225). And in each of these recollections, no reference is made to Piggy's size; instead, it is his spirit rather than his body, his wisdom rather than his flesh, that are emphasized. In this sense, Atayurt seems right to suggest that the book finally plays an implied tribute to Piggy's intelligence and good sense rather than merely stressing his fat. Yet all the mocking references to his obesity throughout the novel—references rarely openly challenged by either Ralph, any other boy, or even the narrator—may still give some readers and some teachers pause as they make their way through the novel, or as they try to lead others through it. Perhaps part of Golding's purpose was deliberately to make readers uncomfortable with all the references to

Piggy's obesity. Perhaps Golding wanted readers to feel twinges of conscience every time Piggy was derided as "fat" or "fatty." Perhaps he wanted readers to ask themselves why prejudice against the obese is so common in our culture, and why obese people themselves often hate their own bodies. Why does our culture treat the "fat" with such contempt? Why do obese persons themselves often suffer from *self-*contempt? These are fascinating questions, but they are ones there is no space left to explore here.

Note
1. For helpful treatments of obesity in literature see, for example, Gilman, Haslam and Haslam, and Levy-Navarro.

Works Cited

Atayurt, Zeynep Z. "'Kill the Pig!': *Lord of the Flies*, 'Piggy,' and Anti-Fat Discourse." In Levy-Navarro, pp. 43-65.

Gilman, Sander L. *Fat: A Cultural History of Obesity*. Polity, 2008.

Golding, William. *Lord of the Flies*. Introduction by Stephen King. 1954. Faber, 2011.

Haslam, David, and Fiona Haslam. *Fat, Gluttony and Sloth: Obesity in Medicine, Art and Literature*. Liverpool UP, 2009.

Levy-Navarro, Elena, editor. *Historicizing Fat in Anglo-American Culture*. Ohio State UP, 2010.

Rings and Flies: Tolkien and Golding, Lords of '54

Nick Groom

Princess Margaret's husband, Anthony Armstrong-Jones, allegedly once told William Golding how much he admired his book *The Lord of the Rings* (Morrison). This foolish (if well-meaning) error got me thinking: Apart from having similar titles, are there further connections between the two works?

Both Golding and Tolkien were comparatively late writers, with no major creative work published until they were in their forties. *The Fellowship of the Ring* (the first volume of *The Lord of the Rings*) was published on July 29, 1954; it was described by C. S. Lewis as "lightning from a clear sky … the conquest of new territory" (Carpenter 222). *Lord of the Flies* was published on September 17, 1954; it in turn was described by C. S. Lewis as a "brilliant success" (qtd. in Carey 165). Tolkien's next volume, *The Two Towers*, appeared the same year on November 11, neatly sandwiching *Lord of the Flies*; *The Return of the King* appeared a little short of twelve months later, delayed by its voluminous appendices (October 20, 1955).

Both books won international acclaim. In 1957, Tolkien was awarded the International Fantasy Award for *The Lord of the Rings*; the runner-up was *The Death of Grass* by John Christopher [Samuel Youd] and third place was shared between Frank Herbert's *Dragon in the Sea* and—*Lord of the Flies* (Hammond and Scull 511). In particular, both *Lord* books became favorites on American campuses: *Lord of the Flies* was christened "Lord of the Campus" by *Time Magazine* in 1962, until it was eventually breathlessly reported that "At Yale the [*Lord of the Rings*] trilogy is selling faster than William Golding's *Lord of the Flies* at its crest. At Harvard it is outpacing J. D. Salinger's *The Catcher in the Rye*" (qtd. in Carpenter 230; see also Ripp). Both quickly inspired interest from filmmakers—*Lord of the Flies* with notably more success at the time than *The Lord of the Rings*.

Both Tolkien and Golding were war veterans—Tolkien having gone "over the top" at the Somme with the Lancashire Fusiliers in the First World War, Golding hunting the *Bismarck* and supporting the D-Day beaches in the Second World War. Such links have led Tom Shippey to argue that Tolkien and Golding—along with C. S. Lewis, George Orwell, and Kurt Vonnegut—could be considered as a group of "traumatized authors": authors who have first-hand experience of some of the most horrific excesses of the twentieth century. These writers were

> bone-deep convinced that they had come into contact with something irrevocably evil. They also ... felt that the explanations for this which they were given by the official organs of their culture were hopelessly inadequate, out of date, at best irrelevant, at worst part of the evil itself. (*J. R. R. Tolkien*, p. xxx)[1]

Interestingly, when Shippey was working on his first study of Tolkien, *The Road to Middle-Earth*, he argued *against* contextualizing Tolkien as a postwar writer, noting in a review that the "idea of putting Tolkien in the 1950s literary scene with Huxley, Orwell, and Golding ignores Middle-earth's enormous gestation" (500). Instead, he recommended focusing on linguistic influences and Old and Middle-English sources. But Shippey subsequently turned to the moment of publication in his follow-up book, *Author of the Century*, and explicitly considered Tolkien as a "post-war" writer. This critical study set *The Lord of the Rings* in the context of Orwell and Golding, plus T. H. White and C. S. Lewis: *Animal Farm* (1945), *Nineteen Eighty-Four* (1949), *Lord of the Flies* (1954), *The Once and Future King* (1958), and *That Hideous Strength* (1945) were "all books insistently marked by war" ("Post-War" 84)—if Tolkien's war was of course the Great War.

This approach led Shippey to propose that

> If one considers the whole history of Tolkien's youth and middle age, from 1892 to 1954, a period marked not only by two world wars

and the rise of Fascism, Nazism, and Stalinism, but also by—I give them more or less in chronological order—the routine bombardment of civilian populations, the use of famine as a political measure, the revival of judicial torture, the "liquidation" of whole classes of political opponents, extermination camps, deliberate genocide and the continuing development of "weapons of mass destruction" from chlorine gas to the hydrogen bomb, all of these absolutely unthinkable in the Victorian world of Tolkien's childhood, then it would be a strange mind which did not reflect, as so many did, that something had gone wrong, something furthermore which could not be safely pushed off and blamed on other people. (*Road* 324-25)

One could add the industrialization of war and killing, the obsession with mass surveillance and internal security, and so forth.... Traditional literary responses were simply inadequate in responding to this "brave new world."

The only way of addressing this horror was, Shippey argues, obliquely, which is why the "dominant literary mode of the twentieth century has been the fantastic" (*J. R. R. Tolkien* vii). More recently, Jed Esty links late Eliot and Woolf with a range of writers and thinkers, from Tolkien to John Maynard Keynes, to the Birmingham school of cultural studies to connect modernist literature with the ensuing turn to romantic nationalism. He writes that "the *anthropological turn* [my italics] names the discursive process by which English intellectuals translated the end of empire into a resurgent concept of national culture—one whose insular integrity seemed to mitigate some of modernism's characteristic social agonies while rendering obsolete some of modernism's defining aesthetic techniques" (2).[2] As J. P. E. Harper-Scott puts it: "Esty's claim is that modernist literature concerns itself with the relationship between the imperial metropolis and its colonial periphery, and that in developing a different focus late-modernist writers were turning their attention away from imperial cohesion towards the need for cohesion at home" (571).[3] Thomas W. Smith has recently broadened this approach to argue that "Fantasy writers as different as Tolkien, Ursula LeGuin, William Golding, George Orwell, Aldous Huxley, J. K. Rowling, C. S. Lewis, Kurt Vonnegut, or Philip Pullman understand their work as a kind of recovery from disillusionment and disenchantment" (81). Whether as "traumatized author" or as late modernists, a consensus is emerging that links Tolkien with Golding, and this can, I think, be developed further by directly comparing *The Lord of the Rings* with *Lord of the Flies*.

I will begin with a reminder of the immediate context. From 1950 to 1953, Britain, as part of the UN, sent troops to fight in the Korean War. In 1951, the state of war between Britain and Germany was officially ended, and coincidentally the Festival of Britain was held. King George VI died in February 1952 and Operation Hurricane, Britain's first atomic weapons test, took place in October of the same year, while a month later the first American hydrogen bomb (fission) was exploded. Stalin died in March 1953; the first Russian hydrogen bomb was tested in August. The coronation of Elizabeth II took place on 2 June 1953; that morning, news of the ascent of Everest by Hillary and Tenzing reached London. Also, postwar rationing ended in Britain on July 4, 1954. All of this bears upon *Lord of the Flies*, a novel set in the nuclear aftermath of a war between Britain and "the Reds" (Golding *Lord* 179)—a novel that investigates how deeply British values are ingrained by education and society, and how leaders take power and maintain order. In the case of Jack, "Power lay in the brown swell of his forearms: authority sat on his shoulder and chattered in his ear like an ape" (Golding *Lord* 165).

Golding's approach was to write his novel as an allegory, describing it as such in his covering letter to Faber and Faber:

> I send you the typescript of my novel
> 'Strangers From Within' [as it was originally titled]
> which might be defined as an allegorical interpretation of a stock situation.
> I hope you will feel able to publish it. (Qtd. in Carey 151)

Golding later described *Lord of the Flies* as a flight from contemporary history:

---

it was an escape to a part of the world I had never seen but wanted to, a tropical island. I made myself a *haliporphuros ornis* ["sea purple bird"; first word taken from Ezra Pound's *Cantos* (750)] and flew away from rationed, broken England with all its bomb damage, flew away across the flowers of foam to where the lianas [woody vines] dropped their cables from the strange tropical trees. (Golding, *A Moving Target* 183)

Yet it turns out that it is impossible to escape England without degenerating into something literally unspeakable; England may be broken, but it is inescapable, and remains far better than the alternatives. Golding's work has consequently been described as *allegory*, although it is not a simple pattern of allegory but a more radical, moving typology, motivated by trying to understand the nature of "humanity." In the essay "Fable," Golding famously commented of the war: "Anyone who moved through those years without understanding that man produces evil as a bee produces honey, must have been blind or wrong in the head" (Golding, *The Hot Gates* 87).

The immediate political and social context speaks to *The Lord of the Rings* as well, with the caveat that the first stirrings of Middle-Earth went back to Tolkien's convalescence during the Great War and the book itself was begun before the outbreak of the Second World War in December 1937, as a follow-up to *The Hobbit* (published September 21, 1937). However, it is clear that warfare, the Home Front, the Cold War, atomic weapons, and the nature of leadership, community, and government saturate the book. Tolkien was less sanguine, however, about historicizing the composition of *The Lord of the Rings* and added a foreword to the second edition of the book (1966) distancing his work from the context of the war, declaring "I cordially dislike allegory in all its manifestations" (1: 12).[4]

Without getting bogged down in Tolkien's specific, mediaevalist meaning of *allegory*, it is worth pointing out that before this he wrote in a letter drafted in April 1956:

Of course my story is not an allegory of Atomic power, but of *Power* (exerted for Domination).... I do not think that even Power or

Domination is the real centre of my story. It provides the theme of a War, about something dark and threatening enough to seem at that time of supreme importance, but that is mainly "a setting" for characters to show themselves. The real theme for me is about something much more permanent and difficult: Death and Immortality: the mystery of the love of the world in the hearts of a race "doomed" to leave and seemingly lose it; the anguish in the hearts of a race "doomed" not to leave it, until its whole evil-aroused story is complete. (246)

What is striking about this statement is that it connects not only with *Lord of the Flies*—"*Power* exerted for Domination"—but also with Golding's earlier novel (if actually published later), *The Inheritors*: "a race 'doomed' to leave and seemingly lose [the world]; the anguish in the hearts of a race 'doomed' not to leave it, until its whole evil-aroused story is complete." But that story is for another time.

More immediately telling for the present instance are Tolkien's problematic and provocative comments on anarchy and governance. On November 29, 1943, he wrote to his son Christopher on his attraction to

Anarchy (philosophically understood, meaning abolition of control not whiskered men with bombs)—or to "unconstitutional" Monarchy. I would arrest anybody who uses the word State (in any sense other than the inanimate realm of England and its inhabitants, a thing that has neither power, rights nor mind); and after a chance of recantation, execute them if they remained obstinate! (*Letters* 63-4: see also 65, 73, 107, 115, 215, 246)

The closing exclamation mark reveals, I hope, that this is tongue-in-cheek banter. But he also admitted to a sympathy for "the growing habit of disgruntled men of dynamiting factories and power-stations" (*Letters* 64). In other words, according to Paul Romney, Tolkien was "simultaneously asserting a contradictory preference for complete absence of government and for the complete centralization of power," but Romney argues that "charismatic leadership is the natural outcome in small groups lacking formal institutions of government, be they biker gangs ... or the stranded schoolboys of William Golding's *Lord of the Flies*" (74; see also Scorville 95). It is a problem that neither writer solved: Golding repositioned himself as an analyst of the plight of the individual in the face of the incomprehensible, more powerfully than any other writer of his time, perhaps of all time; Tolkien went the other way, charting his reconstructed chronicle of the entire history of Faërie in the ultimately unfinished series of cycles that form *The Silmarillion*, the supreme imaginative achievement of the century.

In their themes, both *Lord of the Flies* and *The Lord of the Rings* probe post-Imperial English identity through metaphor and allegory: They are "state of the nation" studies. Both could be seen as versions of travel literature in which the sea plays a mysterious and ineffable role—on Golding's island the sea is unbridgeable until the end of the novel (only navigable by the dead bodies of Simon and Piggy), in Tolkien's Middle-Earth the western sea represents the transit to an afterlife. Both books are haunted by powerful evil forces that have stunning psychological effects (the hallucinations of the beast, Simon's uncanny realization that the beast could be inside "us," Frodo's temptations by the Ring and his supernatural confrontations with the Eye of Sauron, the encounters with the *Palantír*) and physical effects (the collapse of communal order and ensuing bloodshed in both). In this sense, both have been seen as political microcosms, focusing on "the group as a political unit, on the interaction of political units, as well as on the means and ends of political systems," in contrast to individualistic Orwellian heroes attempting to defy such systems (Barnett 383). Both books also focus on artifacts of power: the conch, which symbolically represents power, and the Ring, which is actually an incarnation of supernatural power. And both focus on unlikely groups of protagonists: prepubescent schoolboys, and hobbits—this last eliciting a famously scathing series of reviews of Tolkien from the Orcadian poet Edwin Muir in the *Observer* (and possibly also as the anonymous reviewer for the *Times Literary Supplement*): "The astonishing thing is that all the characters are boys masquerading as adult heroes" (qtd. in Carpenter 223).[5] But this can be countered by considering that both books are studies of camaraderie and male intimacy, evident in the slippery comments the beast makes to Simon and in the palpable love Sam has for Frodo (see Smol).

George Steiner, in an obituary for Tolkien published in *Le Monde* (September 6, 1973), also identified a similarity of style between Tolkien and his contemporaries:

> In England, in contrast to France, the Celtic, Irish, Scottish, and Saxon myths and the Arthurian cycle have made their presence felt in a number of the most significant works of contemporary poetry and prose. It is impossible to appreciate the lyrical genius of Robert Graves, the novelistic force of John Cowper Powys or William Golding, the bestiaries of Ted Hughes whose violent tones current[ly] dominate English poetry, without recognizing the enduring and obsessive presence of ancient epics and legends in the current intellectual climate. (186)

This is an interesting remark as *Lord of the Flies*, at least, is far more classical in its literary style (beginning in medias res, alluding to Circe's Isle, following a Euripidean tragic structure in the deployment of deus ex machina, and so forth) than Tolkien's models drawn from doomy Germanic epics. It is also worth noting some further differences between the works. For instance, Shippey points out that for all its warfare, physical violence in Tolkien is barely described; there is nothing as explicit as the killing of Piggy (*Road* 123-33). One simple reason for this perhaps is that Tolkien and Golding were actually of different generations: Tolkien was a Victorian born in 1892; Golding, born in 1911, grew up under George V—the difference in age between them was just three months short of twenty years.

These differences aside, I think that there is enough to connect the two books beyond their chiming titles. On the other hand, these similarities could merely be coincidence. John Carey's recent biography of Golding has, however, disclosed new directions for research. Carey describes Golding's first teaching job at Michael Hall, a Steiner school in Surrey; Cecil Harwood, one of the backers of the school and effectively the headmaster, had had some contact with the Inklings—Tolkien's literary club in Oxford. Golding was known for telling stories during lessons: "terrifying tales of magicians and sorcerers" (qtd. in Carey 65). These tales don't of course survive, although Carey does describe the unpublished short story "The Mountain Ash" (67-69), a climate-change fable describing the metamorphosis of a man into a tree. So much: so much unprovable.

More significant, perhaps, is *Circle Under the Sea*, an unpublished novel by Golding that predates *Lord of the Flies*. Carey summarizes *Circle Under the Sea* thus:

> Ben Hamilton, its hero, is big, strong, peaceful and unambitious, and makes a modest living writing adventure stories for boys. He has agreed to take two friends, Geoffrey Amoy, a young schoolmaster and amateur archaeologist, and Geoffrey's sister Penelope, who is just down from Oxford, on a boating holiday aboard his thirty-four-foot ketch *Speedwell*. Geoffrey insists on being taken to the Scilly Isles, because he has a theory that the remains of a prehistoric civilization lie under the water offshore, with submerged megaliths of the Stonehenge type, and he intends to search for them. (137)

What follows is an adventure story that Golding himself described as "Arthur Ransome for grownups" (qtd. in Carey 137). But there is a mysterious episode that Carey quotes in which Ben Hamilton dreams that he dives into a tarn and discovers a prehistoric monolith beneath the dark waters. There is an inexplicable encounter with a force called the Man of Authority:

> The Man of Authority took Ben by the right hand and drew him to the edge of the tarn. Ben saw his own arm was black with filth. The Man of Authority was queerly dressed and his movements were a sort of speech, like dancing. The waters of the tarn were a dead and awful black. Ben knew he must dive. The Man of Authority spoke a word that created something of itself and Ben threw himself into the water. At once he was in a green world, rushing through depths where there was no direction but down. Now he was standing in the open and a shock-headed giant was lumbering up the hill towards him. (qtd. in Carey 139)

Circle Under the Sea shares its central idea—and indeed this glimpse of Faërie—with *The Lost Road*, an abandoned sequel to *The Hobbit* in which Tolkien proposed approaching Middle-Earth from a different perspective: from that of the sea off the Cornish coast. *The Lost Road* began as a time-travel fable alongside C. S. Lewis's space-travel narratives that were eventually published as *Out of the Silent Planet* (1938), *Perelandra* (1943), and *That Hideous Strength* (1945). *The Lost Road* begins with the boy Alboin holidaying with his father in Cornwall. Alboin is haunted by the sea, which appears to speak to him in an archaic language through dreams. The fragmentary words and images he receives tell of the fall of *Atalantie*, or *Númenor*—a prehistoric civilization that was deluged by the sea in ages past. *Númenor* survives in linguistic fragments that haunt the languages of England, and it also has some elusive existence in the perilous realm of Faërie. The book, had it been completed, would have had some affinities with Kipling's episodic model of visionary history, *Puck of Pook's Hill* (1906), weaving together mystical linguistics, the history of the Lombards, Alfredian England, and the fall of *Númenor*. Elements of *The Lost Road* were later incorporated into another abandoned novel, *The Notion Club Papers* (written alongside *The Two Towers* in 1944-46), and traces remain in *The Silmarillion*.

Alboin wonders about traveling back in time to the lost lands:

> To walk in Time, perhaps, as men walk on long roads; or to survey it, as men may see the world from a mountain, or the earth as a living map beneath an airship. But in any case to see with eyes and to hear with ears: to see the lie of old and even forgotten lands, to behold ancient men walking, and hear their languages as they spoke them, in the days before the days, when tongues of forgotten lineage were heard in kingdoms long fallen by the shores of the Atlantic. (45)

He meets Elendil, a *Númenorean*, in a dream, and chooses to go back in time with him:

> "You have chosen," a voice said above him. "The summons is at hand."

Then Alboin seemed to fall into a dark and a silence, deep and absolute. It was as if he had left the world completely, where all silence is on the edge of sound, and filled with echoes, and where all rest is but repose upon some greater motion. He had left the world and gone out. He was silent and at rest: a point. (Tolkien, *Lost Road* 51)

Whatever any shared inspiration might have been, Golding took another path as he rewrote *Lord of the Flies*. Simon became increasingly less otherworldly as drafts progressed, and the supernaturalism of the story was submerged into psychological trauma. But the shadows of what I would like to call Faërie remained from *Circle Under the Sea* and its unexpected closeness to *The Lost Road*, and they made themselves felt again, I think, in Golding's 1979 novel, *Darkness Visible*—the provisional title of which was "Here Be Monsters" (see Carey 369).

Notes

1. On Golding, see also pp. 115-17, 119-21, and 156.
2. Qtd. by J. P. E. Harper-Scott, pp. 570-1: "His intention is to offer a post-colonial reading of late-modernism, the argument being that in the throes of imperial decay England's imperializing tendency and discourse was focused inward by an 'anthropological turn.'"
3. See Harper-Scott, p. 571: "That is to say that the early work of Eliot and Woolf is about empire and the later work is not."
4. I have further discussed Tolkien on allegory in "The English Literary Tradition: Shakespeare to the Gothic." *A Companion to J. R. R. Tolkien*, edited by Stuart Lee, Blackwell, 2014, pp. 286-302, especially p. 288.
5. He continues: "The hobbits, or halflings, are ordinary boys; the fully human heroes have reached the fifth form; but hardly one of them knows anything about women, except by hearsay. Even the elves and the dwarfs and the ents are boys, irretrievably, and will never come to puberty" (qtd. in Carpenter 225-6).

Works Cited

Barnett, Malcom Joel. "Review: The Politics of Middle-Earth." *Polity* vol. 1, no. 3, 1969, pp. 383-87.

Carey, John. *William Golding: The Man Who Wrote* Lord of the Flies. Free Press, 2009.

Carpenter, Humphrey. *J. R. R. Tolkien: A Biography*. Allen & Unwin, 1977.

Esty, Jed. *A Shrinking Island: Modernism and National Culture in England*. Princeton UP, 2009.

Golding, William. *The Hot Gates and Other Occasional Pieces*. Faber & Faber, 1965.

_____. *Lord of the Flies*. 1954. Faber, 2011.

_____. *A Moving Target*. Faber, 1982.

Hammond, Wayne C. and Christina Scull. *The J. R. R. Tolkien Companion and Guide, Volume 1*. Houghton Mifflin, 2006.

Harper-Scott, J. P. E. "'Our True North': Walton's First Symphony, Sibelianism, and the Nationalization of Modernism in England." *Music and Letters*, vol. 89, no. 4 (2008), pp. 562-89.

Morrison, Blake. Review of *William Golding: The Man Who Wrote* Lord of the Flies, by John Carey. *The Guardian*, Sept. 4, 2009, https://www.theguardian.com/books/2009/sep/05/william-golding-john-carey-review.

Pound, Ezra. *The Cantos*. 1934. New Directions, 1970.

Ripp, Joseph. "Middle America Meets Middle-Earth: American Discussion and Readership of J. R. R. Tolkien's *The Lord of the Rings*, 1965-1969." *Book History*, vol. 7, 2005, pp. 245-86.

Romney, Paul. "'Great Chords': Politics and Romance in Tolstoy's *War and Peace*." *University of Toronto Quarterly*, vol. 80, no. 1, 2011, pp. 49-77.

Scorville, Chester N. "Pastoralia and Perfectibility in William Morris and J. R. R. Tolkien." *Tolkien's Modern Middle* Ages. Edited by Jane Chance and Alfred K. Siewers, Palgrave Macmillan, 2005, pp. 93-103.

Shippey, Tom. *J. R. R. Tolkien: Author of the Century*. Houghton Mifflin, 2000.

_____. [as T. A. Shippey]. Review of *Vølve: Scandinavian Views on Science Fiction*. Edited by Cay Dollerup, in *Review of English Studies* vol. 31, no.124, 1980, p. 500.

_____. *The Road to Middle-Earth*. Houghton Mifflin, 2003.

_____. "Tolkien as a Post-War Writer." *Proceedings of the J. R. R. Tolkien Centenary Conference*, edited by Patricia Reynolds and Glen H. GoodKnight [sic], Mythopoeic Press, 1995.

Smith, Thomas W. "Tolkien's Catholic Imagination: Mediation and Tradition." *Religion and Literature*, vol. 38, no. 2, 2006, pp. 73-100.

Smol, Anna. "'Oh … Oh … *Frodo!*' Readings of Male Intimacy in *The Lord of the Rings*," *Modern Fiction Studies*, vol. 50, no. 4, 2004, pp. 949-79.

Steiner, George. "Tolkien: Oxford's Eccentric Don." Reprinted in *Tolkien Studies*, vol. 5, 2008, pp. 186-88.

Tolkien, J. R. R. *The Letters of J.R.R. Tolkien.* Edited by Humphrey Carpenter with the Assistance of Christopher Tolkien. George Allen & Unwin, 1995.

_____. *The Lord of the Rings*. 2nd ed. 3 vols. George Allen & Unwin Ltd, 1966.

_____. *The Lost Road and Other Writings*. Edited by Christopher Tolkien. Unwin Hyman, 1987.

Lords of the Flies: Peter Brook, Harry Hook, and Golding's Novel_____

Christopher Baker

In his *Entertainment Weekly* review of Harry Hook's film version of *Lord of the Flies*, Owen Glieberman quipped, "As a novel, *Lord of the Flies* never was much more than a Brat Pack *Heart of Darkness*." Flip one-liners like this may help to sell magazines, but, as decades of Golding's readers and viewers of Hook's and Brook's films attest, it does not do justice to the broad appeal that the novel has had in both written and cinematic form. Hook's filmed version of William Golding's *Lord of the Flies* in 1990 has generally dwelt in the critical shadow of Peter Brook's film of the novel that appeared almost thirty years earlier. In the intervening years, Brook's version established itself as not merely a fine adaptation of the novel but as a remarkable film in its own right. To be sure, each film has had its champions and its detractors. Bosley Crowther found Brook's film "a curiously flat and fragmentary visualization of the original," whereas Penelope Gilliatt, according to J. C. Trewin, felt that Brook's direction "had preserved the book's character with a fastidiousness that was remarkable" (122). Roger Ebert concluded that Hook "seems more concerned with telling the story than showing it," but Stanley Kauffmann declared that "Hook has directed with snap and visual keenness, much more competently than Peter Brook in his 1963 version" (26). However, in seeking to evaluate these films in relation to Golding's narrative, we should be mindful of comparing two productions displaying distinct differences that seem to reveal different directorial intentions, or that do not respond to the novel in identical ways. As George Bluestone pointed out in his seminal work on film adaptation, *Novels into Film*, "Since each film is allowed its own integrity, the novel is considered less a norm than a point of departure" (x); "changes are inevitable the moment one abandons the linguistic for the visual medium" (5). Brook seeks to present us with a filmed version of the novel (it had no shooting script and was shot directly from the book [Wilson 229]), whereas Hook's work was self-described in its opening credits as *"based on* William Golding's *Lord of the Flies"* (emphasis added). Each film departs from the novel differently, at times adding features not present in Golding's book: Brook adds Piggy's talk about the history of Camberly, and Hook replaces Golding's dead airman with an injured pilot who wanders in and out of the action before dying. Brook's version relies more on thematic character relationships and symbols for its effect, whereas Hook renders the story with a plot-driven sense of adventure.

Brook and Hook, both English, have each contributed to contemporary film in distinct ways. Showing an early interest in theatre, Brook (born in 1925) "has been the world's most influential theater director during the second half of the twentieth century and beyond" ("Peter Brook"). He has directed nine opera productions plus numerous stagings of Shakespeare, notably *King Lear* starring Paul Scofield, whom he also directed in a 1971 film version of the play, one of sixteen films and television movies he has directed. Harry Hook (born in 1960) was raised in Africa and has produced eighteen films and documentaries. He has also established himself as a writer, editor, and portrait photographer, especially in his visual record of the native peoples of Kenya, and most recently in his documentary *Photographing Africa* (2014). Brook, who tends to linger over a shot or scene with documentary attention, approaches the novel as a myth of youthful lives increasingly driven by a profound evil, which the boys at first assume to be outside of themselves, but which the more perceptive of them come to realize is within them, a force that cannot simply be externalized, named, and controlled as a "beast." Hook, instead, with what Glieberman termed his "swift yet luxurious hyperrealist camera style" (and which Janet Maslin called "vacuously pretty") moves the plot along more rapidly, making his scenes speak more explicitly and rather less evocatively about the boys' predicament and their response to it. Brook's film unfolds like a poem of linked images and symbols, whereas Hook's conception functions more like the traditional Victorian boy's novel *The Coral Island* to which Golding alludes in the novel's final pages.

The Boys

In 1990, Hook said of his film, "I've got nothing but respect for the original Peter Brook version, and it was not fresh on my mind when we embarked on this. So from my point of view I was just going back to the book. As a director I just wanted to deal with the subject of 25 boys left to their devices, how evil might grow and flourish and all that" (Hicks). But Hook and Brook each go "back to the book" in their own ways. One of the most significant changes Hook makes to Golding's novel, as distinct from Brook's version, is that his boys were all students of an American military academy before they come ashore on the island. As Hook told an interviewer, "When the book was written, England had a huge global responsibility . . . [but now] the way America behaves in world politics is important" (qtd. in Van Gelder). One of Golding's primary fictional achievements was to track the emergence of destructive urges in boys from a civilian upbringing which has imparted to them traditional mores, as suggested in Brook's opening long shot of the boys marching down the beach in their choir robes, Elizabethan ruffs, and church caps, chanting *Kyrie eleison* ("Lord have mercy"). Brook's religious imagery here is obviously and bitterly ironic, but Hook's boys give no evidence of ever having had any contact with religion, a fact that removes a level of moral complexity from his rendition of Golding's story. Their foul language has the faux-macho quality of middle school males who imagine themselves to be far tougher than they are in order to live up to the masculine stereotype of their training. When Piggy shouts at Jack's gang to "shut your goddamn mouths" it seems jarringly out of character. Gratuitous profanity abounds, in contrast to the almost prudish references in Brook's film (and the novel) to the boys' diarrhea (which they refer to as getting "caught short") brought on by their constantly eating ripe jungle fruit. Given their schooling, Hook's boys seem closer to their destined violence right from the start.

As in the novel, Brook's youths revert to a primitive cruelty that emerges from their own untutored decisions, whereas Hook's boys, judging by their uniforms, their habit of calling each other by their student rank, and their shouting of cadence chants as they march, have already been socialized into a militaristic frame of mind; "in reaching the island, none of the prepubescent kids even cries" (Glieberman). We thus miss the spontaneous appearance of evil as a feature of human nature rather than of upbringing; human malevolence is conveyed as a product of nurture rather than originating more deeply within each individual. This difference extends throughout Hook's film in a variety of added details. The boys come ashore in a large survival raft rather than having somehow survived the crash by unknown means as in the novel; more than one boy has a knife, whereas Brook's and Golding's Jack is the only one with a knife, thus establishing him as the first among equals of violence; and the boys are all dressed in blue uniforms that contrast sharply with the green foliage but that stay vividly clean for longer than they should, thus delaying their descent into the grime of the jungle. Hook's Ralph has the conch that represents his authority, but he also brandishes a lime green glowstick that disconcertingly pulls us off the island and into the Star Wars world of Luke Skywalker and his lightsaber. These boys are at ease with the technology on which war depends, whereas Golding's boys are, at least at first, the more innocent victims of their warring elders.

Just as Brook's Simon (Tom Gaman) stands out with his almost angelically white hair, Hook's Simon (Badgett Dale) is more sensitive and perceptive than most of the boys, a quality suggested by his noticeably blue eyes. He carries a pet chameleon that at one point is suddenly knocked to the ground and then speared to death by one of Jack's boys, and later a spiny puffer fish is also pierced by a boy's stick, both in contrast to Simon's lizard in Brook's film that he lovingly pets and cares for. As the chameleon lies skewered into the forest floor, someone mutters "Jesus Christ!"—a fleeting religious link between Simon's love for nature and his own innocent death. But this is the extent of Hook's religious symbolism for a character who carries much greater symbolic weight in Golding and Brook. Hook's Jack Merridew (Chris Furrh) is no taller than most of the other boys; with a slender build and sun-bleached hair, he seems more like an androgynous surfer than the embodiment of a sinister element in human nature; for one critic, he could well be "modeling designer denim" (Maslin). We learn that he had been sent to military school after being arrested for joyriding in a stolen car, so it is not the island experience that coaxes his latent violence to the surface as much as his preexisting love of danger. His ghost story by the campfire is scary but not deeply threatening, his too-frequent cursing reveals a playground bully who leads a "gang" of followers instead of the novel's more evocative "tribe," and, rather than being a personality deeply allied with the beast, he is often merely a shallow, loud-mouthed thug. Ralph's problems with Jack seem to mirror those that Brook had with his own actors, who at times became just too rambunctious to stay focused on the film. John Heilpern recalls an angry Brook telling his actors, "if we cannot work together at every level there is just no *point* in us being here. This isn't a sightseeing tour" (qtd. in Kustow 215). Danuel Pipoly portrays Hook's Piggy with a depth of intensity and range of emotion lacking in the other two leads, a role that earned him two Young Artist nominations. Though less prepossessing physically than Ralph or Jack, he shows a greater self-knowledge than either; when Ralph tries to reassure him by saying that the boys don't really mean to be cruel to him, he knowingly replies that they do.

Contrasting Visions

Hook's film features key details of the novel, but he rarely pauses over them to draw out their implications more fully. Simon gazes at the pig's head more with curiosity than with an understanding stare, and Golding's dead pilot, who arouses such fear in the novel, becomes a badly injured pilot who agonizes under a mosquito net but then ambles off to die in a cave. This flattening of the symbolic dimension of the film pushes it in the direction of an adolescent boy's narrative rather than a moral allegory about human nature. Hook's American boys seem too familiar, most especially to American audiences, and this closing of the dramatic distance between audience and screen tends to reduce their function as instructive, generic types. Piggy sarcastically asks whether the other boys are graduates of the Outward Bound program in Colorado, one cadet eating a roasted lizard says it tastes like chicken, and two others remember watching *Rambo* and *Alf*. Their stranded situation evokes excitement and suspense but not the human potential for evil; we are left feeling that Hook's is more a story of problems to be solved than of mysteries to be pondered.

Brook conveys his story by lingering over visual impressions that carry Golding's themes indirectly yet more persistently. Brook allows Simon to stare at the pig's head with a long, knowing gaze; despite his youth, we sense that Simon comprehends it as the externalization of a central aspect of his, and everyone's, being. As Claire Rosenfield says of him in Golding's novel, "Shaman-like, he holds a silent and imaginary colloquy with [the pig's head]" (292). As in the novel, this perception allows him to state the book's most crucial insight about the beast to Ralph: "Maybe it's only us" (89). Hook's Simon, however, gazes at the pig's head with a fascinated perplexity and never mentions to Ralph that the pig could reflect their own malevolent urges; for him the head is a strange object rather than a stark omen, and, as a character, Hook's Ralph is overall less percipient than Brook's; Balthasar Getty in the later film does not convey the same extremes of emotional intensity that James Aubrey does in the earlier production.

Brook's Jack is likewise more complexly portrayed than Hook's. Tom Chapin's descent into savagery is expressed by his use of more elaborate face paint than Chris Furrh's. Chapin also uses a mask fashioned out of a leaf that at once hides his former schoolboy self while suggesting the beast within. Chapin is noticeably taller than the other boys, lending him a greater air of authority and potential threat. But Jack lacks Simon's deeper understanding of evil, even as it overtakes him. When he screams, "The beast!" and charges down the beach at the head of his tribe to murder Simon, it is clear to us but not to him that he has become the very thing he assumes he is killing. Golding's narrative captures Conrad's threatening sense in *Heart of Darkness* of Europeans who are suddenly plunged into an environment that is not only beyond their native cultural setting but out of their moral depth, a spiritual dimension that Hook's film occasionally touches but does not plumb.

The role of the pilot also differs markedly in the two productions. Brook's dead military pilot, "ironically stifled in the elaborate clothing worn to guarantee survival" (Niemeyer 242), expresses the possible obliteration of humanity by nuclear war. His face is hidden by his black helmet visor, and his parachute lies over him like an entangling net instead of a means of rescue; the technology of safety has become a reminder of death. Hook's pilot, a civilian from the look of his uniform, is badly injured and is crudely looked after the boys, who bandage him as best they can. He appears to Simon in a dream and assures him that they will all return home safely, but he later wanders deliriously into a cave, where his moans are mistaken for the sounds of the beast by Jack's boys, one of whom stabs him with a spear. In contrast to Brook's pilot, Hook's has a less well-defined link to the plot; like Simon and Piggy, he is an innocent victim of Jack's boys who have run amok, and as a civilian he does not offer the vivid antiwar statement of Brook's dead pilot crumpled in his flying gear. Nicola Presley rightly concludes that Hook's pilot destroys the essential premise of children lacking any adult influence: "These boys are not by themselves and the pilot's presence is entirely unnecessary."

The Coral Island

Hook's adaptation of Golding's novel hews closer than Brook's to one of Golding's sources, R. M. Ballantyne's *The Coral Island*, a noted boys' adventure book published in 1858. Like Ballantyne, Hook emphasizes the boys' difficulties in coping with the natural and human challenges of their island life, but unlike Golding, Hook plays down the threat of nuclear war, a prevalent fear during 1954 when the novel appeared. Unlike Ballantyne, Hook's boys make no patriotic declaration to triumph over every difficulty, but, as in the popular Victorian story, they bring with them the values of their culture and use these to surmount the obstacles they face. Ballantyne's Ralph Rover (the narrator gives himself an assumed surname that expresses his love of travel), Jack Martin, and Peterkin Gay are all solid products of the English educational system, "kind, good-natured fellows" (11). In his preface to Ballantyne's novel,

Edward Hower suggests that Peterkin "might be said to be the id of the group, [and] is constantly light-hearted about his predicament"; "Jack, the oldest of the three, the group's superego, if you like, is more British about the situation [and protests] 'we are wasting our time *talking* instead of *doing*'"; "Ralph, the threesome's ego and alter ego . . . spends most of his time observing" (ix). Ralph accepts being regarded by his friends as a "queer [unusual] old-fashioned fellow" (11), but he can't understand this label, even though he admits that he "could never understand the jokes of my companions even when they were explained to me." He "was very fond of inquiring into the nature of things and their causes, and often fell into fits of abstraction while thus engaged in my mind" (12). Being cast ashore on this island seemed to him "the most splendid prospect that ever lay before three jolly young tars. We've got an island all to ourselves. We'll take possession in the name of the king; we'll go and we'll rise, naturally, to the top of affairs. White men always do in savage countries" (27-28).

The imperialist condescension Ralph Rover displays here towards whatever indigenous people he might encounter becomes, in Hook's film, the militaristic, marching, chanting, cursing gang of Jack. Rover's plucky, foursquare outlook is barely dented by his experience on the island, just as Hook's Jack smugly imports his military school swagger into his life as a "hunter." Ralph's glowstick recalls an incident in Ballantyne's book when what seems to be a glowing "heartless monster" (Hook's boys also refer to a monster instead of a beast) is thought to be a "phosphoric light" (151) but is in fact "a stream of light issuing from a cave in the rocks" (154). And, as in both films, a sow is killed, but in *The Coral Island* it is only because Peterkin wants to make new shoes from its hide. Hook's film edges closer to Jack's monochromatic attitude as expressed by Ballantyne than to Golding's evocation of a barely perceived primal threat. Ballantyne's Jack is always self-assured; as he says, in his always impeccable English, "I have generally found that strange and unaccountable things have almost always been accounted for, and found to be quite simple, on close examination" (97). He can also display the raw violence that Hook's Jack shows in beheading the pig. After a native chieftain throws an infant into the ocean and threatens to club a young girl, "Jack uttered a yell that rang like a death-shriek among the rocks. With one bound he leaped over a precipice full fifteen feet high, and before the savages had recovered from their surprise, was in the midst of them. . . . With one blow of his staff Jack felled the man with the club, then, turning round with a look of fury, he rushed upon the big chief with the yellow hair" (231-32). Jack indulges in further acts of violent derring-do, but they are always directed at the boys' enemies rather than at his own companions.

Ballantyne's explicitly Christian tone also drives his book far from Golding's acerbic message. Despite Simon's symbolic function as a Christ figure for Golding and Brook, his role does not approach the missionary zeal present in *The Coral Island*.[1] As Ralph Rover relates, "When the teacher [at the Christian settlement on the island] afterwards told me that the people of this tribe had become converts only a year previous to our arrival and that they had been living before that in the practice of the most bloody system of idolatry, I could not refrain from exclaiming, 'What a convincing proof that Christianity is of God!'" (374). Rover's religious triumphalism is akin to Jack's military determination to dominate the island in Hook's film. In short, there are no problems that cannot be solved by ingenuity and determination in Ballantyne's world of earnest, eager lads. They are not lacking experience of human evil, for the book also includes confrontations with pirates and savages, but these are groups from whom Victorian readers would not likely have expected moral behavior in any case. For Hook's American boys the possibility that the problem-solvers might themselves be the problem is barely suggested, and for Ballantyne's English boys it simply never arises. Far different is Brook's adaptation, where they are more obviously held in the grip of an inexplicable evil.

Another aspect of Hook's film that inclines it more towards the category of adventure than of social commentary is his omission of the larger context of nuclear war that is so central to Golding's conception of the novel. Brook pays close attention to this background, but he does so by displaying under the film's opening credits a series of sepia-toned photographs of English schoolboys and their teachers together with a montage of grainy images of rockets, jet fighters, and military hardware that suggests a worldwide conflict has occurred. This device enables Brook to frame the film within the same historical situation that dominates Golding's novel but without reducing the amount of time he can devote to filming the main plot. When the British officer comes ashore to rescue them at the end, his film is thus bookended by visual references to warfare that underscore Golding's theme of human conflict. Contrastingly, Hook's opening credits, displayed against a dark background with no explanatory text, follow an underwater sequence as the downed boys swim upward towards the ocean's surface. A large, inflated safety raft filled with the boys then floats into a quiet inlet with no indication that they are refugees from a nuclear war, and the rescued pilot whose airliner has presumably crashed into the sea offers no hint of a larger disaster. This makes the later appearance of military helicopters rather puzzling (including one which unaccountably drops a bomb offshore). Perhaps there is a conflict going on, but just as possibly the boys have merely stumbled into a remote, restricted military area. This situational blurriness distances the film from Golding's deeper moral themes, losing the larger backdrop of fear of a nuclear holocaust that was so central to the Cold War ambiance of his novel. As Janet Maslin observes, Hook and his cinematographer, Martin Fuhrer, "can't get a toehold onto what Mr. Golding called his 'attempt to trace the defects of society back to the defects of human nature.'"

Symbol versus Metaphor

The difference between the adaptations of Hook and Brook can perhaps be expressed through the distinction between the functions of metaphor and symbol. The comparative nature of a metaphor means that its significance will necessarily be limited by the relationship existing between its tenor and its vehicle, between the meaning it conveys and the object chosen to convey that meaning. The conch in the novel is, strictly speaking, more of a metaphor than a symbol because its meaning is restricted to the idea of authority it grants to whoever holds it. Piggy's glasses offer a somewhat wider reference, suggesting both his intelligence and the boys' use of technology to help them survive by building a fire. A symbol, in contrast, operates by suggesting both immediate meanings (that can, like a metaphor, be comparative in nature, because a symbol will be "like" something that is immediately apparent) and additional significances that unfold through continued readings over time, in an open-ended, allusive process of meaning that metaphor by its comparative nature tends to forestall. The film versions of Brook and Hook operate in a manner similar to the difference between a symbolic and a metaphoric adaptation of the story Golding tells. This is not to say that Hook never employs symbols or that Brook is without metaphors. For example, the arrival of Brook's naval officer at the film's end is an ironic metaphor centered on the strong probability that the world of grown-ups will again foment a major conflict. However, the pig's head mounted on a stick in both films is a symbol of evil, sin, violence, animalistic human urges, and what Conrad called in *Heart of Darkness* "the fascination of the abomination" (6), plus related ideas that multiply beyond the more rigid structure of an analogy. However, Hook chooses to show Jack actually cutting off the pig's head with his knife, a moment that pulls this image more firmly into the world of physical fact, whereas Brook omits the beheading and depicts the head on its stick, replete with buzzing flies, as a powerful totem whose symbolic import is even more profound than its bloody, rotting presence. The violence of the pig's beheading is implied but not depicted. Brook's film, unlike Hook's, is unified by a strong symbolic structure with clear religious overtones. Choir robes, church caps, the singing of the *Kyrie*, Simon's life and death, the final hellish conflagration, all lend an otherworldly dimension to the film, perhaps even hinting that the pig's head on the stick is a perverse crucifix, the inverse of everything Simon represents. Brook's experience making this film may have influenced his perception of the pig. His film (and part of Hook's) was shot on the Puerto Rican island of Vieques, also the location of a large United States Navy base; life imitated art when, the week Brook began shooting, the Bay of Pigs Invasion began.

The treatment of Simon's death in the films also discloses their differing metaphoric and symbolic approaches to Golding's work. In Hook's version, Simon, having seen the pilot in the cave, runs down the beach waving his glowstick and is immediately set upon by Jack's gang, who viciously kill him with their sharpened sticks. The boys run off, and we see Simon's body in a medium long shot face down in the surf, his inert body covered with vivid, bloody wounds. In Brook's scene, Simon is again spotted, surrounded, and killed by the boys' spears. But, in a closer shot, we then watch him float face up slowly out of the visual frame, followed by rippling points of light that might suggest fireflies, stars, reflections of moonlight, or even the halo of a saint. For an event taking place at night, the image of Simon's floating corpse is startlingly bright; his body might be dead, but the symbolic weight of this moment suggests that something about him—his virtue, his selflessness—still lives. And, amazingly, his body is completely unmarred and unbloody, glistening with clear water. Where Hook offers a murder—graphically colorful, gritty, literal, and fixed viscerally in our vision, an emblem of violence— Brook presents a metamorphosis, perhaps even a transfiguration, as what begins with violence is transformed into a kind of sacrificial offering that is taken into the sea with mythic overtones missing in Hook's homicide on a beach; we are briefly reminded of Golding's dead pilot who is lifted by his parachute and also carried out to sea. As Simon's corpse drifts away in Brook's scene, a choir intones the *Kyrie*, giving the scene an unmistakable religious resonance. Ironically, and perhaps intentionally, "KYR-i-e e-LE-i-son" is practically an exact rhythmic match (a double dactyl) of the chant of Jack's tribe: "KILL the pig, CUT his throat." The demonic and the divine are inextricably mingled.

The death of Piggy is similarly allusive. Each film gives us the crushing impact of a boulder striking his head, but Hook presents him knocked to the ground on his back, his eyes open in death, his head laced with bright blood. This is the visual detail of a crime scene snapshot that captures the death of innocence with photographic realism. In contrast, Brook has Piggy struck off the edge of a cliff; in quick sequence, as with Simon and with no visible signs of injury, he too falls into the ocean. Both boys suffer violent deaths, leave the island, and are taken back in a sense by the sea, the source of life, in a suggestive parallelism that provokes mythic, religious, and psychological meanings that resonate beyond Hook's more graphically precise rendition of an undeserved death. As William Boyd notes, Brook is able to capture Golding's "persistent hypersensitivity to the numinous and immaterial aspects of the world and the human condition."

Pauline Kael has written that "Movies are good at action; they're not good at reflective thought or conceptual thinking" (qtd. in Stam 59). Her first assertion is confirmed by Hook's film, but her second is contradicted by Brook's, who seems as much, or more, concerned about what Golding's novel means and in leading us to confront its meaning than about how "well-constructed" or "convincing" its action is in a self-consciously cinematic way. Brook recognizes the documentary quality of his film, and has commented on the tension between directing the action itself and at the same time allowing the boys to let the action unfold as it will to maintain spontaneity. His black-and-white production thus has both the quality of documentary and the aesthetic dimension that has led to this picture being termed an art film. According to Edward Trostle Jones, Golding's novel "illuminates whatever is latent and dormant in the psyche of civilization and releases it into consciousness. In Brook's film, this end is achieved . . . without recourse to verbalization. . . ." (142). Michael Kustow has stressed the "merciless literalism of the camera which was the bedrock of cinematic experience for Brook" (178), but Brook's literal details also open on to what Irving Wardle calls his darkly suggested "expressions of anthropological despair" (qtd. in Kustow 128). Hook, more content to remain at the level of story and metaphor, likewise offers us documentary particulars but they remain less memorably allusive, more fixed in a comprehensible reality that leaves our complacent self-knowledge less disturbed.[2]

Notes

1.   As Golding told interviewer James Keating, "I intended a Christ figure in the novel, because Christ figures occur in humanity, really,

but I couldn't have the full picture, or as near as full a possible picture of human potentiality, unless one was potentially a Christ figure. So Simon is the little boy who goes off into the bushes to pray" (qtd. in Keating 212).

2.   For a one-hour documentary on the making and history of Brook's production as recalled by the actors at a reunion, see the BBC film *Time Flies* (1996) available on Youtube. https://www.youtube.com/watch?v=V5YnE1pPqfY&t=47s. Tom Gaman (Simon) offers a personal view, also on Youtube: https://www.youtube.com/watch?v=r_QSJSx0UKI.

Works Cited

Baker, James R., and Arthur P. Ziegler Jr., editors. *Lord of the Flies.* Casebook Edition. Perigee, 1988.

Ballantyne, Robert Michael. *The Coral Island.* Garland, 1977.

Bluestone, George. *Novels into Film.* U of California P, 1957.

Boyd, William. "Man as an Island." Review of *William Golding: The Man Who Wrote* Lord of the Flies*: A Life,* by John Carey, *New York Times,* July 18, 2010, p. BR 10. Accessed 26 March 2017.

Conrad, Joseph. *Heart of Darkness.* Fourth edition. Edited by Paul B. Armstrong. Norton, 2006.

Crowther, Bosley. "Agitating Fable of Wild Boys: Savagery is Depicted in *Lord of the Flies.*" Review of *Lord of the Flies,* directed by Peter Brook. *New York Times,* 20 August 1963. https://www.nytimes.com/section/movies. Accessed March 26, 2017.

Ebert, Roger. Review of *Lord of the Flies,* directed by Harry Hook. *RogerEbert.com,* 16 March 1990, http://www.rogerebert.com/reviews/lord-of-the-flies-1990. Accessed January 26, 2017.

Glieberman, Owen. Review of *Lord of the Flies,* directed by Harry Hook. *Entertainment Weekly.* March16, 1990. http://ew.com/article/1990/03/16/lord-flies/. Accessed February 28, 2017.

Hicks, Chris. "Film Review: *Lord of the Flies.*" Review of *Lord of the Flies,* directed by Harry Hook. *Deseret News,* March 16, 1990. http://www.deseretnews.com/article/ 700001085/Lord-of-the-Flies.html. Accessed March 8, 2017.

Hower, Edward. Preface. *The Coral Island,* by R. M. Ballantyne. Garland, 1977, pp. v-xii.

Jones, Edward Trostle. *Following Directions: A Study of Peter Brook.* Peter Lang, 1985.

Keating, James. "Interview with William Golding." In Baker and Ziegler, pp. 189-96.

Kauffmann, Stanley. "Stanley Kauffmann on Films." *The New Republic.* April 2, 1990. 26-27.

Kustow, Michael. *Peter Brook.* St. Martin's Press, 2005.

Maslin, Janet. "Another Incarnation for *Lord of the Flies*." Review of *Lord of the Flies*, directed by Harry Hook. *The New York Times.* March 16, 1990. https://www.nytimes.com/section/movies. Accessed January 14, 2017.

Niemeyer, Carl. "The Coral Island Revisited." In Baker and Ziegler, pp. 217-24.

"Peter Brook." *Europe Since 1914: Encyclopedia of the Age of War and Reconstruction.* Edited by John Merriman and Jay Winter. Charles Scribner's Sons, 2007. *Biography in Context*, link.galegroup.com/apps/doc/K3447000162/BIC1?u=sava66375&xid=74d8d236. Accessed February 16, 2017.

Presley, Nicola. "Lord of the Flies on Film." *William Golding*, March 4, 2013. http://www.william-golding.co.uk/lord-of-the-flies-on-film. Accessed March 3, 2017.

Rosenfield, Claire. "'Men of Smaller Growth': A Psychological Analysis of William Golding's *Lord of the Flies*." In Baker and Ziegler, pp. 261-76.

Stam, Robert. "Beyond Fidelity: The Dialogics of Adaptation." *Film Adaptation.* Edited by James Naremore. Rutgers UP, 2000, pp. 54-76.

Trewin, J. C. *Peter Brook: A Biography.* Macdonald, 1971.

Van Gelder, Lawrence. "At the Movies." *The New York Times.* July 8, 1988: C8. Accessed March 28, 2017.

Wilson, Edwin. "Lord of the Flies in Production." *Peter Brook: Oxford to Orghast.* Edited by Richard Helfer and Glenn Loney. Harwood Academic Publishers, 1998, pp. 227-32.

William Golding's *Lord of the Flies*: A Glimmer of Hope in this Dystopia?

Joan-Mari Barendse

William Golding's novel about a group of boys stranded on an island after a plane crash recalls well-known adventure stories such as *Robinson Crusoe* (1719) by Daniel Defoe, *The Swiss Family Robinson* (1812, originally published in German as *Der Schweizerische Robinson*) by Johann David Wyss, and *Treasure Island* (1883) by Robert Louis Stevenson (George 31). Stuart Manger (among many others) also points to the link between *Lord of the Flies* and R. M. Ballantyne's tale of a group of shipwrecked boys *The Coral Island* (1858) (34). Moreover, *Lord of the Flies* (1954) brings to mind the island utopias which, inspired by the exploration voyages of the time, became popular in the seventeenth century (Moylan, *Demand* 3-4). Unlike these utopian tales of far-off places imagined to be better than the societies of their authors, *Lord of the Flies* is generally described as a dystopia and sometimes also as an anti-utopia (George 32). In this essay, I explore whether *Lord of the Flies* can be read as a critical dystopia, a dystopia that contains at least one eutopian enclave, or the hope that the dystopia can be replaced by a eutopia.

Utopia versus Dystopia

Before discussing *Lord of the Flies*, it is necessary to explain what terms such as *utopia* and *dystopia* mean, and how they will be used in this essay. Thomas More coined the term *utopia* with his work *Utopia* (published in Latin in 1516 and translated into English in 1551). Many critics show that More purposefully created an ambiguous word by combining the Greek words *ou-topos*, meaning no place or nowhere, and *eu-topos*, meaning happy or good place (Jameson 1; Moylan, *Demand* 2; Wegner 81-82). In standard usage, the term *utopia* has come to denote an ideal or perfect place. Referring to the ambiguousness of More's term, Lyman Tower

Sargent argues though that "the word *utopia* or *outopia* simply means *no* or *not place*": "*Topos* means place, 'u' or 'ou' means 'no' or 'not.' Thomas More, inventor of the word, punned on *eutopia* or *good place*, and we have since added *dystopia* or *bad place*" (5, his emphasis). For Sargent, the genre of utopian literature therefore encompasses the eutopia (good place) and the dystopia (bad place). The eutopia portrays a society that is "considerably better" than the society of the contemporaneous reader, while the dystopia sketches a society that is "considerably worse" (Sargent 9). In his paper "The Three Faces of Utopianism Revisited," Sargent discusses different variations of these forms such as the anti-utopia and the critical utopia (9). He defines the anti-utopia as "a non-existent society [...] that the author intended a contemporaneous reader to view as a criticism of utopianism or of some particular eutopia" (Sargent 9). A critical utopia on the other hand, depicts a culture "better than contemporary society but with difficult problems that the described society may or may not be able to solve" (Sargent 9). Sargent later adds another form of the dystopia—namely the critical dystopia, which is a dystopia that contains at least one eutopian enclave or the hope that the dystopia can be replaced by a eutopia (Baccolini and Moylan 7).

Lord of the Flies as Dystopia

Philip E. Wegner claims that most dystopian texts comment on the sociopolitical reality of the time in which they are published (90-91). Raffaella Baccolini and Tom Moylan (1-2) as well as Sargent (26) not only see dystopian literature as commentary on social ills, but also as warnings that things could get worse. While *Lord of the Flies* displays elements of the anti-utopia in being a subversion of the island utopia or eutopia (and therefore criticizes a type of eutopia), it can be classified as a dystopia because it also comments on the sociopolitical context of Golding's time. Usha George considers Golding's disillusionment with humankind after World War II to be the inspiration for the novel (33). Sargent shows that events such as World War I (1914-1918) and World War II (1939-1945) caused the dystopia to become the "dominant utopian form" in the twentieth century (26).

Lord of the Flies can furthermore be described as a dystopia since it portrays a society that is "considerably worse" (Sargent 9) than the society of the author and the contemporaneous reader. Golding is writing in the aftermath of World War II, and in *Lord of the Flies* he depicts a society that is amid an even more horrifying and destructive war: a nuclear war. The details of the world outside the island remain vague throughout the novel, but in Chapter 1 the conversation between Ralph and Piggy about the possibility of rescue gives the reader some insight into what is going on in the outside world when Piggy says: "Didn't you hear what the pilot said? About the atom bomb? They're all dead" (14).

It at first appears as if the boys have escaped from the nuclear dystopia and have found a eutopian paradise on the island. In Chapter 2, Ralph exclaims that "it's like a book": "Treasure Island—Swallows and Amazons—Coral Island [...] This is our island. It's a good island. Until the grown-ups come to fetch us we'll have fun" (38). Here is a direct reference to Ballantyne's *Coral Island*. According to Stuart Manger, Golding modelled *Lord of the Flies* on Ballantyne's book (34). For instance, both novels follow groups of boys stranded on an island, and many of the names of the main characters in Golding's novel (Ralph and Jack) are taken from *Coral Island*. When Golding alludes to *Coral Island* in *Lord of the Flies*, the former work functions as an intertext in the latter work. Manger explains that *Coral Island* is characterized by an "unquestioned acceptance of current political or religious ideologies, social hierarchies-all fuelled by the powerful missionary zeal that drove much mid-nineteenth-century empire-building" (34). *Lord of the Flies*, on the other hand, is written as a reaction to World War II and shows "a whole nation's traumatised postwar pessimism for the human race":

> Since the publication of the Ballantyne novel there had been a century tainted by genocide, tyranny, torture, 'ethnic cleansing'—all of which history now reveals were indeed taking place in Ballantyne's day, but definitions of such atrocities were so different as to make

them unrecognisable to Ballantyne's contemporaries. More or less as Golding published *Lord of the Flies*, the haunting images of the first hydrogen bomb were bleak on the planet's collective retina, and newsreel footage from Belsen and Auschwitz had destroyed any utopian vision of innocence or of a brave new, purged world. (Manger 34)

Considering the context against which *Lord of the Flies* was written, it is not surprising that the boys' island eutopia soon turns into their own dystopia when a power struggle ensues between Ralph and Jack. *Lord of the Flies* therefore also satirizes and acts as critical commentary on Ballantyne's novel.

Despite the bleak dystopia Golding creates, there are, nevertheless, moments of hope. In *Lord of the Flies* hope is symbolized by two objects: the conch shell found by Ralph and Piggy in Chapter 1 (16) and Piggy's glasses, which the boys discover in Chapter 2 can be used to make fire (44). The importance of these objects is already clear from the references made to them in two of the chapter titles: Chapter 1 is titled "The Sound of the Shell" and Chapter 10 is titled "The Shell and the Glasses." In the novel, getting rescued by grown-ups is another premise of hope, and phrases like "until they [the grown-ups] fetch us" (32) echo throughout the boys' conversations. As shown in the discussion below, the glasses and the shell furthermore represent and are connected to the adult world.

Although the critical dystopian form only becomes prevalent in the 1990s (Moylan, *Scraps* 188 and Wegner 92), the present essay explores whether the elements of hope present in *Lord of the Flies*, an older dystopian work, are powerful enough to classify it as a critical dystopia. The discussion will focus on Ralph (after he is replaced as leader by Jack) and his small resistance group holding out against the oppression and control practiced by Jack. Focusing on the themes of leadership and control in the novel, I will look at the function of the two apparent objects of hope (the shell and the glasses). I will then examine whether the rescue scene at the end of the novel offers the hope that the boys' dystopia can be replaced by a eutopia.

Symbols of Hope: A Fair-haired Boy, a Conch Shell, and a Pair of Spectacles

On the first page of the novel, the reader is introduced to "the boy with fair hair" (7) named Ralph (9). The first person Ralph meets after the plane crash is Piggy, and together they discover the first object that plays an important role in the society they create: the conch shell. Referring to the monetary value of the shell, Piggy says that it is "ever so valuable" (16). On the island however, the worth of the shell does not lie in how much it costs, but in the effect it has on the boys. Piggy mentions that he had a friend who used a shell like this to call his mother, and they realize that the shell can be used to make contact with any survivors (17). The plan works and Ralph and Piggy are soon surrounded by other children. It is then that the true power of the shell is made known: "The children gave him [Ralph] the same simple obedience that they had given to the men with megaphones" (19). The "men with megaphones" refer to the men (most likely soldiers or other authority figures) who gave the orders when the children were evacuated due to the war. The shell, like a megaphone in a soldier's hand, thus gives power to the one who holds it. Jack proposes that he should be chief because he is "chapter chorister and head boy" (23). The appeal of the conch shell is too strong, though, and it is decided that Ralph, "him with the shell," "with the trumpet-thing" (24), is chosen as leader instead. Although the shell is a natural object found on the island, its power lies in its connection to the adult world where they come from. The boys know how to use it because of Piggy's experience with a similar shell at his friend's house. Showing the strong hold of the world of the grown-ups on the boys, they furthermore compare the shell to the megaphones of the soldiers.

A negative connotation is initially given to the shell by comparing it to the megaphones used by the men to control the children. Although Ralph assumes a position of authority, he does not use the shell to force his will on the others, but instead he uses it as an instrument to create order and stability in the group. In Chapter 2 it is decided that at meetings whoever holds the conch shell is allowed to speak. Even Piggy, who is from a lower social class than the other boys (as evidenced by his use of nonstandard English and his ill health in general) and is also a social outcast on the island, is given a chance to give his opinion (36-37). Darko Suvin shows that utopian societies (whether they are eutopian or dystopian) are almost always based on class systems (162-90). In Chapter 4 it is explained that the boys' society in *Lord of the Flies* is divided into two groups or classes: the small boys known as the *littluns* and the bigger boys known as the *biguns* (64). Although the littluns do not play a significant part in the decision-making on the island, in Chapter 2 it is shown that under Ralph's rule even they get a chance to have their say while holding the conch (39). That the littluns are the lower class on the island is made clear, however, when their fears of the "snake-thing" are dismissed by the older boys (39-40).

The other object that becomes important in the society created by the boys is Piggy's pair of glasses. Without the glasses, the boys cannot make a fire. As George shows, the boys' ability to make fire with the glasses links this object to "civilization, the adult world and home" (49). They need fire not only for warmth, to cook on, and to scare away potentially dangerous animals, but also as a signal to passing ships (46-47). Piggy's spectacles thus become a symbol of the hope of being rescued. Jack and his hunters are put in charge of keeping the signal fire going. When Jack and his group neglect to look after the fire and it is out while a ship passes, the power struggle between Ralph and Jack intensifies (76).

The fire is initially made on the mountain so that it will be more visible to passing ships. In Chapter 8 the boys decide to move the fire from the mountain because of the presence of the "beast" (143). What the boys think is the beast, however, is in fact a dead man in a parachute who has fallen onto the mountain (Chapter 6, 104). The boys are too scared to maintain the fire on top of the mountain and it is moved to a lower, less visible place, thus decreasing their chances of being rescued. In his essay on *Lord of the Flies* titled "Fable" from the collection of essays in the book *The Hot Gates*, Golding writes that "the figure which is dead but won't lie down, falls on the very place where the children are making their one constructive attempt to get themselves helped" (96). The dead man literally diminishes their hope of getting rescued. On a figurative level, though, it symbolizes the ever-looming presence of the grown-ups' war and the impact thereof. The children cannot escape from the evil the grown-ups have unleashed—it follows the boys to the island, and, as later discussed, they also discover that evil resides in themselves.

Due to the conflict surrounding the "beast" on the mountain and the fire, Jack becomes even more defiant of Ralph's leadership (Chapter 8, 140). He already challenges Ralph's authority and rules in Chapter 6 when he says: "'[W]e don't need the conch any more. We know who ought to say things. What good did Simon do speaking, or Bill, or Walter? It's time some people knew they've got to keep quiet and leave deciding things to the rest of us—'" (111). Baccolini and Moylan consider language as a "key weapon" in the "dystopian power structure" (5-6). With Ralph as the leader, everyone has the right and freedom to speak, while Jack wants to control language. In Chapter 8, Jack finally breaks away from Ralph's group (140). Enticed by Jack's hunting skills, most of the big boys follow him and Jack declares: "'We'll hunt. I'm going to be chief'" (147). Ralph is left with Piggy, the twins Sam and Eric (also known as Samneric), and the littluns. Although the functioning of the society on the island had slowly been deteriorating, it only truly becomes a dystopia when Jack establishes his own rule. In Chapter 9 it is shown that Jack controls the boys in his group with violence and even decides when and how much food is eaten (165).

Baccolini and Moylan explain that in dystopian literature the main character often moves from a state of alienation to a state of resistance against the dystopia in which he/she finds him/herself (5). The narrative can end with the individual's resistance being suppressed, or the individual can facilitate collective resistance by forming a resistance group. The resistance of the group can also be suppressed, or it can lead to a zone of freedom from which the resistance group acts. This enclave functions as the glimmer of hope in the critical dystopia (Moylan, *Scraps* xiii). In *Lord of the Flies*, Ralph experiences alienation when, despite his efforts to keep order, the group disintegrates. Confused by what is causing the island to become "worse and worse" (Chapter 8, 153), he asks Piggy: "[W]hat makes things break up like they do?" (154).

Ralph's resistance group, although small, still tries to hold on to the few objects of hope they possess. When Jack and members of his group come to Ralph's camp to invite them to a feast, Piggy's biggest fear is that they are going to take the conch shell, and he is relieved when they do not: "The group of boys looked at the white shell with affectionate respect. Piggy placed it in Ralph's hands and the littluns, seeing the familiar symbol, started to come back" (156). The little children's response to the shell even suggests that with the help of the conch Ralph might regain his position as leader. Ralph also tries to reinforce the idea of the fire as their only hope of getting rescued: "Can't they see? Can't they understand? Without the smoke signal we'll die here?" (154). That Ralph's group might fail in their resistance is already suggested when in Chapter 8 Ralph realizes that the boys can't even "keep one fire going. And they don't care. And what's more—[…] *I* don't sometimes. Supposing I got like the others—What'ud become of us?" (154). Here one of the last beacons of hope, the fair-haired boy Ralph, is also losing faith in himself. Still, as a last attempt at resistance against the chaos of Jack's dystopian reign, Ralph and Piggy decide to go to Jack's feast to reason with him about the importance of keeping the fire flaming.

That Ralph will not regain power becomes clear when in Chapter 9 Jack refuses to listen to Ralph's argument about the fire and does not even acknowledge the conch shell (166). Ralph's loss of power and the final disintegration of order in the society are further demonstrated by Ralph and Piggy getting drawn into the dystopia of violence that Jack has created when they take part in the ritualistic killing of Simon (167-77). They discover that, just like the grown-ups, they are capable of evil and destructive deeds.

In Chapter 10, after they have left the feast, Ralph, Piggy, and Samneric return to their side of the island. Ralph, still clinging to the hope that fire might save them, has difficulty motivating his small group to start the fire again (180). Later that night, their camp is raided by Jack's group. Still believing in the authority of the conch, Piggy tries to protect it (185). At the feast, Jack and his followers have already shown that they do not respect the conch anymore. It has lost all its power and they are therefore not interested in it. They leave the shell, but they take the other object of hope that Ralph and Piggy had in their possession: "The Chief [Jack] led them, trotting steadily, exulting in his achievement. He was a chief now in truth; and he made stabbing motions with his spear. From his left hand dangled Piggy's broken glasses" (186). Jack has not only taken the glasses, but has broken them, an act that symbolizes the destruction and loss of hope.

A desperate Piggy decides in Chapter 11 to go to Jack with the conch in the hope that the shell will somehow regain some of its former power and that they can convince Jack's group to return his glasses (189). Roger, who is the guard in Jack's group, pushes a huge boulder from a cliff onto Piggy. Piggy is killed and the shell is said to have "exploded into a thousand white fragments and ceased to exist" (200). The last symbol of hope is destroyed.

The resistance of Ralph's group is completely suppressed: Piggy is dead, the twins have joined Jack's group, and Ralph has no option but to hide in the forest (206). The resistance group therefore does not function as the eutopian enclave of the critical dystopia in *Lord of the Flies*. The only hope left for the boys is to be rescued by grown-ups. In the following section of this essay, the rescue scene at the end of *Lord of the Flies* as a possible critical dystopian element in the novel is explored.

When the Grown-ups Come: Can this Dystopia Become a Eutopia?

In Chapter 12, Jack's group set the island on fire to smoke Ralph out (217). A passing naval ship sees the smoke and comes to their rescue. Although being saved is not the intention of Jack's group, the smoke from a fire they make is what eventually gets them rescued. Ralph runs into a naval officer while running away from Jack's group (221). The officer "grin[ing] cheerfully" says: "We saw your smoke. What have you been doing? Having a war or something" (221). The officer jokingly asks: "Nobody killed, I hope? Any dead bodies?" (222). When Ralph replies that two have been killed the officer "whistled softly": "The officer knew, as a rule, when people were telling the truth" (222). Although the officer believes Ralph when he tells him that two boys have been killed, he still sees the boys as children who are playing a game of war rather than being engaged in a true war. He says: "'I know. Jolly good show. Like the Coral Island'" (223). That the officer does not quite realize the seriousness of the situation on the island is shown when he compares what Ralph and the boys have gone through to a fictive adventure tale, *The Coral Island* (once again a direct reference is made to this intertext in the novel). In reality, the boys' war is just as real as the grown-ups' war. Usha George describes the society the boys have created on the island as "microcosmically a human society, related to the 'grown-up' society that occasioned the Original fall from the skies" (32). The boys' society on a smaller scale mirrors the grown-ups' society. Also, the boys would not be on the island, engaged in their own war, if it were not for the war the grown-ups are waging. By putting the word "grown-up" in quotations marks, George suggests that the grown-ups' society is not marked by the responsible behavior one expects from adults. Like the children on the island, the adults have created a violent and destructive dystopia by starting a war. The society of the grown-ups thus does not offer much hope to the children.

Ralph's last act of resistance against the dystopia is when he resumes the leadership role when the officer asks who is in charge (222). This time Jack does not stand in his way, and this fact can be considered a small victory for Ralph (222). By taking responsibility for the chaos on the island, Ralph admits, though, that his actions of resistance were not enough to create a glimmer of hope in the dystopia. The novel ends with Ralph weeping for "the end of innocence, the darkness of man's heart, and the fall through the air of the true, wise friend called Piggy" (223). The dystopian island will never become a eutopia again. During the rescue Ralph has "a fleeting picture of the strange glamour that had once invested the beaches," but then he sees that the island is "scorched up like dead wood" (223).

In Chapter 10, Ralph also has a eutopian vision of home when he imagines that they will be rescued and taken back: "Supposing they could be transported home by jet, then before morning they would land at that big airfield in Wiltshire. They would go by car; no, for things to be perfect they would go by train; all the way down to Devon and take that cottage again. Then at the foot of the garden the wild ponies would come and look over the wall..." (181). Ralph goes back to one of his fondest memories of a holiday with his family and creates a eutopian picture of a world that is perfect, beautiful, and carefree. The reader knows, however, that this world does not exist anymore and has been destroyed in the nuclear war. The boys are being rescued from one scorched space to be taken to another. The last premise of hope, to be rescued by the grown-ups, is also destroyed. The possibility that the dystopia can be replaced by a eutopia, as in the critical dystopia, therefore does not exist in *Lord of the Flies*.

Was There Ever Any Hope?

This essay has shown that the elements of hope present in *Lord of the Flies* are not sufficient to classify the novel as a critical dystopia. The two objects of hope, the conch shell and the glasses, are eventually destroyed. That Golding chose fragile, breakable objects to represent hope in the novel indicates that the chance for the boys to escape from the dystopia never really existed.

The enclave of resistance against the dystopia created by Ralph's group is short-lived. The group disbands when Piggy is killed by Jack's group and when Ralph must also flee for his life. The resistance group fails to create a glimmer of hope in the dystopia.

According to Baccolini and Moylan, critical dystopian texts often have open endings and in this way the eutopian impulse is present in the works themselves (7). In the dystopia on the other hand, hope, if it is present at all, exists outside the text "as a warning that we as readers can hope to escape its pessimistic future" (7). In "Fable" Golding states the following:

Before the second world war I believed in the perfectibility of social man; that a correct structure of society would produce goodwill; and that therefore you could remove all social ills by reorganization of society. It is possible that today I believe something of the same again; but after the war I did not because I was unable to. I had discovered what one man could do to another. (*Hot Gates* 86)

Before the war, Golding still thought that a eutopian, a perfect, society was possible. After the war, at the time he was writing *Lord of the Flies*, he had no hope for humankind. For Golding at this stage, hope did not even exist outside the novel since he did not see the dystopian society he depicted as a warning, but as inevitable.

    Lord of the Flies does to an extent have an open ending. We know that the boys will return to a society ravaged by war, but we do not know what will happen to them there. We do, however, know that the boys have discovered that they harbor evil inside of them. Their actions caused the eutopian island to turn into a dystopia. Just like the grown-ups, they could not maintain order and peace in their society and ended up in a destructive war. Even if the world somehow survives the nuclear war alluded to in *Lord of the Flies*, the novel suggests that humankind is inherently evil and not capable of maintaining a peaceful society. Consequently, there is no hope, and *Lord of the Flies* can only be described as a truly dystopian work.

Works Cited

Baccolini, Raffaella, and Tom Moylan. "Introduction. Dystopia and Histories." *Dark Horizons. Science Fiction and the Dystopian Imagination*. Edited by Raffaella Baccolini and Tom Moylan, Routledge, 2003, pp. 1-12.

George, Usha. *William Golding: A Critical Study*. Atlantic, 2008.

Golding, William. *The Hot Gates*. Faber, 1965.

_____. *Lord of the Flies*. 1954. Faber, 1974.

Jameson, Fredric. *Archaeologies of the Future: The Desire Called Utopia and Other Science Fictions*. Verso, 2007.

Manger, Stuart. "'Maybe it's only us': Stuart Manger Explores the Differences in Language and Kinds of Knowledge in *Lord of the Flies* and *Coral Island.*" *The English Review,* vol. 13, no. 3, 2003, pp. 34+.

Moylan, Tom. *Demand the Impossible: Science Fiction and the Utopian Imagination.* Methuen, 1986.

_____. *Scraps of the Untainted Sky: Science Fiction, Utopia, Dystopia.* Westview Press, 2000.

Sargent, Lyman Tower. "The Three Faces of Utopianism Revisited." *Utopian Studies*, vol. 5, no. 1, 1994, pp. 1-37.

Suvin, Darko. "Utopianism from Orientation to Agency: What Are We Intellectuals Under Post-Fordism To Do?" *Utopian Studies*, vol. 9, no. 2, 1998, pp. 162-90.

Wegner, Philip E. "Utopia." *A Companion to Science Fiction.* Edited by David Seed. Blackwell, 2005, pp. 79-94.

"Fun and Games" and the Sacred in William Golding's *Lord of the Flies*

Gérard Klaus

On the surface, the storyline is simple enough. As the result of evacuation during a nuclear war, a group of British schoolboys get stranded on a desert island. At first, they endeavor to establish a "society" based on what they know of "democracy," but order soon breaks down, and chaos ensues: the once-enchanted island turns into hell on earth.

It is admittedly tempting to read the story as a new version of the Fall, and an allegory of good versus evil: Golding himself did, writing articles, delivering speeches—going as far as touring US campuses!—and scores of critics have since followed suit. But this interpretation, to my mind, falls short of what the novel is really about.

Drawing on Greek mythology, James R. Baker in 1965 was one of the first critics to sense an altogether different polarity: that of Apollo versus Dionysos. He was right, of course, for, as we shall see, if "civilization" does break down on the island, it is to be superseded by a new realm of experience; something akin to the sacred.

But here we are talking about children. So I propose to focus on the children's pattern of play and games in the novel and postulate that while apparently "regressing," the children "naturally" and inevitably revert to the primordial.

"Fun and Games"

"Fun and games"—one of the recurrent phrases in the novel—encapsulates at once both ends of the play patterns: the individual (*fun*), which is clearly disjunctive, and the collective (*games*), conjunctive. At first sight, *fun* does appear idle, spontaneous, and unproductive (see Caillois, *Man, Play, and Games*), but is it "aimless and trivial" (Golding 61) as Golding would have it? Not so, say psychologists, who point out that fun involves a triple mechanism:

(1) compensation, (2) self-fulfillment, (3) conflict resolution.[1] "Games," on the other hand, imply rules that you invent, abide by, and sometimes break. If one keeps that polarity in mind, the novel unfolds neatly in three phases:

> 1. The marooned boys strive to set up a society modeled on the assets of (Western) civilization (Chapters 1-4). Games are the order of the day: they help to maintain safeguards and general cohesion.
> 2. These initial structures break down: disintegration ensues (Chapters 5-9). Rules are gradually desacralized (⇨ broken): fun takes over; censorship (⇨ taboos) recede.
> 3. A new structured group is born (⇨ new games), resulting in transfer from nurture to nature. New cohesion proceeds from dissolution.

From the start, the circle of play/games matches that of the island, whether it be the perimeter that the young "Robinsons" appropriate for themselves, savoring the temporary escape from parent or teacher tutelage, "the delight of a realized ambition" (Golding 2) or the ultimate refuge: the intimate circle of meetings.

It follows that the group's activities fall within the inclusion/exclusion dialectic, as Jack's repeated vexations testify—(sometimes with Ralph's tacit complicity)—: you are *in* if you play [the game]; you are *out* if you are fat or a spoilsport (Piggy), or if you are weird and "batty" (Simon) (Golding 121).

> A storm of laughter arose and even the tiniest child joined in. For the moment the boys were a closed circuit of sympathy with Piggy outside... (Golding 17)
> "Simon? What is it this time?" A half-sound of jeering ran round the circle and Simon shrank from it. (Golding 141)

Once the exhilaration of exploration has faded, the boys elect a chief, Ralph, who, while insisting on the temporary feature of their being stranded, makes a few simple rules to ensure their society will operate soundly.

At first the boys are quite pleased (and probably reassured) to play along with "this toy of voting" (Golding 18), insofar as this

---

socializing game is an exact replica of the world of adults. The conch, which starts off as the instrument for summoning meetings, becomes the (arbitrary) emblem of "democracy" and enables the boys to cling to the two models of society that they all know: school and the family.

Ralph strives to keep a (precarious!) balance between play and work, escapism and the world of adults: "We want to have fun. And we want to be rescued" (Golding 36). Nevertheless, it is clear that the setting up of institutions runs against playing, especially among the younger boys, and soon becomes a constraint. Still, some of the littluns idle their time away building sandcastles or drawing railway lines while showing signs of disruptive behavior.

One would hope that the group would tolerate such marginal activities, but this is not so; jeering and other forms of perverse aggression are soon rife, betraying, no doubt, the first signs of tension and anguish. As a matter of fact, the permanence of the system put in place rests mostly on Ralph's aura; the boys will mumble away their disagreements as long as the chief can guarantee collective safety. Should unknown phenomena creep in, however, the established order will totter, as Ralph himself senses: "faced by the brute obtuseness of the ocean, the miles of division, one was clamped down, one was helpless, one was condemned, one was— . . . . (Golding 121)

The circle of the island, once a refuge/playground, is now turning into a prison—"the taut wire of the horizon" (Golding 42)—, and evil lurking in the dark jungle no doubt underscores the boys' anguish and their phobia of confinement. To name that evil, to give it some kind of representation, is to try to master it. And so the boys comply, but it is noteworthy that their three subsequent representations of the beast belong to the moon bestiary; they are, I believe, avatars of the dragon:

> 1. the snake is the earth-monster: the symbol of quintessential perversion; 2. the octopus is the sea-monster: the one that will swallow you; 3. the big ape is the air-monster, now wingless.

The children are not amused; they are indeed repelled by this polymorphic monster, and this will speed up the dislocation of the first island society. Witness Ralph's own doubts: "Things are breaking up. I don't understand why. We began well; we were happy. And then—" (Golding 87).

It is Jack, of course, his rival from day one, who has been sapping Ralph's authority. But little did Ralph suspect, when he too generously granted his opponent leadership of the hunters, that this would prove a lever, a parallel force that would soon enable Jack to take responsibility for providing meat, and for the children's safety.

All work and no play certainly makes Jack a dull (and dangerous!) boy. See him biding his time, as enthusiasm dwindles for Ralph's kind of game (building huts, making a fire...). The showdown is imminent, as their altercation in Chapter 3 testifies: "We want meat" vs. We need shelters" (Golding 51-52). Even the choice of the verbs is weighted: compulsion ($\Rightarrow$ want) versus necessity ($\Rightarrow$ need).

Breaking the Rules

Jack is first perceived as the trickster, the cheat who breaks the rules while pretending to respect them. Does he not cause the assembly to break down at the end of Chapter 2? Does he not strike Piggy and break his "specs"? Jack's second move is to opt out, to negate the game, when he realizes that he cannot outmatch Ralph within the framework of the established order. But negating the game will not suffice. If Jack is to take over, he has to act out and break the taboo of the old life ($\Rightarrow$ killing), while satisfying the boys ($\Rightarrow$ providing meat), thus turning an evil act into a lawful action recognized as such by all.

Try as he might, Ralph will not be able to keep the boys much longer, for while his "game" is one of representation (many spectators, but few actors), Jack's is one of injunction, contact, action. So the laws are broken—"Bollocks to the rules!" (Golding 99); the elected chief is flouted, then fought; the shelters are copiously ransacked; the conch will soon be smashed to smithereens.

We remember that when Jack (almost accidentally) killed his first pig, the compulsion of hunting was already there: seductive,

---

maddening (Golding 72-73). When he walks away from Ralph's group and sets his mind on tracking and murdering the fat sow, he altogether changes gears. Luring the boys away from Ralph proves to be as easy as he had predicted: "I'm going to get more of the biguns away from the conch and all that. We'll kill a pig and give a feast" (Golding 147).

Pigs (or boars: Golding uses both terms) are plentiful on the island, and by breaking the taboo against killing, the boys sharply switch from a vegetarian diet (⇨ picking) to a meat one (⇨hunting). This is when the mask comes in handy. It is used, first, as camouflage to get as near as possible to the prey, and then, second, to imitate the animal (⇨ principle of similitude). Jack says that the mask will be useful for hunting. "Like in the war—you know—dazzle paint. Like things trying to look like something else—" (Golding 66). The mask also grants Jack a dual personality: "He looked in astonishment, no longer at himself, but at an awesome stranger" (Golding 66). The mask thus ensures anonymity and releases Jack from the anguish of guilt. Yet it is more than an accessory: it becomes an extension of his body (⇨ principle of contiguity) that enables him to venture into foreign territory.

Combine the two processes and you grasp Jack's animal regression: A becomes B as soon as he possesses at least one feature of B (⇨ the part for the whole): "Jack was bent-double... then dog-like, uncomfortably on all fours... he closed his eyes, raised his head and breathed in gently with flared nostrils, assessing the current of warm air for information" (Golding 48).

Now, is it not significant that the chosen victim should be a female, and more significantly a mother? Let's recapitulate: The hunters first injure the sow and decide to chase her to the finish, drawn no doubt by the spilt blood, excited by the female, "wedded to her in lust" (Golding 148). When they catch up with her, an explosion of passion and violence ensues, as the boys submit the mother: "Right up her ass!" (Golding 149)

This outburst of violence is in fact tantamount to the rape (= incest) and murder of the mother, that is, the definitive defiance of the ultimate taboo, signaling the end of the "civilized" world as we understand it. Yet French sociologist Roger Caillois (see *Man and the Sacred*) sees in incest an act of mystic resonance, for to possess one's mother symbolizes the wish to reintegrate with the living mother, and beyond that, the wish to abolish all polarities, and thus restore what Mircea Eliade (in *Images and Symbols*) calls the primitive unity.[2]

Such a "con-fusion" of the life instinct and the death wish transcends the climax attached to the voluptuous destruction of the other, for this outburst leads to the loss of consciousness, that is, the distinction between subject and object. No wonder the hunt intensifies the extreme masculinity of the hunters' experience, as opposed to the stereotypical femininity of Ralph's cautious world. The old (static) assembly is dead and has given way to the dynamic circle of the hunt; the old order (conceived by adults) is defunct.

The (collective) hunt proves to be a great catalyst, of course: Gone now are the democratic principles dear to Ralph and Piggy; in comes the tribe and its territory. The chief, who is no longer elected but a natural leader (Jack), puts forward a demagogical program that falls within the boys' new experience: "We hunt and feast and have fun" (Golding 154). As in so-called primitive populations, the feast adds to the cohesion of the group. It is an event that draws the hunters towards a primal cyclic time, which means it is nonchronological, nonhomogeneous, and alternates moments of relaxation (profane) with moments of tension (sacred): the hunt, the dance, the feast, and the sacrifice.

Like the hunt, the dance reintroduces a collective rhythm that energizes and kills off the sterile circle of assemblies. That it mimics the concentric centripetal movement of the hunt is obvious; that it awaits its victim too: "Then Maurice pretended to be the pig and ran squealing into the center, and the hunters, circling still, pretended to beat him" (Golding 79). The circle of hunters wheels ever faster—"like a steady pulse" (Golding 168)—and obliterates individual consciousness. Jack is "Chief," and some of the boys end up forgetting their own names.

The Sacrifice

The next step has to be the sacrifice. For like the mask, the dance, which starts off as mere imitation of the kill, ends up having its own purpose: the scapegoat. This will lead to the murder of Simon in Chapter 9. Interestingly enough, while "primitive" people generally evolve from human sacrifice to animal sacrifice, the boys, logically in their regression from the state of culture to that of nature, go the other way. This is how they discover the gift: The animal is not sacrificed, and its head is only offered to the beast afterwards—a ritual that resembles an embryonic pagan service, as the center point of the former boys' playground is now sacred ground. This is a propitiatory sacrifice, whose goal is clearly to placate the beast, and in so doing to exorcize the littluns' fears.

However, if we follow G. Frazer (in *The Golden Bough*), the "primitive" hunter often believes that he will be exposed to his victim's vengeance, hence the hunt's double motivation of propitiation and expiation: You try to obtain the victim's mercy in advance, but you also atone for your crime afterwards. Yet this lord, who is hunted and consumed, and is both sacrificed and revered, is now one with the beast, as the incantations reveal:

"Kill the pig. Cut her throat. Spill her blood." (72)
"Kill the pig. Cut her throat. Bash her in." (79)
"Kill the beast. Cut his throat! Spill his blood!" (168)

This sexual ambiguity confirms the confusion between the real animal and the polymorphic monster, which is a product of the boys' unconscious. This of course foreshadows the transfer towards human sacrifice. Thus Simon will be sacrificed by the (human) beast *as* beast and *for* the beast: the final stage of a process that has taken the boys from the imitation of the beast (the principle of similitude) to the ritual identification of the beast (the principle of contiguity).

The process of sacrifice is two-fold: (1) the victim is separated from the group and (2) the victim is then killed. Three boys stand on the margins of Jack's tribe, three witnesses to the old world:

1. Simon, who tacitly rejects Jack's game, Simon, the "idiot," who is prone to epileptic fits and speaks cryptically; 2. Piggy, "a pseudo-species" (see Tiger 49, quoting Eric Erickson) the ultimate killjoy; 3. Ralph finally, who willy-nilly negates Jack's game and cries for peace in vain.

One night, when even Ralph and Piggy have found temporary comfort in Jack's dance, Simon emerges from the dark forest with the revelation about a dead man on a hill, and "stumbles into a horse shoe." The rest is history: "At once the crowd surged after it, poured down the rock, leapt on to the beast, screamed, struck, bit, tore. There were no words and no movements but the tearing of teeth and claws" (169).

Simon, antisocial as he might be, experiences a three-fold quest, namely: (1) the separation, (2) the actual initiation (symbolic death), (3) the return (rebirth). Indeed, his autistic retreat highlights a clean break with the world. For him, the forest is neither a prison, nor monstrous; it is a hiding-place, the ultimate refuge whose secret he will keep to the end.

Piggy is victim number two. That the hunters should kill Simon in pitch dark but later Piggy in broad daylight is a sure sign of their "emancipation." This was to be expected, though: the fat boy is rational to the end; his death is devoid of all mysticism, like the killing of a mere animal: His "arms and legs twitched a bit, like a pig's after it's been killed" (201).

Ralph, the last guardian of the old order, should be the next victim, but, as we know, the British navy land on the island just in time—that fire on the mountain!—and save the day.

The Lord
Now, who is Beelzebub, Lord of the Flies and Prince of Demons? (see Kings I, 2; Luke XI, 15; Mark III, 2), partaking both of teratology—the study of fantastic creatures and monsters—and demonology, and whose male and female attributes remind one of both Baal and Belit? Is it an evil force, or on the contrary, the protector who will in time alleviate the boys' anguish, reducing it finally down to "a quiet terror" (202)? The Lord, by being sacred, enables the boys to

neutralize the evil force, but equally to restore the order disrupted by the murder of the sow, and thus to turn the kill (⇨ impure) into sacrifice (⇨ pure), black magic (⇨ evil and antisocial) into white magic (⇨ positive and socializing).

The Lord's first move is to tempt Simon, to entice him to reintegrate with the world of games: "You'd better run off and play with the others. They think you're batty. You don't want Ralph to think you're batty, do you?" (157)

Next, the Lord confirms his identity ("I'm the Beast") and warns Simon in no uncertain terms: "so don't you try it on, my poor misguided boy, or else—" (158). But Simon, as we know, has an epileptic fit, falls inside the mouth of the Lord, and loses consciousness; the only boy who had not been part of the sow's murder offers himself as sacrifice to the beast. On the strength of that revelation, Simon then climbs the mountain, releases the parachutist's corpse, makes his way down to tell the others, and meets his fate. His mission fails, of course, but through physical death, Simon is granted a genuine rebirth.

Ralph is now the sole survivor of the old order, faced with the elements, the supernatural, and himself. But unlike Simon, he "cannot connect with primal nature" (see Tiger 60). Thus, when in turn he faces the pig's head on a stick, he experiences both terror and rage and attempts to smash the grinning head. In his moment of "madness," Ralph descends into "the darkest hole on the island" (219), goes through various sensory perceptions, and finally grasps at Simon's testament. The beast, which prompted Jack and the hunters to break ranks with Ralph's game, and subsequently initiated the ritual dance and the sacrifice, may well be Man himself.

*   *   *

To what extent, Mircea Eliade wonders (see *The Sacred and the Profane*), can profane be turned into sacred? Golding and a cohort of critics decided to make Simon a saint, thus favoring individual initiation over collective ecstasy. Nevertheless, it is now clear that through the tribe, and in spite of some truly outrageous acts, the boys gain, through the evolution of their "fun and games," a primal perception of time and space. As Caillois (in *Man, Play, and Games* (throughout) writes about vertigo, the object is to reach a kind of spasm, of trance, of blackout, which suddenly obliterates reality. Is this not the path to the sacred?

Notes

1. Witness when Roger wantonly destroys the sandcastles of the littluns and throws stones at them (at first aiming to miss).
2. If you are familiar with Freud, you may remember that in his venture in social anthropology, *Totem and Taboo* (1913), he postulates that incest is related to the development of the clan system.

Works Cited

Baker, James R.. *William Golding: A Critical Study*. St. Martin's, 1965.

Caillois, Roger. *L'Homme et les Mythes* (1939, revised 1950). Translated by Meyer Barash as *Man and the Sacred*. Free Press, 1959.

_____. *Les Jeux et les hommes*. Translated by Meyer Barash as *Man, Play and Games* (1961). Thames & Hudson, 1962.

Eliade, Mircea. *Images and Symbols: Studies in Religious Symbolism*. Princeton, 1961.

_____. *Le Sacré et le profane* (1957). Translated by Willard R. Trask as *The Sacred and the Profane*. Harcourt, Brace, and World, 1959.Frazer, G. *The Golden Bough*. Macmillan, 1922.

Golding, William. *Lord of the Flies*. Faber, 1974.

Tiger, Virginia. *William Golding: The Dark Fields of Discovery*. Boyars, 1974.

"Pig's Head on a Stick": *Lord of the Flies* as a Political and Religious Drama_____

Eric Wilson

> The difference between reason and violence, on which we would like to base the unanimous agreement of members of society, does not precede the action that establishes the political order, but flows from it. (Dumouchel xvii)

Immanuel Kant's jibe concerning the "unsocial sociability" of humankind (Doumechel 14) is the basis of what I argue is the only fully coherent interpretation of *Lord of the Flies* (hereafter *Lord*) possible—the novel is a satire of the influential theory of the social contract laid out in Thomas Hobbes's *Leviathan* (1651).

The first paper I published on William Golding's famous novel (Wilson, "Warring Sovereigns") was devoted to illustrating the relevance of the French literary critic and lay theologian René Girard (1923-2015) to contemporary critical legal theory. Girard's theory of mimesis (the "*mimetic cycle*" [see Palaver vii]) "is based in essence on literary insight into man's [sic] unalterable religious nature" (Palaver 37). For Girard, religion, understood anthropologically, is the basis of social order because its ritualistic practices, most importantly sacrifice, resolve the destructive impulses generated through personal rivalry, which always involves problems of imitation, or mimesis. In a parallel manner the archetypal plot of all literature is an escalating rivalry over mimetic desire that eventually explodes into violence: The Self will model its relationship to the Other (a double) on the basis of imitation (mimetic rivalry) that will narratively culminate in the Self attempting either to replace and/or destroy the double (mimetic conflict; for further details, see below). "Rivalry," according to Girard, "does not arise because of the fortuitous convergence of two desires on a single object; rather, *the subject desires the object because the rival desires it.*" Therefore, in desiring an object—any object—the rival communicates to the subject the desirability of that object by that fact alone; the rival serves "as the model for the subject, not only in regard to such secondary matters as style and opinions but also, and more essentially, in regard to desires" (*Violence* 145). In order to prove the relevance of Girard both to law and to literature, I undertook a dual reading of *Lord*, self-consciously treating it as a commentary upon the nature of law by subjecting it to a parallel Hobbesian and Girardian interpretation. The relevance of Thomas Hobbes (1588-1679) to the novel is obvious—the "constitutional crisis" faced by the boys is an allegorical reenactment of Hobbes's famous concept of the social contract and the resultant division between the democratic commonwealth-by-institution (represented by Ralph and Piggy) and the dictatorial commonwealth-by-acquisition (represented by Jack and Roger). What is far less obvious is the manner in which the struggle over the political order of the island strictly parallels a subtextual imitative rivalry between the two boy-sovereigns, Ralph and Jack. Doubling is one of the unappreciated strengths of the novel, the binary relationship of Self to Other signifying the esoteric union between exoteric opposites. Employing Girard's theory of mimetic rivalry as a supplementary reading to Hobbes's political doubling of democratic with authoritarian rule, a much more challenging interpretation of *Lord* than that typically offered may be formulated: that the mimetic rivalry between the two boys replicates the mimetic dynamic between the competing forms of government that they respectively symbolize, subverting any absolute distinction between liberal and dictatorial forms of the political state. The solution to the "problem" of secular democracy foisted on the boys by the rhetorical ruses of Piggy, the voice of "common sense" ("practical reason" for Kant, "false consciousness" for Marx), is a sacrificial theocracy. In other words, Golding, like Girard, inverts the ideas of Ludwig Feuerbach (1804-1872) holding that religious consciousness is the foundation of social consciousness. The dramatic movement implied in Golding's book is a double arc: the migration from the utilitarian "common-sense" nature of language (Hobbes) to the transcendental language of religion (Girard) and the migration from social contract (symbolized by the conch) to the sacrificial mechanism (the scapegoat, conveyed through the iconic pig's head impaled on a "stick sharpened at both ends").

It is quite remarkable how counterintuitive this reading appears at first glance, a lingering trace, no doubt, of the incessant moralizing that *Lord* has attracted over the years. Just as with Joseph Conrad in *Heart of Darkness* ("...good work was still being done..."), Golding seems to be almost frightened by the radical insight of his own narrative: "The theme [of *Lord*] is an attempt to trace the defects of society back to the defects of human nature. The moral [sic] is that the shape of a society must depend on the ethical nature of the individual and not on any political system ... The whole book is symbolic in nature" (Golding qtd. in Babb 7; for Golding as moralist, see Hynes 13-21). Ever since the time of Charles Dickens, if not Jane Austen, it has been a truism that the English novel can never truly give offence, although it can incite all forms of moralistic tongue wagging. The cultural imperative to never-quite-give-up-on-civilization, broadcast most resoundingly through the incessant critical chant that "the boys" have tragically "regressed" to barbarism narratively stands in unrelieved tension to Golding's masterful depiction of landscape-as-violence; the island is not merely a place where violence happens but violence (and blood) is the metaphysical foundation of the place itself. This interpretation is already implied by the following lengthy passage:

> When Henry tired of his play and wandered off along the beach, Roger followed him, keeping beneath the palms and drifting casually in the same direction.... [Henry] went down the beach and busied himself at the water's edge. The great Pacific tide was coming in and every few seconds the relatively still water of the lagoon heaved forwards an inch. There were creatures that lived in this last fling of the sea, tiny transparencies that came questing in with the water over the hot, dry sand. ... Like a myriad of tiny teeth in a saw, the transparencies came scavenging over the beach. This was fascinating to Henry. He poked about with a bit of stick, that itself was wave-worn and whitened and a vagrant, and tried to control the motions of the scavengers. He made little runnels that the tide filled and tried to crowd them with creatures. He became absorbed beyond mere

happiness as he felt himself exercising control over living things. He talked to them, urging them, ordering them. Driven back by the tide, his footprints became bays in which they were trapped and gave him the illusion of mastery. He squatted on his hams at the water's edge, bowed, with a shock of hair falling over his forehead and past his eyes, and the afternoon sun emptied down invisible arrows. Roger waited too. At first he had hidden behind a great palm bole; but Henry's absorption with the transparencies was so obvious that at last he stood out in full view. ... Roger stooped, picked up a stone, and threw it at Henry—and threw to miss. The stone, that token of preposterous time, bounced five yards to Henry's right and fell in the water. Roger gathered a handful of stones and began to throw them. Yet there was a space around Henry, perhaps six yards in diameter, into which he dare [sic] not throw. Here, invisible yet strong, was the taboo of the old life. Round the squatting child was the protection of parents and school and policemen and the law. Roger's arm was conditioned by a civilization that knew nothing of him and was in ruins. (*Golding* 63-64)

In ruins for having just destroyed itself through nuclear warfare. Readers generally do not appreciate that the boys are imprisoned within parallel apocalyptic universes—the macroapocalypse of the outside world (World War III) and the microapocalypse of the nameless island (the "civil war" between Ralph and Jack that climaxes in an annihilating conflagration).

Contra Piggy's incessant refrain throughout *Lord*, "grown-ups" might not be the best things to imitate.

Personally, I am no great fan of the English novel in general and when I set myself the task to formulate the most subversive interpretation of *Lord* possible (which, unnervingly, proved to be the most law-centric), I settled upon something guaranteed to violate English cultural prejudices; that far from "regressing" towards barbarism, the boys, ultimately led by Jack, are in fact "advancing" towards civilization through their accidental (or unconscious) mimetic imitation of the anthropologically correct process of social formation: the establishment of a religious system predicated upon the ritualistic sacrifice of a formally designated scapegoat (first Simon, then Piggy, and then—almost—Ralph, who gets saved just in time to preserve the fig leaf of moral decorum). Now is the time for the critical reader (or merely one who happens to like Jane Austen or Charles Dickens) to ask the central question: What do I mean by the term "civilization"? Happily enough, I have a definition at hand, one of impeccable academic pedigree and one that is most germane to my purposes, a definition provided by Norbert Elias (1897-1990) in *The Civilizing Process* (first published in German in 1939). For Elias, *civilization* is all about *impulse control*; civilization is a by-product of complexity that both creates and depends upon chaotically emergent patterns of interdependence. As Elias puts it, the

> libidinal energies which one encounters in any living human being are always already socially processed, they are, in other words, sociogenetically transformed in their function and structure, and can in no way be separated from the corresponding ego and super-ego structures. The more animalistic and automatic levels of people's personality are neither more nor less significant for the understanding of human conduct than their controls. What matters, what determines conduct, are the balances and conflicts between people's malleable drives and the built-in drive-controls. (409)

The single most efficacious means of imposing impulse control is through the monopolization of violence (to borrow a phrase from Max Weber) by means of a juridically robust state grounded in executive power. The always potentially anarchic democratic assembly simply will not cut it; we need more Jacks and fewer Ralphs. According to Elias, the

> peculiar stability of the apparatus of psychological self-restraint which emerges as a decisive trait built into the habitus of every "civilized" human being, stands in the closest relationship to the monopolization of physical force and the growing stability of the central organs of society … When a monopoly of force is formed, pacified social spaces are created which are normally free from acts of violence. … Only with the formation of this kind of relatively stable monopoly institutions do societies acquire those characteristics as a result of which the individuals forming them get attuned, from infancy, to a highly regulated and differentiated pattern of self-restraint; only in

conjunction with these monopolies does this kind of self-restraint require a higher degree of automaticity, does it become, as it were, "second nature." (369)

Elias postulates an explicit correlation between the processes of state formation (external environment) and the reconfiguration of the psychic economy (internal landscape), one now founded upon rational calculation, self-denial, impulse control, and the self-censorship of violence, all of which are wondrously conveyed in Golding's mini-allegory of Roger's stalking of Henry on the beach. As Elias comments, the

> moderation of spontaneous emotions, the tempering of affects, the extension of mental space beyond the moment into the past and the future, the habit of connecting events in terms of chains of cause and effect—all these are different aspects of the same transformation of conduct which necessarily takes place with the monopolization of physical violence, and the lengthening of the chains of social action and inter-dependence. It is a "civilizing" change of behaviour. (370)

The achievement of a stable, even if primitive, society is the precondition for the effective censorship of violence—the movement of censorship from the exterior to the interior—which will then yield a "civilized" person at the end of a millennial-long process of incremental transformations. But the very thing that gives us peace is, paradoxically, grounded in violence—it is those selfsame sacrificial rituals and practices that bind us together (*religare*) that serve as a point of intersection between the social and the Absolute (*relegare*), yielding a self-stabilizing community.

We call the thing that gives-us-peace-from-violence Religion (*religio*). But *how*, exactly, does it work? Or, to put it another way—why does the secular commonwealth *require* a transcendental sign system?

Religion and the Mimetic Cycle

We can never be done with religion because we can never be done with the problem of *envy* (see Wilson, "Ballad"). According to

---

Girard, the human subject "does not really know what to desire, in the last resort" (*Things Hidden* 343); thus, the human subject "desires *being*, something he himself lacks and which some other person [the "model"] seems to possess. The subject thus looks to that other person to inform him of what he should desire in order to acquire that being" (*Violence* 146). The entirety of human desire, the libidinal dimension of humanity's social existence, is subsumed under mimesis— "desire itself is essentially mimetic, directed toward an object desired by the model" (*Violence* 46), from which comes rivalry, "the mimetic nature of conflict, which is to say the ultimate absence of any object proper to it" (*Things Hidden* 31). Rivalry is the inverse of a "crisis of distinctions," the collective loss of personal and identifying differences that triggers an avalanche of reciprocal and escalating violence (*Things Hidden* 143-68). "Sameness," Girard asserts, "is the terrible war in which twins [doubles] are personally engaged, right up until the moment when one manages to kill the other....When it spreads it becomes the famous war of all against all of which Hobbes spoke" (*The One* 104-05).

There are two ways to mediate mimetic rivalry: external and internal. Historically, external mediation corresponds to class-based societies: "As long as social difference or any other form of differentiation is present to channel mimetic desire, its conflictual dimension remains contained." Internal mediation, however, is a sign of the egalitarian society in which mimetic conflict is resolved through the direct competition between the role model and the imitating/envious subject (violence, physical or symbolic; see Palaver 25). The true catastrophe is when rigid social hierarchies begin to break down and give way to proliferating "democratic" choices; as "the metaphysical distance between desiring subject and model diminishes—the key component of internal mediation—the potential for rivalry and violence increases. The more negligible this distance becomes, the more probable it is that mimesis will end in rivalry and violence" (Palaver 61). Violence, then, is the outcome not of the repression of desires—according to Girard it is impossible for the peasant to entertain the lord as a mimetic rival—but through their unrestrained expression; the collapse of social differences is "a perquisite for the infectious spread of violent mimesis. The predominance of internal mediation must first be present within the community before mimesis can exert its contagious force. A stable social hierarchy, by contrast, prevents the spread of conflict and violence by restricting desire to external mediation" (Palaver 141). Girard's mimetic cycle offers the true but hitherto concealed explanation of violence by "showing quite simply that the disappearance of difference—physical or metaphysical—results in an increase in the frequency and intensity of conflict between the groups. Conflicts between equals have the greatest risk of turning violent, because the social limitations that normally prevent or channel mimetic desire are missing"—that is, the absence of external mediation (Palaver 66).

In arguably his most audacious move, Girard speculates that the logic of social formation is exchangeable with the logic of literary narrative; every literary depiction of human drama, which is always a form of social phenomena, is ultimately about envy (see *Desire*, generally). As mimetic rivalries are to be proscribed because of their ultimately violent consequences, the mimetic rivals must displace, or discharge, their common violence against a convenient surrogate victim that serves as the transference object of the violence—the scapegoat, the elemental instance of a "form of differentiation present to channel mimetic desire" (*Things Hidden* 93). Girard explains the "magical" efficacy of the scapegoat in terms of two subvariants of mimetic desire: divisive acquisitive mimesis, which leads two or more individuals to desire the exact same object at the same moment in time, and unifying conflictual mimesis, which induces all of the parties to the conflict to settle upon a common rivalry, or enemy, whom they all wish to "strike down" (*Things Hidden* 26). Anthropologically, the ritualistic enshrinement of the scapegoat/ sacrificial mechanism was the domain of religion (*Things Hidden* 48), which was grounded upon the intermediary of the surrogate victim—the one who must die so that the community may live by being spared the "apocalypse of the un-differentiated," the master sign of the mimetic collapse of distinctions. Girard's mimetic cycle, then, is not actually a theory of religion but one of social relations that are literally based upon victimage. As Jean-Michel Oughourlian has observed, Girard's "theory of religion is simply a particularly noteworthy aspect of a fundamental theory of mimetic relations" (44). It is in primitive societies that "the mimetic crisis culminates in a phase of unbearable un-differentiation that is resolved by the violence of the sacrifice" (Michel Treguer qtd. in Girard, *When* 68), and it is religious thought that led early humankind to "make the victim the vehicle and transforming agent of something sacred—mimesis—which is never conflictual or undifferentiated except in so far as it is spread throughout the community; its concentration in a victim makes it a pacifying and regulating force, the positive mimesis found in ritual" (*Things Hidden* 48).

As Golding would put it: In order to survive, hominids must sharpen a stick at both ends.

"Close, Close, Close!" The Apocalypse of the Undifferentiated

The "crisis" posed by the absence of the "grown-ups" is as frequently misinterpreted as it is noted by critics of *Lord*. The problem is not that the boys lack appropriate role models, no matter how flawed (a mimetic crisis), but that there is no superior power to police the necessary differences among them, yielding a "crisis of distinctions." Commenting on Girard, Stefano Tomelleri writes that "where social differentiation has practically disappeared the power of mimesis is most destructive." Hence, while

> the social distance between individuals gradually decreases, the mutual imitation of individual desires grows. In contemporary society, the transition from external mediation to internal mediation increases the person's illusion that he or she has a unique, autonomous, and individual desire, whereas actually differences among people are progressively disappearing. Everyone feels legitimated to compare him- or herself to others and to desire what the other has, independently of any distinction in terms of social role, job or group of reference. (92-93)

Recall that the dramatic action of *Lord* begins with the boys' democratic selection of a chief—with no natural leader, they have to choose among themselves. But since the original act that forms the social contract is an egalitarian one, the political order of the island can be revoked by a countervailing democratic will; which is exactly what happens. The boys' first attempt at public reason, Ralph's and Piggy's democratic assembly, is unable to maintain political hierarchy and it descends into a hedonistic anarchy. In contrast, Jack's commonwealth-by-acquisition does provide political authority through the introduction of the sacrificial mechanism, which is founded directly upon the most primal distinction of all— that between the sacrificer and the sacrificed. If anything, *Lord* is even more relevant in 2017 than when it first appeared in 1954: Golding's reworking of R. M. Ballantyne's *The Coral Island* (1858) highlights like no other English novel the lethal finitude of public reason. Golding's protodeconstruction of Hobbes (and today we would have to add the philosopher John Rawls) directly anticipates Girard's conception of the mimetic cycle as the ontopolitical "remedy" for the eternal failure of the social contract to restrain the paroxysms of mimetic crisis. According to Wolfgang Sofsky, it

> is a misapprehension to assume that human bestialities require social distance or any depersonalization and dehumanization of victims. In Algeria, survivors in many cases recognized former neighbours, friends, and even relatives among their murderers. During the "ethnic cleansing" in the former Yugoslavia, many of the incendiary murderers were particularly brutal with neighbours and co-workers from their villages. Proximity, not anonymity, brings about the most vicious atrocities; far from increasing the threshold of attack, it heightens the passion of violence. (qtd. in Palaver 63)

The epistemological key of the sacrificial mechanism is the logic of substitution: a new victim can always be sacrificed as one member of an unbroken series of copies of the original.

But this same process of substitution—that which reintroduces the "breaking effect" of objective difference into the community through the binary opposition between people and scapegoat—is the same mechanism of political economy that drives *ressentiment*, the foundation of both "middle-class morality" and the politics of modernity. As Tomelleri powerfully expresses it,

> [r]essentiment is a symptom of internal mediation. It arises from the illusion of infinite freedom within a mimetic context. It is an invasive emotion that does not just affect private life, but also dominates the public sphere (94).... Society seems increasingly individualistic, but an analysis of mimetic ressentiment shows that an individualist mentality also arises from the logic that leads to ressentiment. People imagine realizing an individualist and authentic desire when in reality everything needs a mediator in order to find a new desire, a need that is increasingly exaggerated by the paradoxical combination between growing competition among equals and an equally arising social inequality. All are thus condemned to a fundamental dissatisfaction that leads to a desire that finds no rest (Tomelleri 93).[2]

Ressentiment received its classic contemporary expression in the eponymous work published by Max Scheler (1874-1928) in 1912. Scheler there called it

> a self-poisoning of the mind which has quite definite causes and consequences. It is a lasting mental attitude, caused by the systematic repression of certain emotions and affects which, as such, are normal components of human nature. Their repression leads to the constant tendency to indulge in certain kinds of value delusions and corresponding value judgments. The emotions and affects primarily concerned are revenge, hatred, malice, envy, the impulse to detract, and spite. (25)

Scheler views *ressentiment* as seeking natural expression through the antithesis of public reason, the "spirit of revenge," which is the "most suitable source for the formation of *ressentiment*. The nuances of language are precise. There is a progression of feeling which starts with revenge and runs via rancor, envy, and impulse to detract all the way to spite, coming close to *ressentiment*" (25).[3]

In our era of post-Fordist consumerism and the hypercommodification of all forms of social and political

---

relationships (the "system of free competition" as Scheler calls it), the specific form that revenge is most likely to assume will be envy. In Scheler's words,

> [r]essentiment must therefore be strongest in a society like ours, where approximately equal rights (political and otherwise) or formal social equality, publicly recognized, go hand in hand with wide factual differences in power, property, and education. While each has the "right" to compare himself with everyone else, he cannot do so in fact. Quite independently of the character and experiences of individuals, a potent charge of *ressentiment* is here accumulated by the very *structure of society*. (28; emphases in the original)

Important to note here is that Scheler does not reduce envy to the frustrated coveting of "objects" (commodities) alone but extends it equally to the unbridled competition for social capital ("values") now wholly unregulated by external mediation, yielding the ultratoxin of *existential envy*:

> Another source of *ressentiment* lies in *envy, jealousy*, and the *competitive urge*. "*Envy*," as the term is understood in everyday usage, is due to a feeling of impotence which we experience when another person owns a good we covet.... Our factual inability to acquire a good is wrongly interpreted as a positive action *against* our desire—a delusion which diminishes the original tension.... [Paradoxically] Envy does not strengthen our acquisitive urge; it weakens it. It leads to *ressentiment* when the coveted values are such as cannot be acquired and lie in the sphere in which we compare ourselves to others. The most powerless envy is also the most terrible. Therefore *existential envy*, which is directed against the other person's very *nature*, is the strongest source of *ressentiment*.... (29-30)

Even worse, existential envy operates in a wholly mimetic fashion, a near-exact parallel of Girard's concept of violence-as-contagion:

> Through its very origin, *ressentiment* is therefore chiefly confined to those who serve and are dominated at the moment, who fruitlessly resent the sting of authority. When it occurs elsewhere, it is either due

to psychological contagion—and the spiritual venom of *ressentiment* is extremely contagious—or to the violent suppression of an impulse which subsequently revolts by "embittering" and "poisoning" the personality. (Scheler 27)

Girard's relationship with Scheler is complex; although he critiques the latter for his failure to situate the elements of *ressentiment* into a social dynamic, he concedes that "everything becomes clear, everything fits into a coherent structure if, in order to explain envy, we abandon the object of rivalry as a starting point and choose instead the rival himself, i.e., the mediator, as both a point of departure for our analysis and its conclusion" (*Desire* 13). I would suggest that *ressentiment* is most germane to *Lord* because it enables us to identify a hitherto overlooked set of doubles—one which, when identified, completely overturns the convention of the moral(-istic) interpretation of the novel. With both Girard and Scheler in mind, ask yourself one simple question: Of all of the boys, who is the one most vulnerable to the existential envy and, therefore, the one most likely to act as the source of social conflict?

We can exclude the two most obvious suspects, Ralph and Jack. We are likely to identify them as the source of conflict precisely because they are contestants for the position of leadership. But recall the mythology of the sacrificial mechanism: The scapegoat is the one who is identified as bringing harm to the community. Because of their "noble" natures, the rivalry of these two boys is directed solely against each other as existential equals in a manner both narcissistic and homoerotic.

At the return Ralph found himself alone on a limb with Jack and they grinned at each other, sharing the burden. Once more, amid the breeze, the shouting, the slanting sunlight on the high mountain, was shed that glamour, that strange invisible light of friendship, adventure and content.

"Almost too heavy."

Jack grinned back.

"Not for the two of us." (*Golding* 38-39)

As Scheler puts it, the "noble person" enjoys "a completely naïve and non-reflective awareness of his [sic] own value and of his fullness of being, an obscure conviction which enriches every conscious moment of his existence, as if he were autonomously rooted in the universe" (31). This is a very good description of Ralph.

> "Vote for a chief!"
> "Let's vote—"
> This toy of voting was almost as pleasing as the conch. Jack started to protest but the clamor changed from the general wish for a chief to an election by acclaim of Ralph himself. None of the boys could have found good reason for this; what intelligence had been shown was traceable to Piggy while the most obvious leader was Jack. But there was a stillness about Ralph as he sat that marked him out: there was his size, and attractive appearance; and most obscurely, yet most powerfully, there was the conch. The being that had blown that, had sat waiting for them on the platform with the delicate thing balanced on his knees, was set apart. (*Golding* 19)

If Ralph is truly "set apart," then he is the opposite of "common," a situation replete with mimetic significance; the "noble" man "experiences value *prior* to any comparison" whereas the common man (according to Scheler) experiences value "*in* and *through* a comparison. For the latter, the relation is the selective precondition for apprehending *any* value. Every value is a relative thing, 'higher' or 'lower,' 'more' or 'less' than his own. He arrives at value judgments by comparing himself to others and others to himself" (32). *Ressentiment* is nothing more than just this, "a tendency to make comparisons between others and oneself" (30). Hence the "common" person's denigration of value: It cannot be achieved ("Feelings of resentment ... are irritated by the *unattainability* of positive values that others represent" [see Frings 6]) so the values of the high (like hunters or members of the choir) are rejected in favour of the values that express the interest of the commoners, the conveyors of "common-sense."

Employing these criteria, the source of existential envy within the community, externally symbolized as the beast by Golding in a truly unforgettable scene, is the one who abolishes the possibility of external mediation in favor of the catastrophic leveling of internal mediation.

> "There isn't anyone to help you. Only me. And I'm the Beast."
> Simon's mouth laboured, brought forth audible words.
> "Pig's head on a stick."
> "Fancy thinking the Beast was something you could hunt and kill!" said the head…. You knew, didn't you? I'm part of you? Close, close, close! I'm the reason why it's no go? Why things are the way they are?" (*Golding* 158)

So, the question may now be rephrased as: Of all of the boys, who is the one most "common" (or "middle-class")?

The answer, just like Poe's purloined letter, is hiding in plain view.

> "You told 'em. After what I said."
> His face flushed, his mouth trembled.
> "After I said I didn't want—"
> "What on earth are you talking about?"
> "About being called Piggy. I said I didn't care as long as they didn't call me Piggy; an' I said not to tell and then you went an' said straight out—"
> Stillness descended on them. Ralph looking with more understanding at Piggy, saw that he was hurt and crushed. He hovered between the courses of apology or further insult.
> "Better Piggy than Fatty," he said at last, with the directness of genuine leadership…. (*Golding* 21-22)

I dare say.

Conclusion: Not One but Two Pigs' Heads

During the original moment of the democratic social contract, Jack offers up the commonwealth-by-acquisition with these words: "'I ought to be chief,' said Jack with simple arrogance, 'because I'm chapter chorister and head boy. I can sing C sharp'" (*Golding* 18). What is difficult for the liberal (or the American) to come to terms with is that Jack is exactly right; if one applies Girard's cautionary tale of external mediation, Jack is the only one who is able to end the crisis of distinctions—which he does with a vengeance.

"Fatty," however, is an entirely different sort of boy. The significantly nameless Piggy is the only middle class kid on the island, the solitary self-made *arriviste*. Externally, this means that he is damned to eternal social frustration in the (now) unmediated game of social capital. As Scheler explains, the "ultimate goal of the *arriviste*'s expectations is not to acquire a thing of value, but to be more highly esteemed than others. He merely uses the 'thing' as an indifferent occasion for overcoming the oppressive feeling of inferiority which results from his constant comparisons" (32). Internally, he is blocked or psychically constipated; the "immediate reactive impulse, with the accompanying emotions of anger and rage, is temporarily or at least momentarily checked and restrained, and the response is consequently postponed to a later time and more suitable occasion ('just wait till next time')" (25). Together, both aspects of the Self converge in an existential victimage; according to Scheler, this "blockage is caused by the reflection that an immediate reaction would lead to defeat, and by the concomitant pronounced feeling of 'inability' and 'impotence'" (25; or, in Piggy's case, asthma). Predictably, his *ressentiment* will assume the form of the inversion of values: common sense and practical reason—monopolized by Piggy as the bearer of the island's sole pair of "specs"— will be deployed as the (necessarily disguised[4]) means of self-validation. But it is not enough; "even revenge as such, based as it is upon an experience of impotence, is always primarily a matter of those who are 'weak' in some respect" (25). The solution? Simply this: "The desire for revenge disappears when vengeance has been taken ... In the same way, envy vanishes when the envied possession becomes ours" (26). And what is the most envied possession on the island? Piggy shouts out the answer:

> "I got the conch! ...Which is better—to be a pack of painted niggers like you are, or to be sensible like Ralph is? ... Which is better—to have rules and agree, or to hunt and kill? ... Which is better, law and rescue, or hunting and breaking things up?" (*Golding* 199-200)

According to Scheler, the "formal structure of *ressentiment* expression is always the same: A is affirmed, valued, and praised not for its own intrinsic quality, but with the un-verbalized intention of denying, devaluating, and denigrating B. A is 'played off' against B" (42). Piggy and A-Ralph against B-Jack. Piggy, not Ralph, is the one who ends the possibility of external mediation by preempting Jack's (unintentional) attempt to avoid the crisis of distinctions. "He's like Piggy. He says things like Piggy. He isn't a proper chief," cries Jack of his loved/hated double, Ralph (*Golding* 138). How right he is.

We now have the answer to the (optional) essay topic that I always set for my Law and Literature students and which, so far, no one has dared answer: Why do we never learn the real name of "Piggy"?

Because to do so would be to endure that unveiling that is the apocalypse—or at least the end of the liberal faith in secular reason.

For we know now who Piggy's double is.

Piggy's name is *skandalon*.

The Obstacle.

Notes

1. The significance that it is Henry who is selected by the murderer-to-be Roger as "symbolic" victim has gone largely unnoticed; Henry is none other than "a distant relative of that other boy whose mulberry marked face had not been seen since the evening of the great fire…": that is, the primal victim of human violence on the island. (Golding 62)

2. Mimetic rivalry "is always rooted in one of the two following claims: the claim of the self for the ownership of its own desire; and the claim of desire for its anteriority, its seniority over the other's desire, the other desire that has generated it, on which it is modelled" (Oughourlian 43).

3. Compare Bailie on this point: "when I speak of … mimetic desire … the word 'desire' means *the influence of others.* … the mimetic passions include jealousy, envy, covetousness, resentment, rivalry, contempt, and hatred" (112).

4.   "It is of the essence of revenge that it always constrains the *consciousness* of 'tit for tat,' so that it is never a mere emotional reaction" (Scheler 25).

Works Cited

Babb, Howard S. *The Novels of William Golding*. Ohio State UP, 1970.

Bailie, Gil. *Violence Unveiled: Humanity at the Crossroads*. Crossroad Publishing, 1995.

Dumouchel, Paul. *The Barren Sacrifice: An Essay on Political Violence*. Translated by Mary Baker. Michigan State UP 2015.

Elias, Norbert. *The Civilizing Process: Sociogenetic and Psychogenetic Investigations*. Revised Edition. Translated by Edmund Jephcott; edited by Eric Dunnning, Johan Goudsblom and Stephen Mennell. Blackwell, 2000.

Frings, Manfred S. *Max Scheler*, pp. 1-18.

Girard, René. *Desire, Deceit and the Novel: Self and Other in Literary Structure*. Translated by Yvonne Freccero. Johns Hopkins UP, 1976.

_____. *The One by Whom Scandal Comes*. Translated by M. B. DeBoise. Michigan State UP, 2014.

_____. *Violence and the Sacred*. Translated by Patrick Gregory. Johns Hopkins UP, 1977.

_____. *When These Things Began: Conversations with Michel Treguer*. Translated by Trevor Cribben Merrill. Michigan State UP, 2014.

_____, Jean-Michel Oughourlian, and Guy Lefort. *Things Hidden Since the Foundation of the World*. Translated by Stephen Bann and Michael Metteer. Continuum, 1978.

Golding, William. *Lord of the Flies*. Faber, 1954.

Hynes, Samuel. "William Golding's *Lord of the Flies*." *Critical Essays on William Golding*. Edited by James R. Baker. G. K. Hall, 1988, pp. 13-31.

Oughourlian, Jean-Michel. "Desire is Mimetic: A Clinical Approach." *Contagion: Journal of Violence, Mimesis, and Culture*, vol. 3, no. 1, 1996, pp. 43-49.

Palaver, Wolfgang. *René Girard's Mimetic Theory*. Translated by G. Borrud. Michigan State UP, 2013.Scheler, Max. *Ressentiment*. Translated by Lewis B. Coser and William W. Holdheim. Marquette UP, 2010.

Tomelleri, Stefano. *Ressentiment: Reflections on Mimetic Desire and Society*. Michigan State UP, 2015.

Wilson, Eric. "The Ballad of Ed and Lewis: Conflictual Mimesis and the Revocation of the Social Contract in James Dickey's *Deliverance*." *Law and Humanities*, vol. 10, no. 1, 2016, pp. 115-60.

_____. "Warring Sovereigns and Mimetic Rivals: On Scapegoats and Political Crisis in William Golding's *Lord of the Flies*." *Law and Humanities*, vol.8, no. 2, 2014, pp. 147-73.

RESOURCES

Chronology of William Golding's Life and Works

William Golding is the subject of each entry, unless otherwise stated.

1911	William Gerald Golding is born in Cornwall, England on September 19, 1911. His father, Alec Albert Golding, teaches science at Marlborough Grammar School, and his mother, Mildred Mary Agatha (née Curnoe) is a homemaker and suffragette.
1914	World War I begins.
1917	Begins secondary school at Marlborough Grammar School.
1919	Treaty of Versailles concludes World War I.
1921	Begins secondary school at Marlborough Grammar School.
1930	Completes studies at Malborough and enrolls in Brasenose College, Oxford, to study natural science.
1932	Temporarily expelled due to lack of progress towards degree; returned to Oxford and changed his study plan to English literature.
1934	His book of poetry, *Poems*, is published by Macmillan.
1935	Receives diploma in Education and Bachelors of Arts in English from Oxford.
1935-1939	Moves to London to write, produce, and perform plays.

1938-1939	Returns to Oxford and receives teaching qualification; begins teaching at Maidstone Grammar School.
1939	World War II begins. Marries Ann Brookfield on September 30, 1939, just five months after their first encounter. Begins teaching English and Greek literature (in translation) at Bishop Wordsworth's School in Salisbury, Wiltshire. Also teaches at Maidstone Gaol and in Army camps.
1940	Son, David, is born September 9, 1940.
1940-1945	Enlists in the British Royal Navy in December of 1940 and is sent to a secret research center where he is subsequently injured in an explosion. During his time in the Navy, he attends mine-sweeping school, commands a small rocket launching craft, is present at the sinking of the *Bismarck,* and participates in D-Day Campaign.
1945	Daughter, Judy, is born in July 1945. World War II ends; he is released from military service and returns to teaching at Bishop Wordsworth's School, where he continues to teach until 1961.
1954	*Lord of the Flies* is published on September 17, 1954, by Faber and Faber after having been rejected twenty-one times.
1955	*Lord of the Flies* is published in the United States by Coward-McCann with an introduction by E. M. Forster. *The Inheritors* is published on September 16, 1955. Becomes a fellow of the Royal Society of Literature.

1956	*Pincher Martin* is published on October 26, 1956. Contributes novella "Envoy Extraordinary" to the science fantasy anthology *Sometime, Never: Three Tales of the Imagination*, along with John Wyndham and Mervyn Peake, published by Ballantine.
1957	*Pincher Martin* is released in the United States by Harcourt under the title *The Two Deaths of Christopher Martin*. *Lord of the Flies* wins third prize in the International Fantasy Award.
1958	His play *The Brass Butterfly* is produced in Oxford, London, and New York and is published by Faber and Faber. *Pincher Martin* is produced by the BBC as a radio play.
1959	*Free Fall* is published October 23, 1959.
1960	Radio dramatization of *Pulkinhorn* airs. Receives Master of Arts from Oxford.
1960-1962	Writes essays and book reviews for the *Spectator* as well as for *Holiday* magazine, the *Times Literary Supplement*, and *The Listener*.
1961-1962	Serves as a writer-in-residence at Hollins College, Virginia; goes on lecture tour at many US colleges.
1962	Radio dramatization of *Break My Heart* is broadcast.
1963	Peter Brook directs film adaptation of *Lord of the Flies*.

1964	*The Spire* is published. Casebook edition of *Lord of the Flies*, featuring criticism and notes, is edited by James R. Baker and Arthur P. Ziegler Jr. and published by Putnam.
1965	His book of essays, *Hot Gates and Other Occasional Pieces*, is published. He is made a Commander of the Most Excellent Order of the British Empire.
1966	Brasenose College, Oxford, makes him an Honorary Fellow. Radio play *Break My Heart* is broadcast.
1967	*The Pyramid* is published.
1970	Receives honorary Doctorate of Letters from Sussex University.
1971	*The Scorpion God: Three Short Novels* is published.
1974	Receives honorary Doctorate of Letters from University of Kent.
1980	*Darkness Visible* is published and wins James Tait Black Prize for fiction. *Rites of Passage* is published and wins Booker-McConnell Prize for best novel of the year.
1981	Receives honorary Doctorate of Letters from University of Warwick.
1982	His second book of essays, *A Moving Target*, is published.

1983	Receives Nobel Prize for Literature.
	Made a Companion of Literature by the Royal Society of Literature.
	Receives honorary Doctorate of Letters from Oxford University and University of Sorbonne.
1984	*The Paper Men* is published.
	Receives honorary Doctorate of Letters from University of Bristol.
1985	Biographical account of his travels, *An Egyptian Journal*, is published.
1986	In honor of his seventy-fifth birthday, Faber and Faber publish *William Golding: The Man and his Books* as a *Festschrift*.
1987	*Close Quarters*, a sequel to *Rites of Passage,* is published.
1988	Knighted by Queen Elizabeth II at Buckingham Palace.
1989	*Fire Down Below* is published, concluding his sea trilogy about Edmund Talbot.
1990	Harry Hook directs a film adaption of *Lord of the Flies.* Adapts sea trilogy (*Rites of Passage*, *Close Quarters*, and *Fire Down Below*) into a single-volume edition titled *To the Ends of the Earth.*
1993	Dies of a heart attack on June 19, 1993, at his home in Perranarworthal, Cornwall.
1995	His wife, Ann, dies on January 1, 1995.
	The Double Tongue is published posthumously.
	Nigel Williams adapts *Lord of the Flies* as a play.

| 2009 | John Carey publishes biography *William Golding: The Man Who Wrote Lord of the Flies.* |

This chronology draws on previous chronologies by Lawrence S. Friedman, Patrick Reilly, Clarice Swisher, and Harold Bloom as well as biographical entries on William Golding in *Encyclopedia of World Biography* and *Biography in Context.* Furthermore, it is indebted to John Carey's extensive biography of William Golding.

Works by William Golding_____

Poetry Collections

Poems, 1934

Novels

Lord of the Flies, 1954

The Inheritors, 1955

Pincher Martin, 1956 (published as *The Two Deaths of Christopher Martin* in the United States in 1957)

Free Fall, 1959

The Spire, 1964

The Pyramid, 1967

The Scorpion God: Three Short Novels, 1971

Darkness Visible, 1979

Rites of Passage, 1980

The Paper Men, 1984

Close Quarters, 1987

Fire Down Below, 1989

The Double Tongue, 1995

Drama

The Brass Butterfly, 1958

Miss Pulkihorn, 1960

Break My Heart, 1961

Nonfiction

Hot Gates and Other Occasional Pieces, 1965

A Moving Target, 1982

An Egyptian Journal, 1985

Other

"Envoy Extraordinary" in *Sometimes, Never: Three Tales of the Imagination* (anthology), 1956

Talk: Conversations with William Golding (interviews by Jack I. Biles), 1970

Bibliography

Babb, Howard S. *The Novels of William Golding*. Ohio State UP, 1970.

Baker, James R., editor. *Critical Essays on William Golding*. Hall, 1988.

_____. *William Golding: A Critical Study*. St. Martin's, 1965.

Biles, Jack I. *Talk: Conversations with William Golding*, Harcourt, 1971.

_____, and Robert O. Evans, editors. *William Golding: Some Critical Considerations*. UP of Kentucky, 1978.

Boyd, Stephen J. *The Novels of William Golding*. St. Martin's, 1988.

Bryfonski, Dedria. *Violence in William Golding's Lord of the Flies*. Greenhaven Press, 2010.

Carey, John, editor. *William Golding: The Man and His Books*. Faber, 1986.

_____. *William Golding: The Man Who Wrote Lord of the Flies*. Free Press, 2009.

Dick, Bernard F. *William Golding*. Twayne, 1987.

Dicken-Fuller, Nicola C. *William Golding's Use of Symbolism*. Book Guild, 1990.

Dickson, Larry L. *The Modern Allegories of William Golding*. U of South Florida P, 1990.

Firchow, Peter Edgerly. *Modern Utopian Fictions from H. G. Wells to Iris Murdoch*. Catholic U of America P, 2008.

Friedman, Lawrence S. *William Golding*. Continuum, 1993.

Gekoski, R. A., and Peter Grogan. *William Golding: A Bibliography (1934-1993)*. Deutsch, 1994.

Gindin, James. *William Golding*. Macmillan, 1988.

Gregor, Ian, and Mark Kinkead-Weekes, editors. *William Golding: A Critical Study of the Novels*. Faber, 2002.

Grudzina, Douglas. *Teaching William Golding's Lord of the Flies from Multiple Critical Perspectives*. Prestwick House, 2006.

Hodson, Leighton. *William Golding*. 1969. Capricorn, 1971.

Johnston, Arnold. *Of Earth and Darkness: The Novels of William Golding*. U of Missouri P, 1980.

Kinkead-Weekes, Mark, and Ian Gregor. *William Golding: A Critical Study*. Faber and Faber, 1984.

McCarron, Kevin. *William Golding*. 1994. Northcote House, 2006.

Moody, Philippa. *A Critical Commentary on William Golding's Lord of the Flies*. 1964. Macmillan, 1966.

Nelson, Francis William. *William Golding's Lord of the Flies: A Source Book*. Odyssey Press, 1963.

Official Website of William Golding. William Golding Limited, http://www.william-golding.co.uk

Oldsey, Bernard, and Stanley Weintraub. *The Art of William Golding*. 1965. Indiana UP, 1968.

Olsen, Kirstin. *Understanding Lord of the Flies: A Student Casebook to Issues, Sources, and Historical Documents*. Greenwood Press, 2000.

Page, Norman, editor. *William Golding: Novels, 1954-67*. Macmillan, 1985.

Redpath, Philip. *William Golding: A Structural Reading of His Fiction*. Vision Press, 1986.

Reiff, Raychel Haugrud. *William Golding: Lord of the Flies*. Marshall Cavendish Benchmark, 2010.

Reilly, Patrick. *The Literature of Guilt: From Gulliver to Golding*. Macmillan, Basingstoke, 1988.

_____. *Lord of the Flies: Fathers and Sons*. Twayne, 1992.

Smith, Alison, and Peter Buckroyd. *Oxford Literature Companion: Lord of the Flies*. Oxford UP, 2013.

Subbarao, V. W. *William Golding: A Study*. Oriental Academic Press, 1987.

Tiger, Virginia. *William Golding: The Dark Fields of Discovery*. Calder & Boyars, 1976.

Whitley, John S. *Golding: Lord of the Flies*. vol. 42, Edward Arnold, 1970.

About the Editor

Sarah Fredericks is a doctoral candidate in Nineteenth-Century American Literature (with a minor in Rhetoric, Composition, and the Teaching of English) and a Graduate Associate in Teaching in the Department of English at the University of Arizona, where she has held Graduate Access and Graduate College fellowships. She received a Bachelor of Arts in English in 2009 and a Master of Liberal Arts in English in 2011 from Auburn University Montgomery (AUM). Her research has been supported by the Guinevera A. Nance Scholarship, Vanity Tags Academic Scholarships, AUM Alumni Scholarship, Ida Belle Young Graduate Assistantships, Sigma Tau Delta International English Honor Society Graduate Scholarship, Graduate and Professional Student Council Travel Grants, and the English Graduate Union Travel Grants.

She served as the editorial assistant for *The Scriblerian and the Kit-cats*, vol. XLI, no. 1 (2008); the assistant editor for *The American Novel: Understanding Literature through Close Reading,* vol. 1 (Facts on File, 2011); coeditor for *Filibuster* (AUM, 2011); and editorial assistant for *Culture and Society in Shakespeare's Day: Backgrounds to Shakespeare* (Chelsea House 2012). She has contributed numerous articles to Salem Grey House's *Critical Insights* series, including "An Overview of Contemporary Guides to LGBTQ Literature" (*Gay and Lesbian Literature*, 2015); "Maya Angelou and Zora Neale Hurston as Authors of Autobiographies" (*Maya Angelou,* 2016); and "Pow-wows of cussing": Profanity and Euphemistic Variants in Huckleberry Finn" (*Adventures of Huckleberry Finn* 2016). Her essay "The Profane Twain: His Personal and Literary Cursing" was published in 2013 as the cover article for *Mark Twain Journal,* vol. 50, nos.1-2, and her essay "'A great law of human action': Playing at Work and Working at Play in Mark Twain's Writings," coauthored with Alan Gribben, is forthcoming in *Examining the Power of Children's Play in Literature* (Routledge, 2017). Fredericks is currently writing her dissertation, "Mad Mark Twain: Rage and Profanity in the Life and Works of Samuel Clemens and Mark Twain."

Contributors

Christopher Baker is professor of English at Armstrong State University, where he teaches courses in early modern English literature, Shakespeare, Milton, Mythology, and the Bible as Literature. Twice president of the South Central Renaissance Conference, he is author of *Religion in the Age of Shakespeare* (Greenwood 2007), editor of *Absolutism and the Scientific Revolution 1600-1720: A Biographical Dictionary* (Greenwood 2002), and an assistant editor of the forthcoming MLA Variorum edition of *Cymbeline*. His essays have appeared in *Milton Studies, Ben Jonson Journal, Comparative Drama, Studia Neophilologica, John Donne Journal, Journal of Modern Literature*, and elsewhere.

Joan-Mari Barendse received her PhD in Afrikaans literature in 2013 from Stellenbosch University, South Africa. The topic of her research was Afrikaans dystopian novels published after 1999. From 2013 to 2014 she conducted postdoctoral research on dystopian and apocalyptic/postapocalyptic South African literature. She lectured at the University of South Africa from 2014 to 2015. In 2016 she started with a new postdoctoral research project on the representation of insects in South African literature, looking at texts such as the futuristic novel *Nineveh* (2011) by Henrietta Rose-Innes.

Grace Chen received her bachelor's from Syracuse University in 2010 and her master's from CSU San Marcos in 2012. She is currently a doctoral candidate and graduate teaching associate at the University of Arizona. Her master's thesis addressed transgressive femininity in Tennyson's "Lancelot and Elaine," and her research interests include nineteenth-century British literature, poetry, and gender studies.

Robert C. Evans is I. B. Young Professor of English at Auburn University at Montgomery. He earned his PhD from Princeton University in 1984. In 1982, he began teaching at AUM, where he has been named Distinguished Research Professor, Distinguished Teaching Professor, and University Alumni Professor. External awards include fellowships from the American Council of Learned Societies, the American Philosophical

Society, the National Endowment for the Humanities, the UCLA Center for Medieval and Renaissance Studies, and the Folger, Huntington, and Newberry Libraries. He is the author or editor of more than thirty-five books and of more than four hundred essays, including recent work on various American writers.

Nick Groom is professor in English at the University of Exeter, where he teaches topics ranging from the Gothic to cultural environmentalism, as well as a course dedicated to the work of J. R. R. Tolkien. His books include *The Seasons* (Atlantic 2013), *The Gothic* (Oxford University Press 2012), and *The Forger's Shadow* (Picador 2003), and he has edited novels such as *The Castle of Otranto*, *The Monk*, *The Italian*, and *Frankenstein* (all for Oxford University Press). His most recent publications are *Coastal Works*, a collection of essays coedited with Nicholas Allen and Jos Smith (Oxford University Press 2017), and a revised and updated edition of his study *The Union Jack* (Atlantic 2017). He is currently working on the history of vampires.

Kelley Jeans is an independent scholar with extensive background as a college level instructor, counselor, and editor. Previous publications include work on Ken Kesey, Maya Angelou, morality in literature, and multicultural approaches to literature. She has also helped edit volumes on *Othello*, Flannery O'Connor, and on LGBTQ literature.

Brian Ireland is originally from Belfast in Northern Ireland. He did his undergraduate degree at the University of Ulster and on exchange at the University of Wyoming. After completing an MA in American Studies at the University of Ulster, he moved to Honolulu, living there for five years while completing a PhD in American Studies at the University of Hawaii, Manoa. He currently teaches American History and Public History at the University of South Wales, UK. He has written about such diverse topics as the US military in Hawaii, road movies, horror and science fiction stories, and comic books. His latest book is entitled *The Hippie Trail: A History, (1957-1978)* (forthcoming in November 2017 from Manchester University Press). He has received a number of awards, including a Centre for Asia-Pacific Exchange scholarship, an Access to College Excellence award, and the Carl Bode Journal Award for 2003.

Gérard Klaus was a roving working student, getting his BA in English Literature at Lille University, his MA at Aix-en-Provence University, and his PhD at Grenoble University. As a teacher/lecturer, he taught both at secondary and higher education, hopping from London to Rome when still in his twenties, and later to various institutions in France. He specialized in the contemporary British novel, attended various symposiums in France, and published articles on William Golding (*Lord of the Flies*, *The Spire*) and Ian McEwan (*The Cement Garden*). He later reverted to his first love: literary stylistics (*Let's Get Creative: la Grammaire du Roman Anglophone*, pending publication). Now retired, he writes fiction.

Courtney Lane has a BA in English from the University of Mississippi and a Master of Liberal Arts from Auburn University Montgomery. She currently works at Auburn University, and was a contributor to *Critical Insights: The Awakening* (Salem Press 2013).

Rafeeq O. McGiveron holds a BA with Honor in English and History from Michigan State University, an MA in English and History from MSU, and an MA in English from Western Michigan University. He has published several dozen articles, chapters, and reference entries on the works of authors ranging from Ray Bradbury and Robert A. Heinlein to Willa Cather and Shakespeare, including editing *Critical Insights: Fahrenheit 451* (2013), *Critical Insights: Robert A. Heinlein* (2015), and *Critical Insights: Ray Bradbury* (2017) for Salem Press. Currently he works in student services at Lansing Community College, where he has served since 1992. He also dabbles in fiction, occasionally poetry, and mobile art. His website, which includes huge galleries of Heinlein cover art, is www. rafeeqmcgiveron.com, and his novel *Student Body*, the sensual, allusive, and introspective tale of a glib yet secretly troubled young professor-to-be and the women who love him, was released in 2014.

Stephan Schaffrath graduated from the German university-preparatory secondary education track in 1990 at the Gymnasium Olching before fulfilling his military service in Germany and then pursuing higher education degrees in the United States. He graduated with a BA in Psychology and an MA in English from Eastern Kentucky University (1995 and 1997, respectively) and earned his Ph. in English from Indiana

University of Pennsylvania's Literature and Criticism program in 2004. Over the years, he has been holding various positions at Indiana University of Pennsylvania and other universities, most recently as an academic adviser and reading specialist. His academic research interests include reading instructions, intrusive advising, violence, killology, Bakhtinian architectonics, chaotics, vampirism, and the Knights Templar. Much of his academic work has been published in various peer-reviewed journals.

Nicolas Tredell is a writer and lecturer who has published 20 books and more than 350 essays and articles on authors ranging from Shakespeare to Scott Fitzgerald and on key issues in literary, film, and cultural theory. He is Consultant Editor of Palgrave Macmillan's Essential Criticism series and formerly taught literature, drama, film, and cultural studies at Sussex University. His recent books include *C. P. Snow: The Dynamics of Hope* (Palgrave Macmillan 2012), *Shakespeare—The Tragedies: A Reader's Guide to Essential Criticism* (Palgrave Macmillan 2012), *Novels to Some Purpose: The Fiction of Colin Wilson* (Paupers' Press 2015); and a new edition of his interviews with leading literary and cultural figures, *Conversations with Critics* (Verbivoracious Press 2015). His analysis of the work of Martin Amis, *Anatomy of Amis*, comes out this year. A frequent speaker at a wide variety of venues, he gave the keynote lecture on *Ulysses* and *The Waste Land* at the June 2017 conference on "Birth, Death, and Rebirth" at the University of Bucharest and will deliver the Lenora Houchin Memorial Lecture on "Rubens and Rembrandt: Exuberance and Endurance" in Eastbourne, East Sussex, in November 2017.

Eric Wilson is senior lecturer of public law at Monash University, Melbourne, Australia. He received a Doctorate in History from Cambridge University in 1991 and a Doctorate of Juridical Science from the University of Melbourne in 2005. His publications include *The Savage Republic: De Indis of Hugo Grotius, Republicanism, and Dutch Hegemony in the Early Modern World System (c.1600-1619)*, published by Martinus Nijhoff in 2008. He is currently editing a series of volumes on critical criminology devoted to the relationships between covert government agency, organized crime, and extrajudicial forms of governance; the first volume in the series, *Government of the Shadows: Parapolitics and Criminal Sovereignty*, was published by Pluto Press in 2009. The second volume, *The Dual State:*

Parapolitics, Carl Schmitt, and the National Security Complex, was released by Ashgate Publishing in November 2012. Another volume on parapolitics, *The Spectacle of the False Flag: JFK/Dallas; LBJ/Tonkin Gulf; Nixon/Watergate* was published by Punctum in 2015. His most recent monograph is *The Republic of Cthulhu: Lovecraft, the Weird Tale, and Conspiracy Theory* (Punctum 2016). His research interests are radical criminology, critical jurisprudence and the application of the work of René Girard to Law and Literature.

Index

189, 208, 216, 217, 218,
219, 224, 228
point of view *see* perspectives 42,
49, 50, 53, 73, 81, 93, 106,
134, 153, 154, 190
posturing ix, 8, 9, 15

Ralph 64, 116, 164, 170, 172, 205,
206, 207, 210, 211, 221,
223, 227
rape 13, 138, 149, 220
rationalism 61, 115, 126, 128
reef 61, 121
regression xiv, 35, 101, 109, 113,
114, 119, 120, 135, 140,
149, 220, 222
religion(s) 93, 190, 226, 227, 231,
233, 234
rescue xiv, 4, 5, 16, 33, 34, 36,
38, 43, 51, 53, 54, 55, 75,
80, 110, 128, 139, 148, 194,
197, 205, 206, 211, 212, 241
responsibility 94, 98, 100, 101,
102, 133, 172, 190, 212, 219
ressentiment 236, 237, 238, 241,
242
ritual 79, 103, 109, 120, 222, 224,
234
rivalry 140, 226, 227, 232, 233,
238, 242
Robinson Crusoe 32, 94, 117, 132,
133, 143, 203
Roger 7, 9, 12, 14, 79, 95, 102,
103, 109, 116, 128, 129,
135, 173, 188, 201, 211,
221, 225, 227, 228, 229,
231, 242
sadism 95, 103, 109, 129

Romantic Movement and
Romanticism 146
rules 7, 13, 44, 55, 74, 77, 83, 103,
134, 135, 209, 217, 219, 241

sacred xiv, 109, 119, 216, 221,
222, 223, 224, 225, 234
Salinger, J. D. 99, 144, 175
salvation 43, 93, 109, 110, 138,
139, 140
Samneric 48, 63, 64, 69, 105, 209,
210
satire 92, 226
savagery x, xi, 4, 7, 27, 34, 38,
73, 79, 87, 93, 95, 103, 113,
114, 117, 118, 120, 135,
138, 193
scapegoat 98, 103, 127, 128, 222,
228, 229, 233, 235, 238
Scheler, Max 236, 243
science x, xi, 4, 18, 36, 37, 38,
62, 73, 82, 87, 95, 101, 109,
127, 137
science fiction x, xi, 4, 36, 37, 38,
73, 87, 109
self-knowledge xi, 58, 62, 67, 68,
100, 192, 200
sensation xi, 58, 59, 61, 117, 128
sex and sexuality 12, 13, 29, 46,
98, 99, 119, 121, 149
Shakespeare, William 60, 185,
189
sharpened stick and spears 8, 78,
79, 199
Shelley, Percy Bysshe 120, 121
sight and eyes 9, 42, 60, 62, 67,
74, 93, 123, 136, 166, 184,
191, 199, 216, 220, 229

war ix, x, 3, 4, 5, 6, 10, 11, 19, 20, 27, 28, 29, 30, 31, 32, 34, 35, 36, 37, 38, 39, 46, 54, 78, 80, 82, 87, 97, 115, 133, 140, 148, 176, 177, 178, 179, 191, 194, 196, 197, 205, 207, 209, 211, 212, 213, 214, 216, 220, 229, 232

Waste Land, The 63, 72

water 5, 14, 58, 60, 67, 68, 74, 84, 103, 121, 156, 183, 199, 228, 229

weapon 5, 6, 13, 16, 20, 30, 36, 78, 83, 177, 178, 179, 209

World War II ix, x, 3, 5, 6, 16, 20, 27, 28, 35, 36, 37, 54, 99, 140, 150, 156, 204, 205